MADRID

Forthcoming titles include

Chicago • Corfu • First-Time Around the World
The Gambia • The Grand Canyon • The Philippines
Skiing & Snowboarding in North America
South America • Walks In and Around London

Forthcoming reference titles include

Books for Teenagers • Formula One • The Universe

Rough Guides online

www.roughguides.com

Rough Guide Credits

Text editor: Clifton Wilkinson
Series editor: Mark Ellingham
Production: Helen Prior, Julia Bovis
Cartography: Ed Wright and Katie Lloyd-Jones

Publishing Information

This third edition published January 2003
by Rough Guides Ltd,
80 Strand, London WC2R 0RL

Distributed by the Penguin Group

Penguin Books Ltd, 80 Strand, London WC2R ORL
Penguin Putnam, Inc, 375 Hudson Street, New York 10014, USA
Penguin Books Australia Ltd, 487 Maroondah Highway,
PO Box 257, Ringwood, Victoria 3134, Australia
Penguin Books Canada Ltd, 10 Alcorn Avenue,
Toronto, Ontario, Canada M4V 1E4
Penguin Books (NZ) Ltd,
182–190 Wairau Road, Auckland 10, New Zealand

Typeset in Bembo and Helvetica to an original design by Henry Iles.
Printed in Spain by Graphy Cems.

© Simon Baskett
368pp, includes index
A catalogue record for this book is available from the British Library.

ISBN 1-85828-891-6

THE ROUGH GUIDE TO

MADRID

by Simon Baskett

ROUGH
GUIDES

We set out to do something different when the first Rough Guide was published in 1982. Mark Ellingham, just out of university, was travelling in Greece. He brought along the popular guides of the day, but found they were all lacking in some way. They were either strong on ruins and museums but went on for pages without mentioning a beach or taverna, or they were so conscious of the need to save money that they lost sight of Greece's cultural and historical significance. Also, none of the books told him anything about Greece's contemporary life – its politics, its culture, its people, and how they lived.

So with no job in prospect, Mark decided to write his own guidebook, one which aimed to provide practical information that was second to none, detailing the best beaches and the hottest clubs and restaurants, while also giving hard-hitting accounts of every sight, both famous and obscure, and providing up-to-the-minute information on contemporary culture. It was a guide that encouraged independent travellers to find the best of Greece, and was a great success, getting shortlisted for the Thomas Cook Travel Guide Award, and encouraging Mark, along with three friends, to expand the series.

The Rough Guide list grew rapidly and the letters flooded in, indicating a much broader readership than had been anticipated, but one which uniformly appreciated the Rough Guide mix of practical detail and humour, irreverence and enthusiasm. Things haven't changed. The same four friends who began the series are still the caretakers of the Rough Guide mission today: to provide the most reliable, up-to-date and entertaining information to independent-minded travellers of all ages, on all budgets.

We now publish more than 150 titles and have offices in London and New York. The travel guides are written and researched by a dedicated team of more than 100 authors, based in Britain, Europe, the USA and Australia. We have also created a unique series of phrasebooks to accompany the travel series, along with an acclaimed series of music guides, and a best-selling pocket guide to the Internet and World Wide Web. We also publish comprehensive travel information on our website: www.roughguides.com.

Help us update

We've gone to a lot of trouble to ensure that this Rough Guide is as up to date and accurate as possible. However, things do change. All suggestions, comments and corrections are much appreciated, and we'll send a copy of the next edition (or any other Rough Guide if you prefer) for the best letters.

Please mark letters "Rough Guide Madrid Update" and send to:

Rough Guides, 80 Strand, London, WC2R 0RL, or
Rough Guides, 4th Floor, 345 Hudson St, New York NY 10014.

Or send an email to mail@roughguides.com.
Have your questions answered and tell others about your trip at
www.roughguides.atinfopop.com.

Acknowledgements

Special thanks to Trini once again for all her hard work and patience. Thanks, too, go to James, Penny, Andy, Janet, Clifton, Lucy and all those who gave recommendations or advice for this edition.

Readers' Letters

Many thanks to the following who wrote in with useful comments and contributions: Barbara Hatley-Broad, Peter Jenkinson, Analia Kandel, John Montre and Arlene Sadler, John Morrison Milne, Elisa Morillo, Emily Wilson.

Cover Credits

Main front cover photo © Robert Harding
Small front photo © Peter Wilson
Back top photo, Tiopeppe © Peter Wilson
Back lower photo, Madrid city centre © Peter Wilson

CONTENTS

CONTENTS

MAP LIST

Introduction

Madrid became Spain's capital city at the whim of one man, **Felipe II**. Its site possesses few natural advantages – a fierce climate, no harbour and a poor excuse for a river – but it lies exactly in the centre of Spain, and in 1561, Felipe decided to base the formerly itinerant court here to avoid giving too much power and status to any one region. In Madrid he created a symbol of the unification and centralization of the country, and a capital from which he could receive the fastest post and communications from each corner of the nation. However, it was only the determination of successive rulers to promote a strong central capital that ensured the city's survival and development.

Today, Madrid is a large, predominantly **modern** city, with a population of four million and a highly schizophrenic character. There are, in effect, two cities: "Madrid by day" and "Madrid by night"; the capital is freezing in winter, burning in summer; outwardly flamboyant, yet inwardly conservative; seemingly affluent, yet concealing serious levels of poverty. The highest, sunniest and greenest capital city in Europe – despite being choked with traffic and people – its inhabitants, the **Madrileños**, modestly declare, "*Desde Madrid al Cielo*": that after Madrid there is only one destination left – Heaven.

Largely a city of **immigrants**, it's difficult to find a person whose real roots are in Madrid, apart from the *castizos* who proudly exhibit their *Madrileño* heritage during the *San Isidro* festival and the summer *verbenas* (street fairs). As a consequence, the city is a mosaic of traditions, cultures and cuisines and you soon realize that it is the *Madrileños* themselves who are the capital's key attraction: hanging out in the cafés or the summer *terrazas*, packing the lanes of the Rastro flea market, or playing hard and very, very late in a thousand bars, clubs and discos.

The **nightlife** for which Madrid is renowned is merely an extension of the *Madrileño* character. Much of their everyday life is acted out in the streets; they dress up whenever possible, never wanting to be seen at anything but their best; and they are noisy – horns blare, TVs are set at full blast and conversations are conducted at top volume. *Madrileños* consider the nightlife of other European cities positively dull by comparison with that of their own and whatever Barcelona might claim, the Madrid scene, immortalized in the movies of Pedro Almodóvar, remains the most vibrant in the country.

The city which was once accused of provincialism has changed immeasurably in the nearly thirty years since Franco died, initially guided by the late and much-lamented poet-mayor, **Tierno Galván**. His efforts, including the creation of parks and the renovation of public spaces and public life, have left an enduring legacy, and were a vital ingredient of the **Movida Madrileña**, the "happening Madrid", with which the city made its mark in the 1980s. Today, ongoing **improvements** are being made to the transport network, and there are ambitious plans to extend the Paseo de la Castellana – the multi-lane artery road that bisects the city – further north and construct a series of sports facilities as part of a bid for the 2012 Olympics.

The *Movida* may have gone but Madrid has emerged as a

stylish city and important European capital, highly conscious of its image and in better shape than it has been for many years.

What to see

As a **tourist destination**, Madrid has been greatly underrated. It may not boast the outstanding architectural riches of more historic cities in Spain, but it is home to three magnificent museums – the **Prado**, the **Reina Sofía** and the **Thyssen–Bornemisza** – which have long ensured the city a claim to the title of "European capital of art". Apart from these superlative collections, Madrid has a host of other attractions which, when combined with some of the best tapas in Spain, countless bars and legendary nightlife, make it easy to see why so many people get hooked when they visit.

The **layout** of the city is pretty straightforward and the main sights are clustered in a very compact centre where you're likely to spend most of your time. At the heart of the city – and of Spain – is the **Puerta del Sol** and around it lie the oldest parts of the capital, neatly bordered to the west by the **Río Manzanares**, to the east by the park of **El Retiro**, and to the north by the city's great thoroughfare, the **Gran Vía**.

Throughout the guide all street names are abbreviated, using c/ for *calle* (street) and omitting the articles "de", "de la", etc. Calle de Toledo, for example, is c/Toledo and Calle de la Libertad, c/Libertad. Although on Madrid street signs the full name is often used, Spaniards nearly always use the abbreviated form.

The Prado, Thyssen-Bornemisza and Reina Sofía lie in a "golden triangle" just west of El Retiro along the **Paseo del Prado**, and are a must for anyone with even a passing interest in art. Over towards the river are the oldest, Habsburg, parts of town, centred on the touristy but beautiful arcaded **Plaza Mayor**, instigated by Spain's greatest king, Felipe II. The royal theme continues to the west of here with the impressive bulk of the **Palacio Real** (Royal Palace), while to the south lie the cosmopolitan *barrios* of La Latina and Lavapiés, with their fascinating history, myriad eating and drinking options, and the famous **Rastro** flea market.

After **Gran Vía** with its cinemas, shops and monumental architecture, the most important streets are **c/Mayor** and its continuation **c/Alcalá** – which cut through the centre from the **Palacio Real** to **Plaza de la Cibeles** and are home to several quirkier shops and the fine art collections of the **Real Academia de San Fernando** – and the long south–north boulevard beginning as the elegant Paseo del Prado and finishing up as the multi-lane **Paseo de la Castellana**, famous for its summer *terrazas*. Although there's plenty of nightlife in the city centre, especially around **Plaza de Santa Ana** and **Huertas**, you may also find yourself venturing further north to the *barrios* of **Chueca** and **Malasaña** for the hippest bars and clubs.

Day-trips from the city include some of Spain's most splendid historic cities. Above all there's **Toledo**, immortalized by El Greco, which preceded Madrid as the Spanish capital, but other excellent excursions include **Segovia**, with its stunning Roman aqueduct; Felipe II's vast palace-mausoleum of **El Escorial**; **Aranjuez**, a riverside oasis in the parched Castilian plain, famed for its strawberries and lavish Baroque palace; and the beautiful walled city of **Ávila**, birthplace of Santa Teresa. The nearby mountains, the **Sierra de Guadarrama**, with their walking trails and lower temperatures, can also provide a welcome escape if the heat and bustle of the city get too much.

Calling Madrid from abroad, dial your international access code, then 34, followed by the subscriber's number, which will nearly always start with 91.

When to go

Traditionally, Madrid has a typical **continental climate**, cold and dry in winter and hot and dry in summer. There are usually two rainy periods, in October/November and any time from late March to early May. With soaring temperatures in July and August, the best times to visit are often **spring** and **autumn**, when the city is pleasantly warm. The short, sharp **winter** takes many visitors by surprise, but crisp sunny days with clear blue skies compensate for the drop in temperatures.

Although Madrid is increasingly falling into line with other European capitals, much of it still shuts down in **summer**. For around six weeks from the end of July, half the bars, restaurants and offices close, and their inhabitants head for the coast or countryside. Luckily for visitors, and those *Madrileños* who choose to remain, sights and museums stay open and nightlife takes on a momentum of its own. In addition, the council has initiated a programme of summer entertainment, meaning it's not a bad time to be in town, as long as you're not trying to get anything done.

MADRID'S CLIMATE

	F°		C°		RAINFALL	
	AVERAGE DAILY		AVERAGE DAILY		AVERAGE MONTHLY	
	MAX	MIN	MAX	MIN	IN	MM
Jan	47	35	9	2	1.5	39
Feb	52	36	11	2	1.3	34
March	59	41	15	5	1.7	43
April	65	45	18	7	1.9	48
May	70	50	21	10	1.9	47
June	80	58	27	15	1.0	27
July	87	63	31	17	0.4	11
Aug	85	63	30	17	0.6	15
Sept	77	57	25	14	1.3	32
Oct	65	49	19	10	2.1	53
Nov	55	42	13	5	1.9	47
Dec	48	36	9	2	1.9	48

BASICS

Arrival

International **air**, **train** and **bus** arrival points are all some way from the centre. Transport into the city, however, is relatively easy and efficient.

BY AIR

The **Aeropuerto de Barajas** is 16km east of the city, at the end of Avenida de América. It has three terminals: T1 for *vuelos internacionales* (international flights, excluding some Iberia flights to Schengen Treaty countries); T2 for *nacionales* (domestic services, including some Iberia flights to Schengen Treaty countries); and T3 for Iberia regional flights and the Madrid-Barcelona shuttle, the *puente aereo*.

A vast new Richard Rogers-designed terminal building, 3km from the current airport site, is scheduled to open in 2004 and should double the present capacity.

The airport is connected to the **metro** system (line 8; daily 6am–2am, Fri & Sat until 2.30am; €0.95), taking just twelve minutes to reach Nuevos Ministerios station, where check-in facilities are now available. From there it's a fifteen-minute metro ride to most city-centre locations.

There's also a shuttle **bus** that leaves from outside the arrivals terminal every ten to fifteen minutes (daily

5.17am–1.51am; €2.40) and drops you at an underground terminal in the central Plaza de Colón (Metro Serrano; pedestrian entrance from c/Goya). If your plane arrives outside these times, there should be additional connecting bus services. **Taxis** are always available and cost around €17 into the centre, assuming you don't get stuck in traffic. Supplements are charged for baggage, for going outside the city limits (which includes the airport) and for night-trips (11pm–6am). The journey time by bus or taxi into central Madrid is highly variable, depending on rush-hour traffic and can take anything from twenty minutes to an hour.

Half a dozen or so **car rental** companies have stands at the airport, and there's also a 24-hour currency exchange, a post office, a RENFE office for booking train tickets (daily 8am–9pm), a chemist, a tourist office and hotel reservations desk, all in terminal T1.

BY TRAIN

Trains from France and northern Spain arrive at the **Estación de Chamartín**, a modern terminal way out in the north of the city. A metro line connects Chamartín with the centre, and there are regular connections on the commuter train line (Cercanías) with the much more central Estación de Atocha.

The **Estación de Atocha** has two separate terminals: one for Toledo and other local services, the other for all points in southern and eastern Spain, including the high-speed AVE trains to Seville and the soon-to-be inaugurated route to Barcelona. If you're coming from local towns around Madrid you may arrive at the **Príncipe Pío** (aka **Estación del Norte**), near the Palacio Real and connected to the metro network.

BY BUS

Bus terminals are scattered throughout the city, but the largest – used by all international bus services – is the **Estación Sur de Autobuses** on c/Méndez Álvaro at the corner of c/Retama (Metro Méndez Álvaro). Companies and services change frequently so it's worth checking schedules with the Turismo (see p.8) or the information line (℡914 352 266). The largest companies are Auto–Res, Fernández Shaw (Metro Conde Casal; ℡915 517 200, Ⓦwww.auto-res.es) which also has an office on c/Salud just south of Gran Vía (Mon–Fri 10am–1pm & 4.30–8.45pm; ℡902 192 939; Metro Callao/Gran Vía); Continental Auto, Avda. de América 9 (Metro Avda. de América; ℡917 456 300); Herranz, Intercambiador de Autobuses de Moncloa (Metro Moncloa; ℡918 904 100); and La Sepulvedana, Palos de Frontera 16 (Metro Palos de la Frontera; ℡915 304 800, Ⓦwww.lasepulvedana.es).

BY CAR

All the main **roads** into Madrid bring you right into the city centre, although eccentric signposting and even more eccentric driving can be very unnerving. The inner ring road, the M30, and the Castellana are notorious bottlenecks, and virtually the whole city centre can be close to gridlock during the peak rush-hour periods (Mon–Fri 7.30–9.30am and 6–8.30pm).

Be prepared for a long trawl around the streets to find **parking** and even then you'll need to buy coupons from an *estanco* or one of the street-side metres to avoid a fine. A better and safer option is to put your car in one of the many signposted *parkings* or to stay in a hotel with a car park. If you're in Madrid more than a couple of weeks, you can get long-term rates at neighbourhood garages.

With public transport being both efficient and good value, your own vehicle is really only of use for out-of-town excursions.

Information and maps

There are year-round **Turismo** offices at several points around the city (see p.8 for details), whilst in summer, Turismo posts operate at popular tourist spots such as the Puerta del Sol and the Prado. There are also **visitor helpers** (in blue-and-yellow uniforms) on call outside the Palacio Real, Plaza de la Villa and the Prado, and in the Plaza Mayor, Puerta del Sol, Plaza del Callao and the Estación Sur de Autobuses. You can **phone for information** in English on ☎010 within Madrid and ☎915 404 010 from outside Madrid. There's also a tourist information line on ☎901 300 600 (English spoken).

Listings information is in plentiful supply in Madrid.

The newspapers *El País* and *El Mundo* (Ⓦwww.metropoli
.com) have excellent daily listings (in Spanish), and on
Friday both publish sections devoted to events, bars and
restaurants in the capital. If your time in Madrid doesn't
coincide with the Friday supplements, or you want a full
rundown, pick up the weekly listings magazine *La Guía del
Ocio* (€0.90; Ⓦwww.guiadelocio.com) at any newsagent's
stand. The ayuntamiento (city council) also publishes a
monthly what's on pamphlet, *En Madrid* (in English and
Spanish), free from any of the tourist offices. Finally, *In
Madrid* (Ⓦwww.in-madrid.com) is a free monthly magazine
available in many bars, which bills itself as "Madrid's
English monthly for the Hip, Cool and Transient", and features useful reviews of clubs and bars.

One word that might perplex first-timers in Madrid –
and which crops up in all the listings magazines – is
madrugada. This refers to the hours between midnight
and dawn and, in this supremely late-night/early-morning
city, is a necessary adjunct to announcements of important
events. "*Tres de la madrugada*" means an event is due to start
at 3am.

Addresses written as c/Mayor 2, 4° mean
Mayor street (calle) number two, fourth floor.
You may also see izquierda and derecha, meaning
left- and right-hand (apartment or office).

The **maps** in this book should be enough for getting
you round the centre, and free maps of Madrid are also
available from any of the Turismos detailed on p.8.
However, if you intend to do more than just a day's sightseeing, you'd be well advised to invest in the *Almax Madrid
Centro* map (€2), available from just about any newsagent in
the city. This is very clear, 1:10,000 in scale, fully street-
indexed, with a colour plan of the metro on the reverse,

and covers just about everywhere of interest. Almax also produces a 1:12,000-scale *Madrid Ciudad* map (€4.70), which is rather less clear, but goes right out into the suburbs.

TURISMO OFFICES

Barajas International Airport
Mon–Fri 8am–8pm, Sat
9am–3pm; ☏ 913 058 656.

Estación de Atocha Mon–Fri
9am–9pm, Sat & Sun
9am–1pm; ☏ 902 100 007;
Metro Atocha Renfe.

Estación de Chamartín
Mon–Fri 8am–8pm, Sat
9am–1pm; ☏ 913 159 976;
Metro Chamartín.

Plaza Mayor 3 Mon–Fri
10am–8pm, Sat 10am–2pm;
☏ 915 881 636; Metro Sol.

Mercado Puerta de Toledo
Ronda de Toledo 1
Mon–Fri 9am–7pm, Sat
9.30am–1.30pm; ☏ 913 641
876; Metro Puerta de Toledo.

C/Duque de Medinaceli 2
Mon–Fri 9am–7pm, Sat
9am–3pm; ☏ 914 294 951;
Metro Banco de España.

MADRID ON THE INTERNET

Atlético Madrid
ⓦ www.clubatleticodemadrid
Spanish-language official site
for *Los Colchoneros*. Everything from history and fixtures
to the club song and videos.

The British Council
ⓦ www.britishcouncil.es
Useful information if you're
thinking of teaching English,
and for more on the Council's
activities in Madrid.

Listings information
ⓦ madrid. viapolis.com,
ⓦ madrid .lanetro.com,
ⓦ www.softguides.com
/madrid,
ⓦ www.descubremadrid.com
Listings sites covering food,
drink, entertainment and other
activities going on in the city.
The softguide and descubre-
madrid sites are available in
English.

The Madrid City Council

Ⓦ www.munimadrid.es

The city council's official site is available in English, with a variety of information, including forthcoming events. Can be slow to load.

Madrid Regional Government

Ⓦ www.madrid.org

The regional government's website has been recently updated and improved. Click on the button entitled "región" for visitor information (English version available).

Patrimonio Nacional

Ⓦ www.patrimonionacional.es

Information on the Palacio Real, monasteries, convents and other state-owned properties in Madrid and the rest of Spain. Virtual tours of some of the sites. English version available.

The Prado

Ⓦ museoprado.mcu.es

English version available, including sections on news, activities and the history of the Prado, together with in-depth analysis of a number of the museum's most famous paintings.

The Pink 'Un

Ⓦ usarios.lycos.es/cyberpinkun

Homepage for the English five-a-side league in Madrid and a good introduction to the British pub scene.

Real Madrid

Ⓦ www.realmadrid. com

For all the latest information on Ronaldo, Zidane, Figo, Raul and co. English version available.

Terra

Ⓦ www.terra.es

Popular search engine, giving access to most Spanish sites.

The Useful Guide to Madrid

Ⓦ malika.iem.csic.es/~grant/madi.html

A comprehensive index of Madrid-related sites from museums, tourist attractions and fiestas to sport and education. Some links are now out of date.

MADRID ON THE INTERNET

Transport

Madrid is an easy city to **get around**. The central areas are walkable, the metro is modern and efficient, buses serve out-of-the-way districts, and taxis are plentiful. Plus there are several organised **tours** that can whisk you from one sight to another.

If you're using **public transport** extensively and staying long-term, monthly **passes** or *abonos* (which cover metro, train and bus) are worthwhile. They can be bought at stations or *estancos* and you need a photo and identity card or passport. Prices start at €32.30 for a monthly pass for the central zones (reductions for under-21s and pensioners). They must be bought before the calendar month in question starts and put into service before the tenth of that month. If you have an InterRail or Eurail pass, you can use the RENFE urban and suburban trains (Cercanías) for free.

THE METRO

The **metro** is by far the quickest way of getting around Madrid, and the system serves most places you're likely to want to get to. It runs daily from 6am until 2am and the flat fare is €0.95 for any journey – or €5 for a ten-trip ticket (*bono de diez viajes*) – which is valid for buses as well. Lines are colour-coded and numbered, with the direction of travel indicated by the name of the terminus station. The metro is clean and efficient, and most trains are air-conditioned in the summer.

For more information check out the metro website Ⓦ www.metromadrid.es.

See colour map 9 for a plan of the metro.

BUSES

The urban **bus network** is comprehensive and it's best to get hold of a map (see below) to work out your route. **Bus stops** show the numbers of the buses that stop there, along with details of the other stops on the route. There are information booths in the Plaza de la Cibeles, Plaza de Callao and Puerta del Sol, which dispense a huge route **map** (*plano de los transportes de Madrid*) and sell metro/bus passes. Fares and tickets are the same as for the metro, at €0.95 a journey, payable on the bus, or €5 for a ten-trip ticket. When you get on the bus, you punch your ticket in the machine by the driver.

Buses run daily from 6am to midnight. In addition, Búho (owl) **night buses** operate on twenty routes around the central area and out to the suburbs, departing from Plaza de la Cibeles and Puerta del Sol every 35 minutes, midnight–5.30am from Sunday to Thursday, and more frequently on Fridays and Saturdays.

USEFUL BUS ROUTES

#2 From west to east across town: from Argüelles metro station running along c/Princesa, past Plaza de España, along Gran Vía, past Cibeles and out past the Retiro.

#3 From south to north: Puerta de Toledo, through Sol, up

towards Gran Vía and then Alonso Martínez and northwards.

#5 From Sol via Cibeles, Colón and the Paseo de la Castellana to Chamartín.

#27 From Embajadores, via Atocha, up the length of the Castellana to Plaza de Castilla.

#33 From Príncipe Pío out via the Puente de Segovia to the Parque de Atracciones and Zoo in Casa de Campo.

#C The Circular bus route takes a broad circuit round the city from Atocha, via Puerta de Toledo, Plaza de España, Moncloa, Cuatro Caminos, Avenida de América and Goya.

TAXIS

One of the good things about Madrid is that there are thousands of **taxis** – white cars with a diagonal red stripe on the side – and they're reasonably cheap; €5 will get you to most places within the centre and, although it's common to round up the fare, you're not expected to tip. **Supplements** are charged on trips from the airport, bus and train stations, for luggage, journeys between 11pm and 7am, and on holidays. In any area in the centre, day and night, you should be able to wave down a taxi (available ones have a green light on top of the cab) in a couple of minutes. To phone for a taxi, call ☎915 478 200, 914 475 180, 914 051 213 or 914 459 008.

LOCAL TRAINS

The **local train** network or Cercanías is the most efficient way of connecting between the main railway stations and provides the best route out to many of the suburbs and nearby towns. Most trains are air-conditioned, fares are cheap and there are good connections with the metro. Trains generally run every fifteen to thirty minutes from

6am to midnight/1am. For more information go to the RENFE website at Ⓦ www.renfe.es and click on the Cercanías section for Madrid.

SIGHTSEEING TOURS

Several companies offer daily **bus tours** of the main sights in Madrid and day-trip destinations around the capital, which can be worthwhile if your time is limited. Full details from the Municipal Tourist Board, c/Mayor 69, Ⓣ 915 882 900.

Madrid Vision c/San Bernardo 23; Metro Noviciado; Ⓣ 917 791 888, Ⓦ www.trapsa.com/mvision/pagweb/default.html. Bus tours of all the major city sights, with pick-up points including Puerta del Sol, Plaza de España and the Prado. Tickets cost €9.62–10.82 and you can get on and off as many times as you like.

Julià Tours Gran Vía 68; Metro Santo Domingo; Ⓣ 915 599 605. Day-trips to the cities surrounding Madrid. Prices start from €18.

Pullmantur Plaza de Oriente 8; Metro Ópera; Ⓣ 915 411 805. Guided tours of Toledo, Segovia and Aranjuez.

Walking tours of old Madrid are organized by the Municipal Tourist Office, Plaza Mayor 3 (Ⓣ 915 881 636 or 915 882 906, Ⓦ www.descubremadrid.munimadrid.es). The friendly guides are well-versed in local history and provide plenty of interesting anecdotes on the old city. Tours in English are on Saturdays at 10am (€3; meet outside the office thirty minutes before departure).

SIGHTSEEING TOURS

Money, costs and banks

Spain adopted the **euro** at the start of 2002. Like the rest of the euro-zone it has notes in denominations of 5, 10, 20, 50, 100, 200 and 500 euros, and coins in the denominations of 1, 2, 5, 10, 20 and 50 cents and 1 and 2 euros. It's worth noting that many smaller establishments do not accept the 500 notes. The current exchange rate is approximately €1.60 to £1, and €1 to $1.

For the latest currency rates, go to Ⓦ www.xe.com.

Although **prices** have increased significantly over the last few years, Madrid remains relatively cheap in comparison with most other European capitals. If you steer clear of the more obvious tourist traps, **eating** and **drinking** can still be very good value, while **budget accommodation** is widely available. Museums and major sights are all reasonably priced, and public transport is excellent value for money.

On a tight budget you could get by on as little as €35 a day, sharing a double room. Twice that amount is more realistic, while staying in luxurious accommodation and taking in some of the expensive restaurants and nightspots will see costs spiral.

Banks are plentiful throughout the city and are probably the best place to change money. Opening hours are normally Monday to Friday 9am to 2pm, but some banks also open Saturday 9am to 1pm from October to May. Branches of El Corte Inglés have exchange offices with long hours and reasonably competitive rates; the most central is on c/Preciados, close to Puerta del Sol. Barajas airport also has a 24-hour currency exchange office. Although they don't usually charge commission, the rates at the exchange bureaux scattered around the city are often very poor.

For details on American Express and Western Union money transfer services, see "Directory", p.269.

ATM cash machines (*cajeros automáticos*) are widespread and accept most credit and debit cards. They're often the most convenient way to get cash, though it's wise to have a back-up source of funds. **Credit cards** are widely accepted in hotels, restaurants and shops.

Safety and crime

As far as **safety** goes, Madrid gives little cause for concern. Central Madrid is so busy at just about every hour of the day and night that it never seems to carry any "big city" threat. Which is not to say that **crime** is not a problem, nor that there aren't sleazy pockets to be avoided. Madrid has a big drug problem, most evident around Plaza de España and some of the streets just north of Gran Vía. Drugs are reckoned to account for ninety percent of crimes in Madrid, and if you're unlucky enough to be threatened for money, it's unwise to resist.

In recent years parts of the *barrio* of Lavapíes have also been a focus of street crime so stick to the busier streets here. Be aware that the main routes through the Casa de Campo and the Parque del Oeste have been appropriated by prostitutes and their clients so are best steered clear of at night.

Tourists in Madrid, as everywhere, are prime targets for **pickpockets** and petty **thieves** and in all areas it's advisable to keep jewellery, watches and cameras hidden, and to stay away from dark, empty streets at night. The main shopping areas, parks, the metro and anywhere with crowds, are favourite haunts; burger bars and the Rastro market seem especially popular. Be aware that they often work in groups, and associates will try to distract your attention while your pocket is being picked. **Cars** are particularly vulnerable, and drivers may find their vehicles broken into and the radio stolen. The **police** are usually sympathetic and will give you a report form for insurance claims. In an emergency, dial ☎ 112; English is usually spoken on this number.

THE GUIDE

Plaza Mayor and La Latina

Madrid under the Habsburgs was a mix of formal planning – at its most impressive in the expansive and theatrical **Plaza Mayor** – and areas of shanty-town development, knocked up in the sixteenth century as the new capital gained an urban population. The central area of old Madrid, still referred to as *Madrid de los Austrias* after the Habsburg homeland, reflects both characteristics, with its Flemish-inspired architecture of red brick and grey stone, slate-tiled towers and Renaissance doorways set in a twisting grid of streets, alleyways and steps. In fact, the layout of this area has changed little since the Middle Ages, and although there are few traces of the original buildings, you can still spend an enjoyable day exploring the remains of the old city. Most tourists head straight for the Plaza Mayor and leave it at that, but there are other appealing sights scattered throughout the area, especially in the characterful *barrio* of **La Latina**, which stretches south of the square. The delightful **Plaza de la Villa**, with its amalgam of architectural styles, the Baroque excesses of the **Basílica de San Miguel** and the **Capilla de San Isidro**, as well as the decaying splendour of **San Francisco el Grande** are all worth seeking out, as are the culinary delights of the *mesones* (taverns) and tapas bars around **c/Cava Baja**.

The area covered by this chapter
is shown on colour map 3.

PLAZA MAYOR AND AROUND

Map 3, G9. Metro Sol.

The grand **Plaza Mayor** was originally the brainchild of Felipe II, who wanted to construct a more prestigious focus for his new capital. The **Casa de la Panadería** (map 3, G8), on the north side of the square, is the oldest building, begun in 1590. Once housing the city bakery and bakers' guild, it later became a palace. The original building has been almost completely rebuilt, as it and much of the rest of the square were damaged by the many fires that occurred in the plaza in the seventeenth and eighteenth centuries. Its main facade features a balcony from which the royals could watch proceedings below. The present frescoes that adorn the facade and feature a delightful, and highly kitsch, array of allegorical figures, were only added in 1992. Today the palace houses municipal offices and an **exhibition centre** (Mon–Fri 11am–2pm & 5–8pm, Sat, Sun & holidays 11am–2pm; free) displaying temporary exhibits on the history of Madrid.

The real work on the plaza did not get off the ground until the reign of Felipe III (1578–1621), but the city architect, Juan Gómez de Mora, worked quickly and finished it in just two years in 1619. Capable of holding up to fifty thousand people, the square was used for state occasions, autos-de-fé and subsequent executions, jousts, plays and bullfights. The bronze equestrian statue in the middle of the plaza is of Felipe III and dated 1616.

Today, Plaza Mayor is primarily a tourist haunt, full of expensive outdoor cafés and restaurants that advertise themselves as "typical Spanish" – best stick to a drink here. However, an air of grandeur clings to the place, and the plaza still performs public functions. In the summer months, it becomes an outdoor theatre and music stage; in the autumn, there's a book fair; and in the winter, around Christmas, it becomes a bazaar for festive decorations, site of one of the largest *belenes* (cribs) and home to stalls selling all kinds of practical-joke material for Spain's equivalent of April Fool's Day, *El Día de Los Santos Inocentes*, on December 28. Every Sunday, too, stamp and coin collectors convene here to talk philately and rummage through boxes of rare coins in the open-air market. On the whole, though, unless you're a fan of tacky souvenir shops and caricature artists, you'll find more of real interest in the areas surrounding the square.

Around Plaza Mayor

Just to the east, on **Plaza de la Provincia**, the design of the **Palacio de Santa Cruz** (map 3, H10) echoes that of the Plaza Mayor and may also be the work of Juan Gómez de Mora. It was built between 1629 and 1639, was once the city prison and now houses the Ministry of Foreign Affairs.

C/Postas (map 3, H8), a fascinating street linking the northeastern corner of Plaza Mayor with Puerta del Sol, has a selection of good-value bars and shops selling all manner of religious articles, from models of the baby Jesus, rosary beads and icons to dog collars and habits.

Over on the west side of the square, **c/Cava San Miguel** used to be the ditch of the twelfth-century city wall and still retains an ancient feel, lined by towering seventeenth-century houses, whose facades have recently been restored. To the southwest of Plaza Mayor, down the steps by the bar *El Pulpito*, you'll find one of Madrid's more famous institutions, **Botín** at c/Cuchilleros 17, serving classic Castilian fare in traditional surroundings. Mentioned in Galdós's novel, *Fortunata y Jacinta*, and in the *Guinness Book of Records* as the oldest restaurant in Europe, its other claim to fame is that the 19-year-old Goya worked here washing dishes. In typically understated fashion Hemingway merely described it as the "best restaurant in the world".

For more on *Botín* see p.167.

In this and the other *mesones* you'll no doubt be serenaded by passing **tunas** – musicians and singers dressed in traditional knickerbockers and waistcoats who wander around town playing and passing the hat. These men-only troupes are attached to various faculties of the university and are a means for students to supplement their grants.

Finally, leading south from the square down to San Isidro (see p.30), **c/Toledo** has a host of idiosyncratic little shops, specializing in fortress-like corsetry and hairpins. Casa Hernanz, at no. 81, is a must if you're a fan of espadrilles. The king reputedly buys his here and you can purchase models of every description, with prices ranging from €6 to €21.

CALLE MAYOR

North of Plaza Mayor, **c/Mayor** (map 3, B9–I8) is one of the most ancient thoroughfares in the city, along which religious processions from the Palacio Real to the Monasterio de Los Jerónimos passed for centuries. The street is home to a whole host of intriguing little shops and bars and is flanked by the facades of some of the most characterful buildings in the city, their grimy exteriors concealing an array of treasures. Heading west from the entrance to Plaza Mayor, you soon pass the decorative ironwork of the **Mercado de San Miguel** (map 3, F9), built in 1916. Further along, it's worth pausing at the gloriously antiquated **Farmacia de La Reina Madre**, at no. 59, where, according to legend, Isabel de Farnese, second wife of Felipe V, preferred to purchase her medicines rather than in the royal pharmacy in the palace, because she feared being poisoned by her stepson Fernando VI. The decoration dates from 1914 and inside are over three hundred sixteenth- and seventeenth-century ceramic and glass jars.

Slightly further along, it's worth stopping off at no. 84, the **Casa Ciriaco** (see p.167), for a wine or a coffee. A favourite meeting place for the intelligentsia, politicians and bullfighters, this traditional *taberna* is full of memorabilia, detailing the colourful history of the building, in particular the notorious attack on the royal wedding procession of Alfonso XIII and his English bride, Victoria Eugenie, in 1906. A bomb secreted in a bunch of flowers was thrown from one of the second-floor balconies, killing 23 onlookers, but leaving the royal couple unscathed. The assassin, Mateo Morral, was executed a few days later, and a bronze angel commemorating the victims can be seen on the opposite side of the street in front of the Iglesia Arzobispal Castrense.

To the north, up c/San Nicolás, stands the oldest surviving church in Madrid, **San Nicolás de los Servitas** (map 3, D8; Sun & Mon 8.30am–1.30pm & 5.30–9pm, Tues–Sat 6.30–9pm), with its twelfth-century Mudéjar tower featuring Arabic horseshoe arches. The rest of the church was rebuilt between the fifteenth and seventeenth centuries and houses a very small, but interesting, display on the history of Muslim Madrid.

Continuing along c/Mayor you'll pass the **Italian Institute of Culture** on the right. It stands on the site of

CALLE MAYOR

the house of the Princess of Eboli where Juan de Escobedo, Don Juan de Austria's secretary, was murdered by three assassins in March 1578, a murder in which King Felipe II himself was implicated. Opposite is the grand **Palacio de Uceda**, originally built by one of the favourites of Felipe III in the early seventeenth century and now home to the Capitanía General (Military Headquarters).

On the corner of c/Bailén, the wonderful music shop,
Garrido Bailén, is crammed full of musical
instruments and accessories (see p.260).

PLAZA DE LA VILLA AND AROUND

Map 3, E9. Metro Sol.

Plaza de la Villa, south off c/Mayor, is the oldest square in the city and reflects three centuries of Spanish architectural development. It was originally the old market square of Muslim and medieval Madrid, and today the centre is marked by a statue of the Marquis of Santa Cruz, an admiral under Felipe II and hero of the great naval battle of Lepanto in 1571. The battle involved over 100,000 men – including Cervantes, who lost an arm in the engagement – with the Spanish navy vanquishing the Turks off the Greek coast to the relief of Christendom.

The oldest ensemble of surviving buildings is the simple but eye-catching fifteenth-century **Torre y Casa de los Lujanes** (map 3, E9), where Francis I of France is said to have been imprisoned in 1525 after his capture at the Battle of Pavia. The fine Mudéjar tower has been substantially restored, and the characteristic arched doorway bears the original coat of arms of its owners, the powerful Lujanes family. On the southern side of the square is the **Casa de Cisneros** (map 3, E10), constructed for the nephew of the celebrated Cardinal Cisneros (Inquisitor-General from 1507 to 1517 and Regent of Spain after Fernando's death in 1516) in the sixteenth-century Plateresque style, incorporating the intricate techniques of silversmiths or *plateros*. The building was acquired by the Ayuntamiento of Madrid in 1909, and now houses the Mayor of Madrid's offices.

The Casa de la Villa

The west side of the square is taken up by the **Casa de la Villa** (map 3, D9), one of the most important and emblematic buildings of Habsburg Madrid. It was constructed in fits and starts from the mid-seventeenth century in order to house the offices and records of the council. The initial design by **Juan Gómez de Mora** wasn't completed until 1693, 45 years after his death, and was mellowed by the addition of Baroque details in the eighteenth century.

The weekly **tour** (5pm every Mon) is normally only in Spanish but is still well worth it. Inside, the **Salón de Goya** contains a copy of Goya's *Allegory of Madrid* – the original being in the Museo Municipal (see p.118) – a testament to the turbulent political history Madrid experienced in the nineteenth century. The painting underwent no fewer than seven alterations in order to satisfy the sensibilities of the various rulers of Madrid during this period, and the final version shows the story of "*Dos de Mayo*", commemorating the heroic resistance of the city against the French in 1808 (see "Contexts", p.326). Also here is the monumental canvas by Palmorli, *The Morning of May 3rd*, in which you can see the dawn panorama of Madrid featuring the Palacio Real and the dome of San Francisco El Grande. The **Patio de los Cristales** contains a stunning stained-glass roof depicting some of the most celebrated city sights and houses busts of famous *Madrileño* writers, painters and playwrights, including Tirso de Molina, Lope de Vega, Claudio Coello and Quevedo. The highlight of the tour is the **Salón de Plenos** or Assembly Room, where meetings of the council still take place. The chamber is dripping with gold leaf and lavishly decorated with burgundy velvet curtains, red leather benches and frescoes by Antonio Palomino.

The Convento de Las Carbonera and the Basílica de San Miguel

Just before the Torre de los Lujanes, a small alleyway on the left, c/Codo (Elbow Street), leads out of the square down to c/Sacramento. On the right as you walk down and just before Plaza del Conde de Miranda, an unassuming wooden door hides the **Convento de las Carboneras**. The convent, whose official name is the Monasterio del Corpus Christi, was founded in the early seventeenth century and belongs to the closed Hieronymite Order. The more commonly used name of Las Carboneras originates from a painting of the virgin found in a coal bunker and donated to the convent. The convent also makes and sells its own cakes – a tradition that has existed in Spanish convents since the time of St Teresa of Ávila, who gave out sweetened egg yolks to the poor of her city. The cakes can be purchased every day 9.30am–1pm and 4–6.30pm. Ring the bell above the sign saying *venta de dulces* to be let in, then follow the signs to the *torno*; the business takes place by means of a revolving drum to preserve the closed nature of the order.

For more on Ávila, see p.307.

At the end of the alleyway you reach the **Basílica de San Miguel** (map 3, E10; Mon–Sat 11am–2pm & 5.30–7pm) on **c/Sacramento**, a beautiful, well-preserved and quiet street, crowded with municipal buildings. The church itself was designed at the end of the seventeenth century for Don Luis, the precocious five-year-old Archbishop of Toledo and youngest son of Felipe V. It's one of the few examples of a fully-blown Baroque church in Madrid, showing the unbridled imagination of Italian architect Santiago Bonaviá, and features an unconventional convex façade with four recesses, each containing a statue, variously representing Charity, Strength, Faith and Hope.

LA LATINA

Immediately to the south of c/Sacramento, and bordered to the west by c/Bailén and to the east by c/Toledo, is the area known as **La Latina**, which repays a leisurely stroll with some of the city's most intriguing and atmospheric streets. The district gets its name from the hospital and convent founded here in 1507 by Beatriz Galindo, tutor and friend to Queen Isabella, whose scholarly reputation saw her christened "La Latina".

Half-way up c/Segovia is the **Plaza de la Cruz Verde** (map 3, D10), one of the sites of the notorious autos-de-fé and executions organized by the Inquisition. From here the Costanilla de San Andrés leads up into the old Muslim quarter, **La Morería**. Keep an eye out on your left for the Mudéjar tower of the second oldest church in Madrid, **San Pedro El Viejo** (map 3, E11; Mon–Thurs & Sat 9am–noon & 5–8pm, Fri 8.30am–9pm, Sun 9am–1pm), said to have been founded in the fourteenth century by Alfonso XI on the site occupied by the old mosque, although the rest of the church was largely rebuilt in the seventeenth century. Halfway up the costanilla you reach one of the real gems of old Madrid, the **Plaza de la Paja** (map 3, D11). This sloping, acacia-shaded plaza was the commercial and civil hub of the city before the construction of the Plaza Mayor and was once surrounded by a series of mansions owned by local dignitaries. Recently remodelled, with the restored houses beaming down on the former market square, this is one of the few areas in the city where you can get a break from the interminable Madrid traffic.

There's a selection of bars in and around Plaza de la Paja, and the square is also home to one of Madrid's most pleasant vegetarian restaurants, *El Estragón* (see p.177).

La Iglesia de San Andrés, Capilla del Obispo and Capilla de San Isidro

On the southern side of Plaza de la Paja stands the **Iglesia de San Andrés** (map 3, D12). The church was badly damaged by an anarchist attack in 1936, and the adjoining **Capilla del Obispo** is still undergoing a long-running restoration programme. However, the main church, whose brick cupola has now been restored to its former glory, and the Baroque **Capilla de San Isidro** (Mon–Sat 8–11.30am & 5.30–8pm, Sun 9am–2pm) are open to visitors and can be reached by walking round the building into Plaza de San Andrés and into the courtyard. Note that it's particularly strict about not letting people in with short sleeves or shorts. The chapel was built in the mid-seventeenth century to house the remains of San Isidro, patron saint of Madrid, which were later transferred to the Catedral de San Isidro in c/Toledo (see p.33). The interior is richly decorated, with a beautifully sculpted dome in pink, green and yellow, depicting angels laden with fruit. The lower level, inspired by the pantheon in El Escorial, features a red-marble backdrop, fronted by black columns with gold leaf and sculptures of saints.

LA LATINA

Museo de San Isidro

Map 3, D12. Jan–July & Sept–Dec Tues–Fri 9.30am–8pm, Sat &
Sun 10am–2pm; August Tues–Sat 9.30am–2.30pm, Sat & Sun
10am–2pm; free. Metro La Latina.

Plaza de San Andrés also contains one of the city's newest
museums, the **Museo de San Isidro**, housed in a reconstructed sixteenth-century mansion on the supposed site of
the saint's and his wife Santa María de la Cabeza's home. It
includes an informative permanent exhibition on the **history of the city** from prehistoric times up until 1561,
when Felipe II moved the court to the city on a permanent
basis. The municipal archeological collection, with relics
from the earliest settlements along the Manzanares river, is
in the museum basement, while the rest of the mansion has
been given over to the patron saint himself, with displays
relating to his life and his miraculous activities. It also claims
to contain the well that was the site of one of his most
famous exploits (see box), and the seventeenth-century
chapel built on the spot where the saint was said to have
died in 1172.

La Morería

To the west of Plaza de la Paja you can explore the narrow,
labyrinthine streets of **La Morería**, still clearly laid out on
the old Moorish lines.

On Plaza Gabriel Miró, *El Ventorrillo* (aka *Las Vistillas* – Little
Views) is a good place for a drink with a view (see p.205).

North, towards the cathedral, you'll reach the **Cuesta de
la Vega** (map 3, A9–B9), the former site of one of the
main entrances to Muslim Madrid. In the adjoining Parque
Emir Mohammed I, a rather scruffy patch of sandy open

SAN ISIDRO

The life of Madrid's patron saint San Isidro is shrouded in mystery. Tradition has it that the humble agricultural labourer, renowned for his pious devotion and generosity, lived together with his wife María de la Cabeza and their son Millán in the mansion of their master Iván de Vargas inside the city walls in the second half of the twelfth century.

Popular accounts later claimed that Isidro had demonstrated God-given powers on several occasions during his life. It was said that when he took time off from his labours in the fields to pray, his work was completed by a band of angels, and that he possessed the power to multiply harvests and to cause water to spring from the ground with a simple tap of his staff.

His most famous miracle of all was when he managed to rescue his young son who had plunged headlong into a deep well. Calmly standing by the well, Isidro prayed hard until the water level rose, bringing the child to the surface once more.

Shortly after his death in 1172, a cult – remarkable for the fact that it revered someone of such modest origins – developed in his honour. But it still took 450 years for Isidro to be canonised, during which time his body was exhumed and transferred to new, and more exalted, resting places on no less than four different occasions. His wife and son were subsequently canonized too, making them what must be the most saintly family on record.

San Isidro's feast day is celebrated on May 15 and is one of the biggest events on the city's impressive calendar of festivals (see p.233).

land, are some of the few remaining fragments of the **city walls**, dating back to the ninth and twelfth centuries.

Calles Cava Baja and Cava Alta

Map 3, E12–F11. Metro La Latina.

Heading south from the San Andrés complex you'll come to a series of plazas, variously named San Andrés, Puerta de Moros, Los Carros and Humilladero, which now effectively merge into one. They form an excellent site for summer *terrazas* and tapas bars which are always crowded with locals at the weekends. The web of streets running northeast out of the square back towards Plaza Mayor – calles Almendro, **Cava Baja** and **Cava Alta** – are also well worth investigating and are where you'll find some of the best places to eat and drink in all of Madrid. C/Cava Baja, once full of workshops, is now famous for its *mesones,* serving traditional Castilian and *Madrileño* fare, and its wide selection of bars.

For details of bars and restaurants
see "Eating", p.154 and "Drinking", p.181.

Iglesia-Catedral de San Isidro

Map 3, G11–12. Mon–Sat 8am–noon & 6–8.30pm, Sun & public holidays 9am–2pm & 6–8.30pm. Metro La Latina.

North of La Latina metro station on c/Toledo stands the massive church of **San Isidro**. It was built from 1622 to 1633 as part of the Colegio Imperial – the centre of the Jesuit Order in Spain – according to the express wishes of Felipe IV's wife, Mariana de Austria, who left a very large legacy to the Jesuits, and its illustrious alumni include the writers Lope de Vega, Calderón de la Barca, Quevedo and Góngora. After Carlos III fell out with the Jesuits in 1767, the church was dedicated to San Isidro (see opposite), and his remains – and those of his wife – were brought here in 1769. The church was the city's provisional cathedral from

LA LATINA

1886, when Madrid was given its own diocese, until 1993 when the new Catedral de la Almudena (see p.41) was finally completed. It contains a single nave with large, ornate lateral chapels and an impressive altarpiece.

San Francisco El Grande

Map 3, B14. Tues–Sat: June–Sept 11am–1pm & 5–8pm; Oct–May 11am–1pm & 4–7pm; €0.60 with guided tour. Metro Puerta de Toledo/La Latina.

From Plaza Puerta de Moros there's a splendid view of the Neoclassical exterior of the huge domed church of **San Francisco El Grande**. Tradition has it that St Francis of Assisi came to Spain in 1214, on a pilgrimage to the tomb of St James in Santiago and built a humble home next to a **monastery** on this site. The monastery was enlarged and enriched over the years, but was demolished in 1760 in order to build a still more beautiful one. Plans were ambitious and included a great dome with radial chapels crowned by a cupola, modelled on the Pantheon in Rome. The building was finally completed in 1784, its magnificent **dome** exceeding that of St Paul's in London by a metre in diameter. In 1837, the church was converted into a national mausoleum, reverting to the control of the Franciscan friars in 1926.

After a painfully slow twenty-year **restoration** pro- gramme it's now possible to appreciate this magnificent church in something close to its original glory. Each of the six **chapels** is designed in a distinct style ranging from Mozarabe and Renaissance, to Baroque and Neoclassical, and all contain something of interest. Look out for the early Goya, *The Sermon of San Bernadino of Siena*, in the Plateresque chapel on your immediate left as you enter, which contains a self-portrait of the 36-year-old artist (in the yellow suit on the right of the painting). The

LA LATINA

breath-taking scale and beauty of the frescoed **cupola** has now been revealed and is worth the visit in itself. Even if your Spanish is not that good, try following the guided tour to get a glimpse of the ante-sacristy with its seventeenth-century Plateresque benches carved from Spanish walnut, and the church's art treasures, including paintings by José de Ribera and Zurbarán.

LA LATINA

The Palacio Real and Ópera

The compact area around Ópera metro station, bounded by c/Mayor to the south, Cuesta de San Vicente to the north, Paseo Virgen del Puerto to the west and Puerta del Sol to the east, contains a rich array of architectural and artistic treasures. The main sites date from the sixteenth to the eighteenth centuries, although the area itself only became really fashionable from the mid-nineteenth century onwards. The imposing **Palacio Real** dominates the area, bordered by the somewhat disappointing **Catedral de la Almudena** to the south and the tranquil gardens of the **Campo del Moro** to the west. The restored **Teatro Real** and **Plaza de Oriente** have brought some of the original nineteenth-century sophistication back to the area, while the two monastery complexes, **La Encarnación** and **Las Descalzas Reales**, conceal an astounding selection of artistic delights behind their modest exteriors. You'll have to plan your itinerary carefully to dovetail the opening times of the sights, as the hours of the monasteries are restricted.

The bulk of the area covered by this chapter
is shown in detail on colour map 3.

THE PALACIO REAL

Map 3, B6. April–Sept Mon–Sat 9am–6pm, Sun & holidays
9am–3pm; Oct–March Mon–Sat 9.30am–5pm, Sun 9am–2pm;
closed occasionally for state visits and on Jan 1 & 6, May 1 & 15,
Dec 24 & 25; guided tours €6.91, unguided €6, concessions €3;
Wed free for EU citizens. ⓦwww.patrimonionacional.es. Metro
Ópera.

The **Palacio Real** (Royal Palace) scores high on statistics.
It claims more rooms than any other European palace; a
library with one of the biggest collections of books, manuscripts, maps and musical scores in the world; and an
armoury with an unrivalled collection of weapons dating
back to the fifteenth century. Guided tours are no longer
compulsory, which leaves you to wander the fixed route
yourself, though bear in mind that the rooms are not that
well labelled and the visitors' guide books (€3.35–€6.95),
while beautifully illustrated, are badly translated. Not all the
rooms are open to the public – some are closed for restoration, while unfortunately, others, such as the King's Library,
can only be visited by prior arrangement for research pur-
poses. The palace also contains an impressive temporary
exhibition space, the **Galería de Pinturas** (same opening
hours; €3, concession €1.50).

The Palacio Real has a gift shop and café by the entrance.

The palace stands on the site of the old **Alcázar**, erected
by the Arabs in the ninth century to defend the route to
Toledo. This became the royal residence of Felipe II when

he moved his court to Madrid in 1561. However, on Christmas Eve 1734, the Alcázar burned down after some curtains caught **fire**, destroying, in the process, some of the great works of Velázquez and Rubens. Felipe V, a Bourbon who had been brought up in the considerably more luxurious surroundings of Versailles, took the opportunity to order the construction of an altogether grander palace. However, he did not live to see the completion of his project; the palace only became habitable in 1764 during the reign of Carlos III. It remained the principal royal residence until Alfonso XIII went into exile in 1931, and both Joseph Bonaparte and the Duke of Wellington also lived here briefly. The **present-day royals** prefer the modest Zarzuela palace located some 10 kilometres out of the city near El Pardo.

A planned new museum between the cathedral and the palace to house the royal collections of carriages, tapestries, paintings and glassware is on hold after excavations there revealed remains of the old city walls.

Inside the palace

To enter the palace, you first cross the vast shadeless **Plaza de la Armería**, used for state parades and the changing of the guard (noon, first Wed of each month, except July & Aug). From the plaza there are superb views of the vast colonnaded southern facade, the Cathedral, Casa de Campo and the Sierra. As you enter the building you're directed up the magnificent main staircase with golden stucco work and epic frescoes by Corrado Giaquinto. In the **Salón de los Alabarderos** (Halbardiers' Room), Tiepolo's masterpiece fresco, *Venus commanding Vulcan to forge arms for Aeneas*, features billowing clouds, heroic military figures and majestic gods, while the **Salón de las Columnas** (Hall of Columns) contains several excellent Flemish tapestries woven with wool, gold, silver and silk. It was in this room that Spain signed the treaty to join the European Community in 1985 and where the Middle East Peace Conference was held in October 1991.

One of the highlights is the **Salón del Trono** (Throne Room), with its magnificent celestial fresco by Tiepolo, *The Grandeur and Power of the Spanish Monarchy*. The walls are decorated in red velvet, with ornamental framed mirrors exaggerating the size of the room, while gold drips from the furniture, stucco work and bronze lions guarding the thrones – an ostentatious display of wealth and power at odds with Spain's declining status at the time.

The **Antécamara de Gasparini** (Carlos III's Conversation Room) contains two pairs of Goya masterpieces: one portraying Carlos IV and his wife Queen María Luisa of Parma in formal style, with the king wearing the uniform of a Royal Guard colonel and the queen dressed in court clothes; the other, more casual, with the king in hunting attire and the queen dressed as a *maja* in a black skirt and mantilla. The exotic fancy of the **Salón de Gasparini** (the Gasparini Room), decorated in an incredible oriental style by Carlos III's court painter, features a swirling marble floor, gold and silver embroidered wall hangings and beautiful stucco plants, animals and fruits. There are yet more fantastic frescoes, ornate furniture and lavish decoration in the **Salón de Carlos III** (Carlos III's bedroom).

One of the palace's real treats is the marvellous **Sala de Porcelana** (Porcelain Room), decorated with one thousand gold, green and white pieces, made in the Buen Retiro porcelain factory in the eighteenth century and depicting cherubs, garlands and urns. The **Comedor de Gala** (State Dining Room) is a truly massive affair, again blessed with a selection of superb frescoes and adorned with golden French candelabras and sixteenth-century tapestries. The table seats 145 and is still used for official banquets. Other rooms display royal silverware from the nineteenth century (Joseph Bonaparte ordered the original silver dinner service to be melted down to meet war needs), crockery and a very impressive collection of musical instruments, including a number of Stradivarius's creations and a fantastic jewelled guitar by José Frias. The tour of the main building is completed with the **Capilla Real** (Royal Chapel) and Queen María Cristina's official apartments, which are more modest in scale, but still lavishly decorated.

The Armería Real, Farmacia and Jardines de Sabatini

The palace outbuildings and annexes include the recently remodelled **Armería Real** (Royal Armoury), a huge room full of guns, swords and armour, with such curiosities as El Cid's sword and the suit of armour worn by Carlos V in his equestrian portrait by Titian in the Prado. Especially fascinating are the complete sets of armour, with all the original spare parts and gadgets for making adjustments, and the suits designed for children, horses and dogs. Also open to visitors is the eighteenth-century **Farmacia** (pharmacy), which served the royal family and employees at the palace; it's a curious mixture of alchemist's den and laboratory, and the walls are lined with jars labelled for various remedies. Immediately north of the palace, the **Jardines de Sabatini** (Sabatini Gardens; daily April–Sept 9am–10.30pm, Oct–March 9am–9pm) contain an ornamental lake, some fragrant magnolia trees and well-manicured hedges, and make an ideal place from which to view the northern facade of the palace or to watch the sun go down.

THE CATHEDRAL

Map 3, B8–9. Daily 9am–9pm. Not open for visits during mass: Mon–Sat 10am, noon, 6pm & 7pm, Sun and Hols 10.30am, noon, 1.30pm, 6pm & 7pm. Metro Ópera.

Facing the Palacio Real to the south is Madrid's cathedral, **Nuestra Señora de la Almudena**, its bulky Neoclassical facade designed to match the palace. Planned centuries ago, the building was plagued by lack of funds, bombed out in the Civil War and eventually opened for business in 1993 by Pope John Paul II. Its cold Gothic interior is uninspiring, though the garish ceiling designs, the sixteenth century altarpiece in the Almudena chapel and the boutique-like Capilla Opus Dei dedicated to José María Escrivá de Balaguer – the founder of the movement in Madrid – are all worth a look. The cathedral crypt (daily 10am–8pm; entrance on c/Mayor to the south) with its forest of columns and dimly lit chapels is far more atmospheric than the main building itself.

Outside, nestling on the south wall behind the cathedral, facing the Parque Emir Mohammed I, is a figure of the **Virgin of the Almudena**, marking the site of the first recorded miracle in Madrid. The figure was said to have been brought to Spain by St James and concealed in the wall of the old castle here by early Christians to protect it during the conquest of the city by the Muslims. When the city was reconquered by Alfonso VI at the end of the eleventh century, he was anxious to unearth the virgin to re-establish the city's Christian credentials. He organized a huge procession appealing for divine help, and when the faithful arrived, a woman offered her life in return for the statue's reappearance. The wall crumbled away to reveal the virgin in all her splendour and the woman immediately dropped dead.

THE CATHEDRAL

MADRID'S FREEBIES

Madrid's premier attractions allow free entrance at certain times. Sites classed as *Patrimonio Nacional* – Palacio Real, the Convento de la Encarnación, El Pardo and the Monasterio de las Descalzas – are free to EU citizens on Wednesdays (bring your passport). Many museums also grant free entry on the following dates: October 12 (Fiesta Nacional), October 18 (International Museums Day) and December 6 (Día de la Constitución), and the majority have the usual concessionary rates (bring ID in all cases). In addition, the following are free at the times given:

Centro de Arte Reina Sofía Sat 2.30–9pm & Sun 10am–2.30pm.

Ermita de San Antonio de la Florida Wed 10am–2pm & 4–8pm, Sun 10am–2pm.

Museo de América Sat 2–3pm & Sun 10am–2.30pm.

Museo Arqueológico Sat 2.30–8.30pm & Sun 9.30am–2.30pm.

Museo de Artes Decorativas Sun 10am–2pm.

Museo Cerralbo Sun 10am–2pm & Wed 9.30am–2.30pm.

Museo del Ejército Sat 10am–2pm.

Museo del Ferrocarril Sat 10am–3pm.

Museo Lázaro Galdiano Sat 10am–2pm.

Museo Municipal Sun 10am–2pm & Wed 9.30am–8pm.

Museo del Prado Sat 2.30–7pm & Sun 9am–2pm.

Museo Romántico Sun 10am–2pm.

Museo de San Isidro Tues–Fri 9.30am–8pm, Sat & Sun 10am–2pm; August Tues–Sat 9.30am–2.30pm, Sat & Sun 10am–2pm.

Real Academia de Bellas Artes Sat & Sun 9am–2.30pm.

Templo de Debod Wed April–Sept 10am–2pm & 6–8pm, Oct–March 9.45am–1.45pm & 4.15–6.15pm; Sun 10am–2pm.

EL CAMPO DEL MORO
AND THE PUENTE DE SEGOVIA

Map 2, B5–6. Metro Príncipe Pío.

North of the Jardines de Sabatini, the Cuesta San Vicente leads past the partly restored **Estación del Norte** and the modern replica of the eighteenth-century Puerta de San Vicente to the **Campo del Moro** (April–Sept Mon–Sat 10am–8pm, Sun 9am–8pm; Oct–March Mon–Sat 10am–6pm, Sun 9am–6pm; occasionally closed for state visits; entrance on Paseo de la Virgen del Puerto). One of the most underused and beautiful of Madrid's parks, it was the site of the Moors' encampment, from where, in 1109, they mounted their unsuccessful attempt to reconquer Madrid and the Alcázar. It later became a venue for medieval tournaments and celebrations. After the building of the Palacio Real plenty of plans to landscape the area were put forward, but it wasn't until 1842 that Pascual y Colomer got things under way. Based around two monumental fountains, *Las Conchas* and *Los Tritones,* the grassy gardens are very English in style, featuring shady paths and ornamental pools, and provide an excellent refuge from the summer heat, as well as a splendid view of the palace.

The Campo del Moro first opened to the public during the Second Republic in 1931, but was closed under Franco and not reopened until 1983.

A short walk south along Paseo de la Virgen del Puerto is the early eighteenth-century **Ermita de la Virgen del Puerto**, Pedro de Ribera's Baroque-style fairytale chapel with its original octagonal slate cupola. Set in grounds right beside the River Manzanares, the Ermita stands alongside the oldest bridge in Madrid, the **Puente de Segovia**, designed by Juan de Herrera and completed in 1584. The bridge is an imposing structure, but the river below doesn't really match up. A French aristocrat once remarked, "with such a fine bridge, they really ought to get a river", while the German ambassador Rhebines called it the best river in Europe because it had the advantage of being "navigable by horse and carriage".

PLAZA DE ORIENTE AND BEYOND

Map 3, C5–D5. Metro Ópera.

Since the completion of a major pedestrianization project, entailing the diversion of the busy c/Bailén beneath the square, the aristocratic **Plaza de Oriente** has become one of the most pleasant open spaces in Madrid. The days when Franco used to address crowds here from the balcony of the royal palace now seem a distant memory, although a small number of neo-Fascists still gather here on the anniversary of his death on November 21. The showpiece **fountain** in the centre was designed by Narciso Pascual y Colomer, who also transferred the bronze equestrian statue of Felipe IV here from the garden of the Buen Retiro Palace near the Prado. Pietro de Tacca's statue, which was based on designs by Velázquez, is reputedly the first ever bronze featuring a rearing horse. Galileo is said to have helped with the calculations to make it balance. Other **statues** depict Spanish kings and queens, and were originally designed to adorn the palace facade, but were too heavy or, according to one version, were removed on the orders of Queen Isabel of Farnese, second wife of Felipe V, who dreamt they had fallen on her during an earthquake.

There is a very French feel to the buildings facing the Palacio Real, with their glass-fronted *terrazas* and decorated balconies, underlined by the elegant neo-Baroque **Café de Oriente**, whose summer *terraza* is one of the stations of

Madrid nightlife. The café looks as traditional as any in the city, but was in fact opened in the 1980s by a priest, Padre Lezama, who ploughs his profits into various charitable schemes.

The bulky, rather squat **Teatro Real** (map 3, D5; open for visits Tues–Sun & holidays 10.30am–1.30pm; €3; tickets on sale from 10am at the box office) straddles the area between Plaza de Oriente and Plaza de Santa Isabel. Designed by Antonio López Aguado and opened in 1850, it was the hub of fashionable Madrid and staged highly successful operas by Verdi and Wagner. Plagued by municipal wrangling and pure incompetence, the opera house was finally reopened in October 1997 after a ten-year refurbishment that should have lasted four and which ended up costing a mind-boggling $150 million.

For more information on opera in Madrid see p.214.

Calle de Arenal

Map 3, F6–I7. Metro Ópera/Sol.

C/Arenal, stretching from the Teatro Real to Puerta del Sol, was once a stream which frequently dried up to leave a sandy channel (*arena* means "sand"). Today it's lined with shops, but does contain a few, easily missed sights. The Palacio de Gaviria (no. 9) was originally an ornate palace constructed in 1851 by the Marquis of Gaviria, and now houses a disco, nightclub, dance school and cocktail bar all rolled into one. Further along, the *Joy Madrid* disco occupies the site of the former Teatro Eslava, established in 1872 to provide popular light entertainment. Behind it, the **Chocolatería San Ginés**, a Madrid institution, which at one time catered for the early-rising worker, now churns out *churros* and hot chocolate for the late nightclub crowd

PLAZA DE ORIENTE AND BEYOND

(see box p.202). Nearby stands the ancient church of **San Ginés** (Fri–Sun 7–10pm), one of the original ten parishes included in the 1202 Madrid charter, which granted Madrid its own *fueros* – legally established privileges – and divided the city into parishes. The neighbouring seventeenth-century **Capilla de Cristo** (daily during services 9am–1pm & 6–9pm, but opening hours are unpredictable; entrance in c/Bordadores) contains an El Greco canvas showing the moneychangers being chased from the temple.

CONVENTO DE LA ENCARNACIÓN

Map 3, D5. Compulsory tours (some in English) Tues, Wed, Thurs & Sat 10.30am–12.45pm & 4–5.45pm, Fri 10.30am–12.45pm, Sun 11am–1.45pm; €3.46, concessions €1.80; joint ticket with Monasterio de las Descalzas €6/€3.31, valid for a week; Wed free for EU citizens. Metro Ópera.

North of Plaza de Oriente, the **Convento de la Encarnación** is worth a visit for its reliquary alone – one of the most important in the Catholic world. Founded in 1611 by Felipe III and his wife Margarita de Austria, the convent was intended as a retreat for titled women. The solemn granite facade is the hallmark of architect Juan Gómez de Mora and was modelled on the Iglesia de San José de Ávila, built by his uncle, Francisco de Mora. Much of the painting contained within is uninspiring artistically, but there are some interesting items, including an extensive collection of royal portraits and a highly prized collection of sculptures of Christ, with an extremely gory post-crucifixion one by Gregorio Fernández. The library-like **reliquary** is lined with a cupboard full of more than 1500 sixteenth-to eighteenth-century saintly relics from around the world: skulls, arms encased in beautiful ornate hand shaped containers, and bones from every conceivable part of the body.

The most famous relic of all is a small glass bulb said to contain the blood of St Pantaleón, a fourth-century doctor martyr whose blood supposedly liquefies at midnight on the eve of his feast day (26 July). Great tragedies are supposed to occur if the tour fails to liquefy, and it's said that the miracle didn't happen during the two world wars or the Spanish Civil War. The tour ends with a visit to the Baroque-style church which features a beautifully frescoed ceiling by Bayeu and the González Velázquez brothers, depicting scenes from the life of the monastery's patron, St Augustine, and a jasper- and marble-columned altarpiece.

Note that visitors with rucksacks and large bags are not allowed into the Convento de la Encarnación or the Monasterios de las Descalzas, and there's nowhere to leave them.

MONASTERIO DE LAS DESCALZAS REALES

Map 3, H6. Compulsory tours (some in English) Tues–Thurs & Sat 10.30am–12.45pm & 4–5.45pm, Fri 10.30am–12.45pm, Sun & holidays 11am–1.45pm, closed Easter; €4.81, concessions €2.40; joint ticket with Convento de la Encarnación, €6/€3.31, valid for a week; Wed free for EU citizens. Metro Ópera/Sol.

Just north of c/Arenal in Plaza de las Descalzas, behind an unobtrusive wooden door, stands one of the hidden treasures of Madrid, the **Monasterio de las Descalzas Reales** (Monastery of the Barefoot Royal Ladies). Originally the site of a medieval palace, then the residence of Emperor Carlos V's royal treasurer, Alonso Gutiérrez, the building was transformed by Juana de Austria, born here in 1535, into a convent in 1564, and the architect of El Escorial, Juan Bautista de Toledo, was entrusted with its design. Juana was the youngest daughter of the Emperor

Carlos V, sister of Felipe II, and already, at the age of 19, the widow of Prince Don Juan of Portugal. The original nuns were from Gandía, near Valencia, but were later joined by a succession of titled ladies, who, not wanting to leave behind all evidence of earthly delights, brought with them a whole array of artistic treasures. As a result, the *monasterio* accumulated a fabulous collection of paintings, sculptures and tapestries. The place is unbelievably opulent and is still in use as a convent, housing 23 shoeless nuns of the Franciscan order. Unfortunately, the quality of the guides is variable, with some intent on doing the tour at record speed, so you'll have to do your best to slow them down if you want a chance to properly admire the monastery's treasures.

The **main staircase**, connecting a two-levelled cloister lined with small but richly embellished chapels, is truly magnificent, with floor-to-ceiling frescoes painted at the end of the seventeenth century by José Ximénez Donoso and Claudio Coello. Felipe IV and his family are pictured gazing down at visitors from a balcony at the very top.

The **Coro** (Choir) contains the tomb of Empress María of Austria, sister of Felipe II and Juana, who had fifteen children and later died in the convent. Juana de Austria herself is also buried here. Look out for the moving sculpture of the *Doloroso*, with its incredibly realistic tears and misty eyes. There is also a waist-high chapel built especially for the children of the ladies. One of the most outstanding features of the monastery is the **Tapestry Room**, containing a magnificent collection of early seventeenth-century Flemish tapestries based on designs by Rubens – now in the Prado – and representing the Triumph of the Eucharist. A mass of royal portraits and beautiful, painted wooden sculptures, most of which are of unknown origin, decorate other rooms. Keep an eye out for the little spiked slippers worn by the nuns to mutilate their feet; for the works by Rubens,

Brueghel the Elder and Titian; and for a marvellous painting by an artist of the Bosch school, *Ship of Salvation*, full of devilish mutant figures. On your way out you pass screened windows hiding the orchard and gardens still tended by the nuns.

MONASTERIO DE LAS DESCALZAS REALES

The Rastro, Lavapiés and Embajadores

The areas south of Plaza Mayor have traditionally been tough, working-class districts, with tenement buildings thrown up to accommodate the huge expansion of the population in the eighteenth and nineteenth centuries. In many places these old houses survive, huddled together in narrow streets, and the city's early industrial and commercial centre, now known as the **Rastro**, was concentrated here, its inhabitants known as **castizos** – authentic *Madrileños* – and renowned for their sharp wit and fierce pride.

The character of these areas has changed in recent years as the inhabitants become younger and the districts more fashionable. **Lavapiés** and **Embajadores**, built on land sloping down towards the River Manzanares, were traditionally the *barrios bajos* (lower districts) and developed their own identity. The former is now Madrid's most **racially-mixed** *barrio*, with Chinese, North African and Asian

Most of the area covered by this chapter
is shown in detail on colour map 4.

communities bringing teahouses, kebab joints and textile shops to the area, along with some of the best-value and most original **bars and restaurants** in the city. Petty crime has been a problem but the reality is not nearly as dramatic as the papers would suggest. More noteworthy is an ongoing rehabilitation scheme which will no doubt lead to higher prices and another change in the *barrio*'s identity.

CASTIZO

The word castizo is used to signify anything authentically *Madrileño*, and bears many similarities to the Cockney tradition in London, with the inhabitants of the *barrios* of Lavapiés and La Latina, as well as Chamberí, all laying claim to the label. Community life in these working-class districts was based around corrales (balconied tenement blocks with a central courtyard), and it was here that the strong sense of *castizo* identity began to develop. Quick-witted, sarcastic, sharp dressers, intensely proud, and often described as being *chulo* or "cocky", the *castizos* were immortalized in many of Goya's paintings and are celebrated in Zarzuelas, Madrid's own form of operetta (see box on p.54). Today, their traditional dress of black-and-white-checked caps, waistcoats and black trousers for the men, embroidered dresses, petticoats, shawls and headscarfs plus red carnation for the women, is most likely to be seen during the festivals of San Isidro, the summer *verbenas* of San Cayetano, San Lorenzo and La Paloma or at the *zarzuela*. Also associated with the *castizos* is the chotis, a sort of upbeat Wild-West saloon type of music played on a barrel organ and said to be descended from the Scottish jig.

THE RASTRO

Map 4, C5. Metro La Latina/Puerta de Toledo.

The best starting point for an exploration of the **Rastro** is the church of San Isidro on c/Toledo (see p.33). From here take the signposted route down c/Estudios to Plaza de Cascorro where the main thoroughfare **c/Ribera de Curtidores** begins. This area was formerly the site of two large slaughterhouses and the resulting blood that flowed down the hill gave the area its name (*rastro* means stain). The establishment of the slaughterhouses acted as a magnet for other traders and craftsmen: tanners, after whom Ribera de Curtidores is named, leather workers and food sellers all soon set up in the area. These days, c/Ribera de Curtidores is lined with furniture shops, antique dealers (some extremely upmarket) and outdoor pursuits equipment suppliers, but the best day to visit is Sunday, when it's taken over by Madrid's most famous market, **El Rastro** (see box opposite).

At the southern end of Ribera de Curtidores on your right, you'll see a large arch, the **Puerta de Toledo**, an eloquent testament to the political vicissitudes that Madrid endured in the nineteenth century. Originally commissioned by Joseph Bonaparte to commemorate his accession to the Spanish throne, the arch ended up being a celebration of his defeat when it was completed in 1827.

Just in front of the arch, the **Mercado Puerta de Toledo** (map 4, A6), once the city's fish market, has pretensions to being a stylish arts, crafts and antiques centre, but in fact much of it remains empty, apart from an under-used tourist office. Below, past the lines of anonymous apartment blocks, lies the **Puente de Toledo**, a pedestrian bridge designed by Pedro de Ribera for Felipe V and built between 1718 and 1732. The arched construction spanning the rather sad-looking River Manzanares and the hopelessly

THE RASTRO

THE FLEA MARKET

Madrid's flea market, El Rastro, is as much part of the city's weekend ritual as Mass or a *paseo*. This gargantuan, thriving shambles of a street market sprawls south from Metro La Latina along Ribera de Curtidores to the Ronda de Toledo. Crowds flood through the market between 10am and 3pm every Sunday and increasingly on Friday, Saturday and public holidays too. On offer is just about anything you can imagine, from Taiwanese radios and T-shirts to canaries and coke spoons, though the serious antique trade has now mostly moved off the streets and into the adjacent shops, and the real junk is found only on the fringes. The atmosphere is always enjoyable and the bars around these streets are as good as any in the city.

One warning, however: keep a tight grip on your bags, cameras (best left at the hotel) and jewellery. The Rastro rings up a fair percentage of Madrid's tourist thefts.

congested M30 ring road can still be crossed to reach the summer *terraza* on the other side. As you cross, on your right you'll see the M30 disappearing underneath the main stand of the huge **Vicente Calderón** football stadium, home to Atlético Madrid.

LAVAPIÉS AND EMBAJADORES

Lavapiés and **Embajadores** stretch south and east from Plaza Tirso de Molina (Metro Tirso de Molina). Just to the south of the plaza at c/San Pedro Mártir 5 is the house where the young Pablo Picasso stayed during his visits to Madrid when painting *Woman in Blue* (now hanging in the Reina Sofía, p.97). From here, follow colourful and cosmopolitan **c/Mesón de Paredes**, stopping for a drink at the darkly panelled *Taberna Antonio Sánchez* at no. 13, which dates back to 1830. Now owned by an ex-*torero* (bullfighter), it's decked out with two bull's heads and numerous taurine paintings.

Halfway down c/Mesón de Paredes is **La Corrala** (map 4, E5), built in 1839 and restored in the 1980s, one of many traditional *corrales* (tenement blocks) in the quarter, with balconied apartments opening onto a central patio. The cramped housing means that much of the drama of everyday life is played out on the balconies or in the courtyard below – neighbours conducting long-distance conversations with each other, children crying, dogs barking, old men arguing over the football. The ruined building alongside was a church and religious school, destroyed in the Civil War and left as a monument, although it has now been decided to turn it into a municipal library. Plays, especially farces and **zarzuelas**, used to be performed regularly

THE ZARZUELA

Madrid is the birthplace of the zarzuela, Spain's very own brand of opera, incorporating features of classical opera, as well as the more bawdy elements of music hall. The name originates from the royal palace and hunting lodge just to the north of Madrid where entertainments were laid on for Felipe IV. The *zarzuela* developed in the early nineteenth century and is usually centred on a local community, with small-time protagonists, minor romances and soap-opera type plots. The most famous work is *La Revoltosa* ("The Rebellious Daughter") by Ruperto Chapí which tells the story of a young girl who refuses to desert her true love to marry for money. The season runs throughout the summer (June–Sept), with performances taking place at several venues in the city (see p.215 for details).

in Spanish *corrales*, and the open space here usually hosts a number of performances in the summer as part of the Veranos de la Villa cultural programme (see "Festivals", p.232). Some of the audience come dressed up in traditional *castizo* costume (see box on p.51) and sit, eating, drinking and chatting at the tables set up in the courtyard here.

Running parallel and to the west of Mesón de Paredes is **c/Embajadores**, one of the oldest streets in Madrid, brimming with traditional traders, shops and markets. The name of the street originated in the fifteenth century, when a number of ambassadors fled to the area in order to escape an outbreak of the plague in the city centre. The elaborately sculpted and ornamented church of **San Cayetano** (map 4, C4), patron of one the area's most important festivals in August, dominates the upper part of the street. José de Churriguera and Pedro de Ribera, both renowned for their extravagant designs, were involved in the design of the facade, constructed in 1761. Most of the rest of the church was destroyed in the Civil War and has since been reconstructed. The remainder of the street is a jumble of traditional shops, many with tiled frontages, and dilapidated dwellings, while at the bottom is the oldest **tobacco factory** (map 4, E6–7) in Europe. Originally built as a distillery, but modified to produce tobacco in 1809, its austere, unornamented facade is a classic example of early nineteenth-century industrial architecture. Its workforce was overwhelmingly female and constituted, by the end of the century, about twenty percent of Madrid's working population. The flamboyant *cigarreras*, as they were called, were renowned for their independence, solidarity and strength. They bargained with the management to achieve the establishment of special schools, crèches and better working conditions.

Just east of here, along c/Miguel Servet, you'll reach **Plaza Lavapiés** (map 4, E4–F5). This district was the core of the **Jewish quarter** in medieval Madrid, with the synagogue situated on the site now occupied by the Teatro Olimpia. In 1492, the Jews were given the choice of expulsion or conversion to Christianity by the fanatically Catholic Spanish monarchs; those that converted took Christian names, traditionally using Manuel for the eldest son, which led to the area being dubbed "*El Barrio de los Manolos*". Meanwhile, the converted Muslims (*Moriscos*) tended to congregate around c/Ave María. With its Chinese, Arabic and African inhabitants, Lavapiés remains a cosmopolitan place to this day, and the plaza is an animated spot, with a variety of bars and cafés in various states of decay. There are *terrazas* and more bars along the cool, tree-lined c/Argumosa, which leads out to Atocha and the Centro de Arte Reina Sofía (see p.95).

Calle de Atocha

Map 4, E1–I4. Metro Tirso de Molina/Atocha.

Lavapiés is bounded to the northeast by **Calle de Atocha**, one of the old ceremonial routes from Plaza Mayor to the *basílica* at Atocha. At its southern end it's a mishmash of fast-food and touristy restaurants, developing, as you move north up the hill, into a perverse mixture of cheap hostels, fading shops, bars, lottery kiosks and sex emporia. The huge sex shop, El Mundo Fantástico, at no. 80, with its brash neon lighting and shiny black facade, stands unashamedly opposite a convent and the site of an old printing house that produced the first edition of the first part of *Don Quixote*. Further up, just before Plaza Antón Martín, you pass Pasaje Doré, a narrow alley on the left, bordered by an indoor market crammed with miniature stores. At the end is the **Cine Doré** (map 4, F2), the oldest cinema in Madrid, dating from 1922 with a later *modernista*/Art Nouveau facade. It's been converted into the

Filmoteca Nacional, an art-house cinema with bargain prices and a pleasant, inexpensive café/restaurant (Tues–Sun 1.30pm–12.30am).

For more information on Madrid's cinemas see p.228.

Back on c/Atocha, **Plaza Antón Martín** (map 4, F2) is named after the founder of a sixteenth-century hospital for venereal diseases, once situated here, and now the site of the Teatro Monumental, where Prokofiev premiered his second violin concerto in 1935. Around the plaza are a variety of great-value bars, cafés and flamenco joints, including *Casa Patas* in c/Cañizares (see p.218).

Further up the road opposite Plaza Jacinto Benavente and behind a suitably anonymous door at c/Doctor Cortezo no. 2 is the **Museo Erotico de Madrid** (map 4, D1; Mon–Thurs & Sun 11am-11pm, Fri & Sat 11am-midnight; €5.11; ⓦwww.museoerotico.com; Metro Tirso de Molina). The hefty entry fee means that thrills certainly don't come cheap in this X-rated museum, and in any case you would need to be a serious fanatic of sex-related paraphernalia to get your money's worth.

LAVAPIÉS AND EMBAJADORES

Sol, Santa Ana and Huertas

The **Puerta del Sol** marks the western tip of the **Santa Ana/Huertas** area, into which Madrid expanded in the 1560s during Spain's golden age. A triangle bordered to the east by the Paseo del Prado, to the north by c/Alcalá, and along the south by c/Atocha, this *barrio de las letras* (literary neighbourhood) was home to many of the great Spanish authors and playwrights, including Lope de Vega, Cervantes and Góngora. Theatres, bookshops and literary cafés proliferate and the *barrio* also contains the **Ateneo** (literary, scientific and political club), **Círculo de Bellas Artes** (Fine Arts Institute), **Teatro Nacional** and the **Congreso de los Diputados** (Parliament). Just to the north, there is also an important museum and art gallery, the **Real Academia de Bellas Artes de San Fernando**. For most visitors, though, the major attraction of the district is its beautiful **bars** and *tascas* (tavern-type bars) – some of the best in the city – particularly concentrated around the picturesque **Plaza de Santa Ana**.

The area covered by this chapter is
shown in detail on colour map 5.

PUERTA DEL SOL

Map 5, A3–B3. Metro Sol.

The best place to start exploring this part of Madrid – and
many other areas of the centre – is the **Puerta del Sol**
(Gateway of the Sun). This square marks the epicentre of
the city – and, indeed, of Spain, as it's from here that all dis-
tances in the country are measured. On the pavement outside the clock-tower building on the south side of the
square, a stone slab shows Kilometre Zero. In front of the
department store El Corte Inglés stands a statue of the
city's emblem, the bear and *madroño* (arbutus or straw-
berry) tree, and an equestrian bronze of King Carlos III.
For most *Madrileños*, however, the square's most renowned
landmarks are the Tío Pepe sherry sign perched above the
buildings to the east and the sweet-smelling Mallorquina
cake shop, just outside the metro station entrance to the
west.

Puerta del Sol's most important building, the **Casa de
Correos** (map 5, A4), was built in 1766 by Jaime Marquet
and served as the city's post office until 1847, when it
became home to the Ministry of the Interior and later the
headquarters of the much-feared security police under
Franco. It now houses the main offices of the Madrid
regional government, the Comunidad de Madrid. The
Neoclassical building is crowned by the nation's most
famous **clock** which officially ushers in the **New Year**: on
New Year's eve, *Madrileños* pack into the square below and
attempt to scoff twelve grapes, one on each of the chimes
of midnight to bring themselves good luck for the

succeeding twelve months. There was a national outcry some years back when the chimes were mistimed so that the majority of Spain was left holding its grapes.

The square has been a popular **meeting place** since the mid-sixteenth century, when the steps of the former monastery San Felipe (on the site now occupied by *McDonald's*) acted as one of the officially recognized *mentideros* or gossip mills. Citizens came here to catch up on all the latest news and scandals. Later, the square was the site of the *Café Pombo*, where regular *tertulias* (see box on p.188) were held in the 1920s.

A typical *tertulia* session is portrayed in José Gutiérrez Solana's famous painting *La Tertulia del Café Pombo*, now hanging in the Reina Sofía (see p.97).

The square has also witnessed several events of national importance. On May 2, 1808, troops of Napoleon's marshal, Murat, aided by the infamous Egyptian cavalry (the "Mamelukes"), cold-bloodedly slaughtered a rioting crowd, an event depicted in Goya's canvas *Dos de Mayo*, now hanging in the Prado. Just off Puerta del Sol, in c/Carretas, the liberal prime minister of Spain, José Canalejas, was assassinated in 1912 while browsing in a bookshop. The communist Julián Grimau also met his end here in 1963 in even more sinister fashion: he was thrown out of a window of the Casa de Correos and later finished off by a firing squad. Just north of the plaza, on c/Tetuán, is *Casa Labra*, famous for its tapas of fried *bacalao* (cod) and where the Spanish Socialist Party, the PSOE, was founded in 1879 (see p.159).

The road leading from the southeast corner of Puerta del Sol is **Carrera de San Jerónimo** (map 5, B3–E4), a route laid out in 1538 to provide access to the San Jerónimo Monastery. Although now a rather anonymous street, it does contain the marvellous **Lhardy** restaurant and shop, founded by Frenchman Emilio Lhardy in 1839. Entering the shop you take a step back into the nineteenth century – the shelves are packed with ancient preserves, patés and soups; crystal decanters and glasses grace silver salvers; and customers are greeted by impeccably mannered ancient staff dressed in aprons. Help yourself to the consommé from the giant silver urn, select a savoury cake or vol au vent from the octagonal glass display case and pay at the till on your way out. The restaurant upstairs is famous for its *cocido madrileño* (meat and chickpea stew), but is only for those with large wallets.

PLAZA SANTA ANA

Map 5, C5. Metro Sol.

Recently renovated, **Plaza Santa Ana** was one of the series of squares created by Joseph Bonaparte, whose passion for open spaces led to a remarkable remodelling of Madrid in the six short years of his reign. The plaza is dominated by two distinguished buildings at either end: to the west, the *Reina Victoria*, a giant cream cake of a hotel which looks as though it would be more at home in Nice or Cannes, and to the east, the nineteenth-century Neoclassical **Teatro Español** (map 5, D5). The theatre, the facade of which is decorated with busts of famous Spanish playwrights, is the oldest in Madrid and there has been a playhouse on the site since 1583. The main reason for visiting the area, however, is to explore the mass of **bars**, **restaurants** and **cafés** on the square itself and in the nearby streets.

Plaza Santa Ana lies southeast of Puerta del Sol;
head along c/San Jerónimo and take any of the streets off
to the right. Places to eat and drink in the plaza are
reviewed on pp.160–161 and 182–187.

HUERTAS

The **Huertas** area, east of Plaza Santa Ana, has a highly schizophrenic identity. By day, it's rather dull and sleepy with doors closed, windows shuttered and the odd stray cat roaming the empty streets, but at night, the buildings metamorphose into an astounding variety of **bars** – cocktail, classical, jazz, karaoke, disco – and the place is a hive of activity, with people thronging the streets and car horns hooting until 2 or 3am. Plans to pedestrianize the street are likely to make it an even more attractive night-time destination. North of c/Huertas, and parallel to it, are two streets named after the greatest figures of Spain's seventeenth-century literary golden age, **Cervantes** and **Lope de Vega**. Bitter rivals in life, both are probably spinning in their graves now, since Cervantes is interred in the Convento de las Trinitarias on the street named after Lope de Vega, while the latter's house finds itself at c/Cervantes 11 (see below). Two sites that have played a significant role in the political history of the city are also to be found in this area. The **Ateneo** was the focus of political debate and discussion in the early nineteenth century, while the **Congreso de los Diputados** was the scene of the most dramatic event in recent political history: the Tejero Coup attempt (see p.64).

Casa de Lope de Vega

Map 5, E5. Tues–Fri 9.30am–2pm, Sat 10am–2pm; €1.50, concessions €0.90, Sat free. Closed mid-July to mid-Aug. Knock if the door is closed. Metro Antón Martín.

The reconstructed home of the great golden age Spanish dramatist merits a visit if only for what it shows of life in seventeenth-century Madrid. **Lope de Vega** lived here for 25 years until his death in 1635 at the age of 48. He was a prolific writer and had a tangled private life. His first wife died in childbirth, his second also died and he had five children with his actress mistress. His ordination as a priest in 1614 did not diminish his appetite for romantic liaisons, and one of his mistresses moved into the house after the death of her husband. Gradually turning blind and then insane, she remained here, cared for by the playwright, until her death in 1632. The house itself has been furnished in authentic fashion using the inventory left at the writer's death. A number of family possessions have survived, preserved by Lope de Vega's daughter, who became a nun at the nearby Convento de las Trinitarias. Other pieces of period furniture in the house are from the Prado and other museums. The highlights include a chapel containing some of Lope de Vega's original relics, the writer's study with a selection of contemporary books, and an Arabic-style harem complete with silk cushions and a *brasero* (an open pan in which hot coals were placed to warm the room). The garden, with its orange tree, vine, well and courtyard, has been replanted and designed according to references found in the writer's correspondence.

Cervantes lived and died at no. 2 on the street that now bears his name, up the hill from Lope de Vega's house. The original building has long gone and all that remains is a plaque above the shop that occupies the site.

Ateneo Artístico, Científico y Literario

Map 5, D4. Mon–Sat 9am–12.45am, Sun & public holidays 9am–9.45pm. Metro Sevilla.

The **Ateneo** (literary, scientific and political club), c/Prado 21, was founded after the 1820 Revolution and provided a home for some of the new liberal political ideas circulating at that time. It was accordingly closed down by the myopically conservative Fernando VII, who had been reinstalled on the throne on his return from exile after the French occupation. However, it reopened after his death on its present site in 1835, once again establishing itself as one of the focuses of cultural and political life in nineteenth-century Madrid. The exterior is Neoplateresque in style, while the inside (currently being restored) features a neo-Greek lecture theatre, a wooden panelled corridor with portraits of past presidents of the club and a splendid reading room, with individual desks, lights and green leather writing boards. There's also a good-value cafeteria.

El Congreso de los Diputados

Map 5, E4. Sat 10.30am–1pm. Closed Aug & public holidays.
Metro Sevilla.

A short stroll down c/Prado from the Ateneo to Plaza de las Cortes, takes you past an unprepossessing nineteenth-century building where **El Congreso de los Diputados** (the lower house of the Spanish parliament) meets. Sessions can be visited by appointment only, though anyone can turn up (with a passport) and queue for a tour on Saturday mornings – this takes in several of the most important rooms and the chamber itself where the bullet holes left by mad Colonel Tejero and his Guardia Civil associates in the abortive coup attempt of 1981 are pointed out (see "Contexts", p.330).

CALLE DE ALCALÁ AND PLAZA DE LA CIBELES

Calle de Alcalá, the original road to the Roman university town of Alcalá de Henares, runs west–east from Puerta del Sol to Plaza de la Cibeles, at the junction with Paseo del Prado, and on past the Retiro park. Lined with gargantuan buildings, its architectural highlights include the colonnaded Neoclassical **Banco Central Hispano** designed by Antonio Palacios and Joaquín Otamendi in 1910, the more severe **Banco del Comercio** and the **Ministry of Education and Culture**. The red-brick **Iglesia de San José**, near the junction with Gran Vía, dates back to the 1730s and was the last building designed by the prolific Pedro de Ribera. Inside is the splendidly ornate Baroque Capilla de Santa Teresa de Ávila, and an impressive collection of colourful images of Christ and the Virgin Mary.

South American independence hero Simón de Bolívar
got married in San José church in 1802.

Heading past the elegant cylindrical facade of the **Edificio Metrópolis** (map 5, E2) you come to the pastel-pink **Iglesia de las Calatravas** (map 5, D2; Mon–Fri 8am–1pm & 6–8pm, Sat & Sun 11am–1pm & 6–8pm; free), a seventeenth-century church built for the nuns of the Calatrava, one of the four Spanish military orders, and containing a fantastically elaborate gold altarpiece by José Churriguera. Look out for the splendid early- twentieth-century wedge-shaped **Banco Español de Crédito**, adorned with elephant heads and plaques listing all the branches of the bank in Spain; the **Banco de Bilbao Vizcaya**, with its Neoclassical concave facade complete with charioteers on top; and the classic Baroque **Ministerio de Hacienda** (Inland Revenue). Yet more delights await with the **Casino de Madrid**, constructed according to the design of Luis Esteve after an international competition in 1903, organized by the business and intellectual elite who wanted a more upmarket setting for their meetings. It has a suitably opulent central staircase and main salon – ask the doorman if you can have a look.

CALLE DE ALCALÁ AND PLAZA DE LA CIBELES

Museo de la Real Academia de Bellas Artes de San Fernando

Map 5, C2. Tues–Fri 9am–7pm, Mon, Sat, Sun & public holidays 9am–2.30pm; €2.40, concessions €1.20, free Wed. Free guided visits 5pm on Wed, Oct–June. ⓦrabasf.insde.es. Metro Sevilla.

Two hundred metres east of Puerta del Sol, art buffs should head for the **Real Academia de Bellas Artes de San Fernando**, c/Alcalá 13. One of the most important art galleries in Spain, it has sections dealing with sculpture, architecture and music, and its extraordinary, but chaotically-displayed collection of **Spanish painting** includes work by El Greco, José de Ribera, Velázquez, Murillo, Zurbarán, Goya, Sorolla and Picasso, as well as interesting French and Italian work. The Real Academia was set up by Felipe V at the request of his state secretary and his court sculptor, with the present building being acquired in 1773. The Goya section includes, among other gems, two revealing self-portraits, several depictions of the despised royal favourite *Don Manuel Godoy*, the desolate representation of *The Madhouse* and *The Burial of the Sardine* (a popular procession that continues to this day in Madrid, see p.233).

The museum's collection contains a self-portrait of Goya's brother-in-law, Francisco Bayeu, who, as court painter to Carlos III and a member of the Real Academia, gave his relation a helping hand in his early career.

Look out, too, for the bizarre *Spring* by Giuseppe Arcimboldo, López Enguidanos's curious *Family of Skeletons* and the penetrating, rather haunting, portrait of *Haile Selassie* by Delgado. There are some supremely ugly royal portraits such as De la Calleja's *Carlos III*, and a variety of interesting sculptures scattered throughout the museum, including a brutally graphic set that comprises the *Massacre of the Innocents* by eighteenth-century sculptor José Ginés. The gallery is also home to the national chalcography collection (Mon–Fri 10am–2pm, Sat 10am–1.30pm; free), which includes some Goya etchings and a selection of the copper plates used for his *Capricho* series now on show in the Prado.

Círculo de Bellas Artes

Map 5, E2. Café daily 8am–2am; exhibitions Tues–Fri 5–9pm, Sat 11am–2pm & 5–9pm, Sun 11am–2pm; €1. Metro Banco España.

As c/Alcalá descends towards Plaza de la Cibeles, you pass, on the right, the **Círculo de Bellas Artes** at c/Marqués de Casa Riera 2, a strange-looking 1920s Art Deco building designed by Antonio Palacios and crowned by a statue of Pallas Athene. This is probably Madrid's best arts centre, and includes a theatre, music hall, exhibition galleries, cinema and a very pleasant café – all marble and leather decor, with a nude statue reclining in the middle of the floor. For many years a stronghold of Spanish culture, it attracts the city's arts and media crowd, but it's not in the least exclusive, nor expensive, and there's an adjoining *terraza*, too. The Círculo is theoretically a members-only club, but it issues day membership on the door, for which you get access to all areas. Pick up the centre's *Minerva* magazine to find out what's on or ask the helpful staff.

PLAZA DE LA CIBELES

Map 5, G1. Metro Banco de España.

Encircled by four of the most monumental buildings in Madrid – the Palacio de Comunicaciones (the Post Office), Banco de España (the Central Bank), the Palacio de Buenavista (the Army HQ) and the Palacio de Linares (the Casa de América) – **Plaza de la Cibeles** is the most glorified roundabout in the city. Awash with a sea of traffic, the centre is dominated by a **fountain** and statue of the goddess Cibeles, riding in a chariot drawn by two lions, built in the late eighteenth century to commemorate the city's first public water supply. It survived the Civil War by being swaddled in sandbags, but was damaged in celebrations after one of the victories of the national football team in the 1994 World Cup. Fully repaired, it still hosts celebrations for victorious Real Madrid fans (Atlético supporters bathe in the fountain of Neptune just down the road).

- -

The fountain in Cibeles and the two other fountains gushing magnificently on the Paseo del Prado were all designed by Ventura Rodríguez, who has a metro station and street named after him for his efforts.

- -

The wedding cake building on the eastern side of the square is Madrid's main post office, the aptly named **Palacio de Comunicaciones** (map 5, H2). Constructed between 1904 and 1917, and designed by the prolific architect partnership of Antonio Palacios and Joaquín Otamendi, it is vastly more imposing than the parliament and runs the Palacio Real pretty close. A fabulous place, flanked by polished brass postboxes for each province, it preserves a totally Byzantine system within, with scores of counters each offering a particular service, from telegrams to string, and, until quite recently, scribes. To the rear of the building is a small museum (Mon–Fri 9am–2pm & 5–7pm, Sat 9am–2pm, free; entry on c/Montalbán) detailing the history of the postal service and communications. The **Casa de América** (Tues–Sat 11am–7pm, Sun 11am–2pm; Ⓦwww.casamerica.es) is used for concerts, films and exhibitions of Latin American art and has a good bookshop and fine café/restaurant.

The Museo del Prado

Map 5, H6. Tues–Sat 9am–7pm, Sun & hols 9am–2pm (July & Aug till 7pm); closed New Year's Day, Good Friday, May 1 and Christmas Day. €3.01, concessions €1.5; free Sat after 2.30pm & all day Sun. Ⓦmuseoprado.mcu.es. Metro Banco de España/Atocha.

The **Museo del Prado**, or the Prado, is Madrid's premier tourist attraction, and one of the oldest and greatest collections of art in the world. It houses all the finest works collected by Spanish royalty – for the most part avid, discerning and wealthy buyers – as well as Spanish paintings gathered from other sources over the past two centuries. The museum, however, is desperately short of space, with only about ten percent of its artistic holdings actually on permanent display (still a pretty daunting tally). A controversial plan is currently under way to modernize and extend the museum, adding three existing nearby buildings, which will enable the Prado to double the number of works on show (see box on p.71). The plan on p.73

outlines the positions of the major schools and collections, though it's worth bearing in mind that paintings are sometimes moved to accommodate temporary exhibitions; changes are detailed on the free maps available on your way in.

The museum's highlights are its Flemish collection – including almost all of **Bosch**'s best work – and its incomparable display of Spanish art, especially paintings by **Velázquez** (including *Las Meninas*), **Goya** (including the *Majas*) and **El Greco**. There's also a huge collection of Italian painters – **Titian**, notably – collected by Carlos V and Felipe II, both great patrons of the Renaissance, as well as a strong showing of later Flemish pictures collected by Felipe IV. Even in a full day you couldn't hope to do justice to everything here, and it's perhaps best to make a couple of focused visits. In summer and at weekends, the crowds can become oppressive, with the incursions of large tour groups; it's best to hang back and let them sweep by on their whirlwind progress.

There are two main **entrances** to the museum: the **Puerta de Goya**, which has an upper and a lower entrance opposite the *Hotel Ritz* on c/Felipe IV, and the **Puerta de Murillo** on Plaza de Murillo, opposite the Botanical Gardens, which often has shorter queues. The upper entrance of the Puerta de Goya takes you to the first floor, where the seventeenth-century Flemish and Dutch art gives way to the main Spanish collections, while the lower entrance is the one to take if you want to embark on a chronological tour. The Puerta de Murillo is a ground-floor entrance which steers you towards the classical sculpture and on to the Italian Renaissance galleries. Thankfully, there is no prescribed or obvious route, which helps ease congestion, and rooms are now numbered more clearly. Most paintings have informative captions explaining their history, but nearly all of these are only in Spanish.

THE MUSEO DEL PRADO

THE PRADO EXTENSION

With a mere tenth of the Prado's holdings crammed into the original eighteenth-century buildings, an extension to the museum has long been on the cards. After years of procrastination and internal wrangling, Navarran architect Rafael Moneo, who refurbished both the Estación de Atocha and the Museo Thyssen-Bornemisza, eventually won the competition to design the first stage of the plan. His controversial designs entail the construction of a glass-fronted cube on the three hectare site once occupied by the eighteenth-century cloisters of the church of San Jerónimo situated to the rear of the main museum building. The extension will be reached via an underground passage and include two new galleries housing temporary exhibitions, a library and reading room, a restoration centre and a café.

The plan caused an outcry from local residents who claimed "Moneo's cube" would destroy the architectural coherence of the zone and from conservationists concerned about the fate of the cloisters. Work has, however, already begun and the €42 million extension is due to be completed by 2004. In stage two of the extension plans the Prado is due to take over the buildings occupied by the nearby Museo del Ejército, which is to be relocated to Toledo, although this idea has also encountered stiff opposition. The Museo del Ejército buildings once formed part of Felipe IV's Palacio del Buen Retiro and the plan is to relocate Velázquez's equestrian portraits of the Habsburg monarchs and paintings such as *The Surrender at Breda* in the main *Salón de Reinos* (Throne Room) which is where they were originally designed to hang.

As well as the extension programme, the museum also aims to break with direct government control and boost its €25 million budget with funds from the private sector, a move it is hoped will secure the Prado's future well into the 21st century.

Illustrated **guides** and **catalogues** describing and explaining the paintings are on sale in the two museum **shops**, one on each floor. Particularly helpful is the Quick Visit Guide (€8.45), which explains the background to about fifty of the most important works. Useful colour booklets (€0.90) on Velázquez, Goya, El Greco, Titian and Bosch are also available in their respective galleries. The museum has a decent **café** and restaurant in the basement.

If you plan to visit all three art museums around the Paseo del Prado (the Prado, the Reina Sofía and the Thyssen-Bornemisza), it's worth buying the Paseo del Arte ticket (€7.66), on sale at all three. It's valid for a year and allows one visit to each museum.

SPANISH PAINTING

The Prado's collections of **Spanish painting**, not surprisingly the largest in the world, begin on the ground floor. Room 51c houses twelfth-century **Romanesque frescoes**, reconstructed from a pair of churches from the Mozarabic (Muslim rule) era in Soria and Segovia. In the rooms that follow, the remarkably well-preserved **early panel paintings** – exclusively religious fourteenth- and fifteenth-century works – include a huge *retablo* by Nicolás Francés, the anonymous *Virgin of the Catholic Monarchs*, Bermejo's ornate portrayal of *Santo Domingo de Silos*, Pedro Berruguete's *Auto-de-Fé* and depictions of the lives and tortuous deaths of a variety of saints.

The golden age

The Prado's collections from Spain's golden age – the late sixteenth and seventeenth centuries under Habsburg rule –

MUSEO DEL PRADO

N

Legend:
- Spanish painting
- Flemish, Dutch and German painting
- Italian painting
- French and British painting
- Classical and Renaissance sculpture
- Temporary exhibits

Second Floor

80
81
82
83
84
79
78
77
76

Drawing collection

First Floor

Goya's Cartoons

85
90
91
92
93
94
89
88
87
86

Goya

Goya drawing collection

Goya

19 20 21 22 23
32
34 35 36 37 38
39

Goya's Black Paintings

15a 16a 17a 18a
15 16 17 18
16b
14
29
28
27

Velázquez

12
11
10a 10b
10
9a 9b
9
8a 8b
8
7a 7b
7

Rubens

26
25
24

1

El Greco

Bosch

Giftshop

Cloakroom

Puerta alta de Goya

Ground Floor

Titian

64 65 66 67
74
72 73
71
70

Puerta de Murillo

To Basement, the Dauphin's Treasure & Cafetería

60a 61a 62a 63a
60 61 62 63
62b 63b
61b
60
59
75

Goya

Bookshop

Salón de actos

47

Puerta de Velázquez

54 55 55a 55b
56a 56 56b
57a 57 57b
58a 58
49

Giftshop

50
51c
51b
51

Cloakroom

Puerta baja de Goya

are prefigured, on the ground floor (rooms 60a, 61a and 62a), by a collection of paintings by **El Greco** (Domenikos Theotokopoulos, 1541–1614), the Cretan-born artist who worked in Toledo from the 1570s. You really need to see the collection of El Greco's works in Toledo to fully appreciate his extraordinary genius, but the portraits and religious works here are a good introduction. The development of his Mannerist style can be traced from the richly coloured, Italian-influenced *Trinity*, in which there is little sign of the distortions and exaggerations that characterize his later work, to the visionary *Adoration of the Shepherds*, painted 35 years later for his own burial chapel, with its ghostly elongated bodies and sombre oily colouring. His skills as a portrait painter are amply demonstrated in *The Nobleman with his Hand on his Chest*, where the depiction of the Mayor of Toledo with his pointed beard, austere black dress and stern expression has become an archetypal image of the sixteenth-century Spanish nobleman.

See p.288 for details on visiting the city of Toledo.

Nearby, in Room 63a, is a fine collection of imperious portraits of Felipe II's family by **Alonso Sánchez Coello** (1531–88), among them a portrait of *El Príncipe Don Carlos*, the half-mad son of Felipe II's first marriage who died mysteriously in prison in 1568.

Upstairs on the first floor (rooms 12, 14, 15, 15a and 16), you confront the greatest painter of Habsburg Spain, **Diego Velázquez** (1599–1660). Born in Seville, in 1623 he became court painter to Felipe IV, whose family is represented in many of the works. "I have found my Titian," Felipe is said to have remarked of the artist's appointment. Velázquez's masterpiece, **Las Meninas** (*The Maids of Honour*, 1656), is given pride of place in the large central gallery in Room 12.

SPANISH PAINTING

- -

Manet remarked of Velázquez's *Las Meninas*,
"After this I don't know why the rest of us paint";
the French poet Théophile Gautier asked, "But where
is the picture?" because it seemed to him a continuation
of the room; while the Italian painter, Luca Giordano,
identified it as "the Theology of Painting".

- -

The work captures a moment in the artist's study, featuring the artist himself, the Infanta Margarita, the court dwarves, ladies-in-waiting, a butler, the palace marshal watching from the stairs at the back, and Felipe IV and his wife Mariana of Austria standing in the viewer's footsteps and reflected in the mirror on the wall. Velázquez's superlative brushwork and his mastery of colour, light and perspective mark the painting out as one of the all-time great works of art.

The painter's other canvases also merit attention. With the aid of light and loose brush strokes in *Las Hilanderas* (The Tapestry-Weavers), Velázquez again plays with simultaneous action in the foreground and background, depicting the story of Minerva, the goddess of the arts, challenging Arachne to see who can weave the most beautiful tapestry. In the foreground, yarns are being prepared for the weaving of the tapestries, while in the background Minerva is preparing to turn Arachne into a spider for producing a work of superior quality to her own. Velázquez's portraits of Felipe IV are sympathetic and intimate representations of the monarch, with his childlike features and tired eyes, while that of the dwarf, *Don Sebastián de Morra*, focuses on his morose, pensive expression. Further magnificent works include *Christ Crucified*, with his bowed head and shimmering halo; *Los Borrachos* (The Drunkards), a clever corruption of which can be seen in *Los Gabrieles* bar (see p.183); *Vulcan's Forge* and *The*

SPANISH PAINTING

Surrender of Breda. In fact, almost all of the fifty works on display (around half of the artist's surviving output) warrant close attention. Note also the two small panels of the *Villa Medici*, painted in Rome in 1650, in virtually Impressionist style.

In the newly refurbished adjacent rooms are examples of just about every significant Spanish painter of the seventeenth century, including many of the finest works of **Francisco Zurbarán** (1598–1664), **Bartolomé Esteban Murillo** (1618–82), **Alonso Cano** (1601–67) and **Juan Carreño** (1614–85). Murillo's soft, vaporous, almost mystical style is seen to best effect in *The Immaculate Conception of Soult* and *The Good Shepherd*. Look out for Carreño's portrait, rendered with terrible realism, of the last Habsburg monarch, the mentally retarded *Carlos II*, a product of chronic inbreeding. The contemporary obsession for the bizarre is also amply illustrated in Carreño's pair of paintings of a grossly overweight six-year-old girl *La Monstrua Vestida* and *La Monstrua Desnuda* (Room 18), forming an interesting contrast with Goya's *Majas* displayed upstairs. Here, too, are the Prado's holdings of **José Ribera** (1591–1652), who worked firstly in Rome, where he was influenced by Caravaggio, and then in Naples, where local fishermen and beggars acted as models for many of his works. His masterpieces are considered to be the dark, realist portrait of *Saint Andrew* and *The Martyrdom of St Philip*, where the artist uses light and shade to dramatic effect, highlighting the naked body of Philip who is being prepared for his ordeal of being skinned alive.

Goya

The final suite of Spanish rooms (32–39 and 85–94) which spans the first and second floor at the Puerta de Murillo-end of the building, provides an awesome and fabulously complete overview of the works of **Francisco de Goya** (1746–1828), the largest and most valuable collection of his works in the world, with some 140 paintings and 500 drawings and engravings. Goya was the greatest painter of Bourbon Spain and a chronicler of contemporary Spanish life, an artist whom many see as the inspiration and fore-runner of Impressionism and modern art.

After an apprenticeship in Zaragoza, Goya studied in Italy in 1770–71, returning to Spain to draw cartoons for the Royal Tapestry Workshop and later, in 1789, became court painter to Carlos IV. Illness in 1792 made him deaf and from then on his paintings became more intense, introverted and stylized. He left for France in 1824 and died there four years later.

Goya was an enormously versatile artist: contrast the voluptuous *Maja Vestida* and *Maja Desnuda* (The Clothed and Naked Belles) with the horrors depicted in *Dos de Mayo* and *Tres de Mayo* (on-the-spot portrayals of the rebellion against Napoleon in the streets of Madrid and the subsequent reprisals). Then again, there are the series of pastoral cartoons – designs for tapestries – and the extraordinary Black Paintings, a series of murals painted by the deaf and embittered painter in his old age. His many portraits of his patron, Carlos IV, are remarkable for their lack of any attempt at flattery, while those of Queen María Luisa, whom he despised, are downright ugly.

The **tapestry cartoons** (rooms 85–94) include a series dedicated to the seasons of the year; others feature toothless, starving peasants, dainty playful aristocrats, mischievous boys and a hunchback bridegroom. Most are produced in clearly separated pastel colours to help the weavers and are set against the Madrid landscape.

Nearby is the museum's most recent Goya acquisition, *The Countess of Chinchón*, painted in 1800, eight years before her premature death. Goya brilliantly conveys the glazed, melancholy expression of the 20-year-old niece of Carlos III, who had recently become pregnant following her marriage to Manuel de Godoy, the most powerful and hated man in Spain.

The two **Majas** (Room 89) are further evidence of Goya's masterful portraiture skills. They were painted at different times – the brushwork used in each of the paintings is quite different – and may have formed part of a game whereby the clothed figure was placed over the naked one. *The Family of Carlos IV*, hanging in the octagonal Room 32 alongside preliminary studies for the painting, provides a rather sardonic commentary on Goya's patron: the domineering María Luisa is clearly in charge, while the well-fed Carlos is pictured staring into space. In a clear tribute to Velázquez, Goya places himself staring out at the viewer from the left-hand corner. The two canvases portraying the events of the **Second and Third of May, 1808** (Room 39), and painted six years later, have immortalized the heroic resistance to the Napoleonic invasion of Spain, and also allowed Goya to reaffirm his somewhat compromised patriotic credentials, having worked for Joseph Bonaparte. Both works are incredibly powerful condemnations of the violence. *The Colossus*, or *Panic*, is also said to refer to the upheavals inflicted by the Napoleonic invasion, some claiming that the giant figure represents Napoleon wreaking havoc on Spain, while others claim it symbolizes Spain rising against her oppressor. The disillusioned *Self Portrait* in Room 89 bears a passing resemblance to that other famous deaf artist, Beethoven, with his deeply troubled demeanour and penetrating eyes.

The Black Paintings (1819–23), now displayed in the suitably gloomy rooms 36–38, were originally painted straight on to the wall of Goya's house, known as "*Quinta del Sordo*" (The Deaf Man's Villa), beside the Manzanares. The haunting series of works were transferred to canvas in 1873 and donated to the Prado in 1881; they were given

THE HISTORY OF THE ROYAL COLLECTION

The Paseo del Prado originally ran along the edge of the city by the *prado* ("meadow") of San Jerónimo. During the reign of Carlos III, plans were made to develop the area as a showcase for scientific knowledge, embodying the ideas of the Enlightenment, and a botanical garden, observatory and natural history museum were to be sited here. The latter was to be housed in the Prado building, begun in 1785 and designed by Juan de Villanueva in matchless Neoclassical style. Work continued until 1808 when, during the Napoleonic invasion, it was ransacked by the French, who used it as a barracks and stables. The building was restored by Fernando VII, who decided to move the royal painting collection here. It was opened in 1819, becoming the property of the state in 1868. The collection's holdings were greatly enlarged by the incorporation of the Museo Nacional de la Trinidad, which contained works confiscated from dissolved ecclesiastical properties. During the Civil War, over 350 paintings were taken first to Valencia and then to Geneva under the protection of the League of Nations, but were returned at the beginning of World War II. Once democracy was restored after the death of Franco, the museum became home to the Picasso legacy, including *Guernica* (now in the Reina Sofía).

The nucleus of the Prado collection, however, is made up of paintings from the Spanish royal family, many of whom were enthusiastic collectors and dedicated patrons of the fine arts. Consequently, the – at times – rather eccentric collection is best viewed as a faithful reflection of the changing tastes of the Spanish monarchs. Carlos V's favourite painter was Titian, and his son, Felipe II, continued to acquire his works, but also showed a penchant for Hieronymus Bosch. Felipe III favoured Rubens and Felipe IV Velázquez, while one of the few redeeming features of Carlos IV's reign was his patronage of Goya.

SPANISH PAINTING

titles after Goya's death by people who had known him. The thoroughly disconcerting canvases are often hard to penetrate, but both their style and their ability to shock mark Goya out as an artist well ahead of his time. They also provide a vivid image of an isolated, bitter and seriously ill old man living out his last years in a world of anguished silence. *Saturn Devouring One of His Sons* symbolizes the destruction of everything by time; *The Cudgel Fight* illustrates a fight to the death by two men; others feature ghoulish skull-like faces, witches and devils and a half-submerged dog.

ITALIAN PAINTING

The Prado's early **Italian galleries** (in the ground floor rooms 49, 56b, 60–63, 63b & 75) are distinguished principally by **Fra Angelico**'s (1387–1455) devout and mystical *Annunciation* (c.1445), which originally hung in the Monasterio de las Descalzas (see p.47), and by a trio of panels by **Botticelli** (1444–1510). The latter illustrate a story from the *Decameron* about the strange vision experienced by a young man who has been rejected by his lover. In his vision he sees a woman hunted by hounds and caught by a nobleman who tears her heart out and feeds it to his dogs; when the young man shows the prophetic vision to his disdainful lover she changes her mind and marries him. The wedding is shown in a fourth panel which is in a private collection in the US.

With the sixteenth-century Renaissance, and especially its Venetian exponents, the collection really comes into its own. The Prado is said to have the most complete collection of Titian and painters from the Venice school in any single museum. There are major works by **Raphael** (1483–1520), including a fabulous *Portrait of a Cardinal*, and masterpieces by **Tintoretto** (1518–94), including the beautifully composed *Lavatorio*, one of many masterpieces bought by Felipe IV when Charles I of England was beheaded and his art collection was auctioned off by Cromwell's Commonwealth. **Veronese** (1528–88) and **Caravaggio** (1573–1610) are also represented. The most important group of works, however, is by **Titian** (1487–1576) and includes portraits of the Spanish emperors, *Carlos V* and *Felipe II*. The magnificent equestrian portrait, *The Emperor Carlos V at Mühlberg*, depicts his triumph in 1547 over the Protestant armies of Germany, with Carlos resplendent in his armour – the suit is preserved in the Palacio Real – astride a huge black charger. Ironically, however, by the time Titian painted his subject some years later, he could hardly sit on a horse because of his gout. The collection also features a famous, and much-reproduced, piece of erotica, *Venus, Cupid and the Organist* (two versions are displayed here), a painting originally owned by a bishop.

FLEMISH, DUTCH AND GERMAN PAINTING

The biggest name in the extremely rich early **Flemish** collection (rooms 55–58A) is **Hieronymus Bosch** (1450–1516), known in Spain as "El Bosco". The Prado has several of his greatest triptychs. The early-period *Hay Wain* features fish-headed monsters devouring humans. The middle-period *Garden of Earthly Delights* begins on the left with the Creation of Man, then in the centre, worldly pleasures and sins and, finally, Hell on the right, where fantasy animals, sexual imagery and satanic visions abound. These, and the late *Adoration of the Magi*, are all familiar from countless reproductions, but infinitely more chilling in the original. Bosch's hallucinatory genius for the macabre is at its most extreme in these triptychs, but is reflected in many more of his works, including three versions of *The Temptations of Saint Anthony* (though only the smallest of these is definitely an original). Don't miss the amazing table-top of *The Seven Deadly Sins*, showing devils roasting, spanking and tormenting peasants, while ghostly skeletons creep around in the background. The Latin inscription reads "Beware, beware, God sees you."

Bosch's visions find an echo in the works of **Pieter Brueghel the Elder** (1525–69), whose *Triumph of Death* must be one of the most frightening canvases ever painted. Death is pictured riding on a wizened horse hauling cart-loads of skulls, driving humanity against an army of skeletons shielded with coffin lids and dragging bloated bodies from the water, whilst a wretched figure on a hill is about to be beheaded. The grim unrelenting image is emphasized by the use of dark shades of brown and black and by the burning smoke in the background.

Another elusive painter, **Joachim Patinir** (1480–1524), precursor of landscape painting, is represented by four of his finest works, including the dreamlike blue-green-toned *Crossing the Styx Lake*. From an earlier generation, **Roger van der Weyden**'s (1400–64) dramatic *The Descent from the Cross* is outstanding, its monumental forms making a fascinating contrast with his miniature-like *Pietà*. There are also important works by Memling, Bouts, Gerard David and Massys, as well as a dramatic series of panels by Van der Stockt. The arresting portraiture work of **Mor**, or "**Antonio Moro**" (1519–67), as he was known when he worked in the Spanish court, is displayed amongst the royal portraits on the ground floor in rooms 55 and 55b, and includes his fine representation of the haughty gaze of *Mary Tudor*.

The collection of more than 160 works of **later Flemish and Dutch** art has been imaginatively rehoused in a new suite of twelve rooms on the first floor (rooms 7–11). Grouped by themes, such as religion, daily life, mythology and landscape, the rooms have been tastefully decorated, while many paintings have been given a new lease of life by restoration of their original colours.

Rubens (1577–1640) is extensively represented, though he supervised rather than executed the series of eighteen mythological subjects designed for Felipe IV's hunting lodge in El Pardo. The gruesome horror of his *Saturn Devouring a Child* clearly influenced Goya, whose version can be seen with the Black Paintings. Typically, there is plenty of pearly white female flesh set amongst sensual landscapes in works such as *Nymphs and Satyrs*, *The Judgement of Paris* and the beautifully restored *Three Graces*.

There is, too, a fine collection of works by his contemporaries; for example, **Van Dyck**'s (1599–1641) dramatic *Piedad* and magnificent portrait of himself and Sir Endymion Porter. The minute detail of **Jan Brueghel**'s representations of the five senses and **David Teniers**' (1610–90) scenes of peasant lowlife also merit a closer look. For political reasons, Spanish monarchs collected few works painted in seventeenth-century Protestant Holland; an early **Rembrandt** (1606-69), *Artemisia*, in which the artist's pregnant wife served as the model is, however, a notable exception.

The **German room** (54) on the ground floor is dominated by **Dürer** (1471–1528) and **Lucas Cranach the Elder** (1472–1553). Dürer's magnificent *Adam and Eve* was saved from destruction at the hands of the prudish Carlos III only by the intervention of his court painter, Mengs. The most interesting of Cranach's works are a pair of paintings depicting Carlos V hunting with Ferdinand I of Austria. The work of **Anton Raphael Mengs** (1728–79), who worked on the ceilings of the Royal Palace and directed the Royal Tapestry Factory, is to be found in the European galleries on the second floor. His portraits of the royal family are meticulous in their detail and possess an almost photographic quality.

FLEMISH, DUTCH AND GERMAN PAINTING

CHAPTER FIVE

FRENCH AND BRITISH PAINTING

Most of the **French** work held by the Prado is from the seventeenth and eighteenth centuries (rooms 2–4 on the first floor and rooms 76–84 on the second floor). Royal marriages and the establishment of the Bourbon royal house helped establish closer links between the two countries, although a large part of the collection was lost in the Peninsular War. Among the outstanding painters represented is **Nicolas Poussin** (1594–1665), with his classical Baroque style and intense colours, shown to best effect in *Triumph of David, Bacchanal, Landscape with St Jerome* and *Mount Parnassus*. The romantic landscapes and sunsets of **Claude Lorraine** (1600–82) are well represented by *The Port of Ostia with the Embarcation of Santa Paula Romana* and *Landscape with Tobias and the Archangel Raphael*. Look out, too, for the outrageously imperious portrait of Louis XIV by **Hyacinthe Rigaud** (1659–1743).

British painting is poorly represented – a result of hostile relations between the Spanish and English from the sixteenth to nineteenth centuries. There are, however, some examples of the aristocratic portraiture of Joshua Reynolds (1723–92), Thomas Gainsborough (1727–88) and Thomas Lawrence (1769–1830) in Room 83.

SCULPTURE AND THE DAUPHIN'S TREASURE

Various pieces of **sculpture**, from the classical era to the nineteenth century, are grouped around the entrance halls and scattered throughout the museum. The classical work is well preserved, and the marble representations of gods, goddesses and emperors are undeniably impressive. There's an interesting selection of busts of Carlos V and Felipe II by **Leone Leoni** and his son **Pompeo Leoni**. One of their most arresting works is a statue of *The Emperor Carlos V*

FRENCH AND BRITISH PAINTING • SCULPTURE AND THE DAUPHIN'S TREASURE

84

Subduing Rage (Room 1), from which the emperor's Roman armour can be removed to reveal his nude figure.

The basement houses a display of part of the **collection of jewels** that belonged to the Grand Dauphin Louis, son of Louis XIV and father of Felipe V, Spain's first Bourbon king. The collection features goblets, cups, trays, glasses and other pieces richly decorated with rubies, emeralds, diamonds, lapis lazuli and other precious stones. It was taken back to France during the Napoleonic invasion, but returned to Spain in 1815. One of the highlights is the onyx saltcellar with a gold mermaid.

CASÓN DEL BUEN RETIRO

Currently closed for restoration and likely to remain so until the end of 2003. Admission is included in the entrance ticket to the Museo del Prado.

Just east of the Prado is the **Casón del Buen Retiro** which used to be a dance hall for the palace of Felipe IV, but is now devoted to **nineteenth-century Spanish art**, in which Neoclassical, romantic and historical themes dominate. The Realist work of **Eduardo Rosales** in the melodramatic deathbed scene of *Queen Isabella's Will* and **Francisco Pradilla** in *Doña Juana la Loca (Joanna the Mad)* are perfect examples of this style. The latter depicts Carlos V's grief-stricken mother, Joanna, accompanying her dead husband's coffin on the long march from Burgos to Granada. **José de Madrazo Agudo**'s (1781–1859) *The Death of Viriato* is a characteristic epic piece; **Vicente López**'s portrait of the ageing *Goya* is certainly worth a look for its impressive depiction of the old master, looking rather disapproving, as is the luminescent Impressionist work *Children at the Beach* by **Joaquín Sorolla** (1863–1923; see p.126 for the Museo Sorolla).

Museo Thyssen-Bornemisza

Map 5, F4. Tues–Sun 10am–7pm; extended summer times (hours vary). Permanent collection €4.80, concessions €3, under-12s free; temporary exhibitions €3.60, concessions €2.40; combined ticket €6.60/€3.60. ⓦwww.museothyssen.org. Metro Banco de España.

J ust across the street from the Prado is another exceptional museum, the **Museo Thyssen-Bornemisza**, an ideal complement to the former establishment, as the Thyssen tends to excel in the areas in which the Prado is particularly deficient. The Thyssen collection houses important German Renaissance works, seventeenth-century Dutch painting, Impressionist, German Expressionist and Russian Constructivist art, Abstract and Pop Art. Although both museums are essentially personal – the Prado reflecting the tastes of the Spanish monarchy and the Thyssen those of the late baron and his father – the Thyssen also provides an unprecedented excursion through the history of Western art from the fourteenth to the late-twentieth century.

Begun in the 1920s by German–Hungarian industrial magnate **Baron Heinrich Thyssen-Bornemisza**, on his death in 1947, the works were distributed amongst his heirs. His son, Hans Heinrich, tried to reunite the collection by buying back the paintings and later expanding it with the purchase of additional old masters and modern art. As his own Villa Favorita in Lugano in Switzerland could only accommodate about three hundred pictures, the baron sought a new home for his collection. Despite stiff competition from other suitors, including Prince Charles, the Swiss and German governments, and the Getty Foundation, Spain managed to secure the display of the collection for a knock-down $350m (£230m) in June 1993.

The baron died in April 2002 aged 81, shortly after an acrimonious law suit with his eldest son Georg to regain the family's $2.7 billion fortune was settled out of court. The trial cost an estimated $100 million in legal fees and left Georg in control of the Thyssen empire.

The museum operates as a private institution, administered by the Thyssen Foundation, and proceeds from the entrance fees of the 700,000 visitors each year are ploughed back into its running. It occupies the mid-eighteenth-century Neoclassical **Palacio de Villahermosa**, which was brilliantly remodelled by architect Rafael Moneo, who redistributed the rooms and changed the ceilings in order to make the most of the natural light available. Without a doubt, the availability of this prestigious site played a large part in Spain's successful bid, while another trump card was Baron Thyssen's last (fifth) wife, "Tita" Cervera, a former Miss Spain, who steered the works towards her home country. A kitsch portrait of Tita in fairy-like winged dress hangs in the great hall of the museum, alongside her husband, plus King Juan Carlos and Queen Sofía. Tita, in fact, has her own separate collection of some eight hundred works of art, including masterpieces by Monet, Gaugin, Van Gogh, Cezanne and Picasso, and though these are not yet on public display, about half of them are due to be given a permanent home if a proposed extension plan finally comes off.

The basement houses a handy **café/restaurant** which can be entered separately from the museum, and there's also a temporary exhibition space. The museum **shop** sells an informative and well-illustrated guide (€10.90), as well as the first instalments of the fifteen-volume catalogue of the Baron's collection. It also has a good selection of postcards and children's art books. Audio guides (€3) are available at the desk in the main hall. Re-entry to the museum is allowed as long as you get your hand stamped at the exit desk.

See p.72 for details on the Paseo del Arte ticket which gets you into all three art museums on the Paseo del Prado.

EUROPEAN OLD MASTERS: SECOND FLOOR

Cross to the far side of the building and take a lift or the stairs to the **second floor** and you find yourself at the chronological beginning of the museum's collections: European painting and some sculpture from the fourteenth to eighteenth centuries. The core of these collections was accumulated in the 1920s and 1930s by the late Baron's father, Heinrich, who was a friend of the art critics Bernard Berenson and Max Friedländer.

Heinrich was clearly well advised. The early paintings include incredibly good, rare devotional panels by the Siennese painter **Duccio di Buoninsegna** and the Flemish artists **Jan van Eyck** and **Roger van der Weyden**. In rooms 1 and 2 the pilgrimage through the history of Western art begins with a fine exhibition of the evolving styles that prefigured the Renaissance. The development of spatial depth, inclusion of gestures and the increasing repertoire of artistic skills can be seen in the differences between the Master of Magdalen's *Madonna and Child* and Duccio's *Christ and the Samaritan Woman*, both painted in the first half of the fourteenth century. The International Gothic style is well represented by Johann Koerbecke's expressive *Assumption of the Virgin* (1457) and the eight panels dedicated to the four evangelists by Gabriel Maelesskircher (1478). In Room 3 **Jan van Eyck**'s highly original and remarkable *Annunciation Diptych* (c.1434–1441), in which he depicts the Angel, Virgin and Holy Spirit, draws the eye, as does Petrus Christus's *Our Lady of the Tree* (c.1450), where the Virgin is shown as a flowering shoot bringing life to the dry tree. One of the highlights in the room dedicated to the Italian Quattrocento is the haunting, translucent *Resurrected Christ* by **Bramintino** (c.1465–1530).

Moving on to Room 5, you come to a fabulous array of Early Renaissance portraits, showing a change from the portrayal of the supernatural to more worldly matters. **Ghirlandaio**'s *Portrait of Giovanna Tornabuoni* (1488) – said to be the Baron's favourite painting – captures the serene beauty of the subject, the Latin epigram in the painting stating, "If the artist had been able to portray the character and moral qualities there would not be a more beautiful painting in the world." **Hans Holbein**'s portrait of the self-confident *Henry VIII* (1534–36), the only one of many variants in existence which is definitely genuine, is accompanied by the austere, melancholic *Spanish Infanta* (1496) by **Juan de Flandes**, which may represent the first of Henry VIII's wives, Catherine of Aragón. The technical advancement in the art of portraiture and the beginnings of real characterization are seen to good effect in the *Portrait of a*

EUROPEAN OLD MASTERS: SECOND FLOOR

Stout Man by Robert Campin (c.1425). Among the sixteenth-century Italian paintings, **Raphael**'s delicate and subtly coloured *Portrait of a Young Man* and **Titian**'s *Portrait of the Doge Francesco Vernier* stand out, while the *Young Knight* by **Carpaccio** (Room 7), with its symbolic plants and animals and various allegorical figures, is one of the earliest known full-length portraits. Beyond these, a collection of **Dürers** and **Cranachs** rivals that in the Prado, and includes the former's *Jesus Among the Doctors*, showing an effeminate-looking Christ hounded by decrepit old men. As you progress through this extraordinary panoply, display cases along the corridor contain scarcely less spectacular works of sculpture, ceramics and gold- and silverwork.

Next in line, in Room 11, is **Titian**, ushering in a stylistic revolution with his greater range of tones and almost Impressionistic brushwork, as evidenced in his masterpiece *St Jerome in the Wilderness*. The influence of Titian can be seen in the work of **Tintoretto** – his massive canvas of *Paradise* is exhibited in the central gallery on the ground floor – and in *The Annunciation* by **El Greco**, in which Mannerist influence is also apparent. The stylistic changes in El Greco's work are illustrated clearly with a comparison of the two versions of this painting that are on show in this room. More defined forms and pastel shades in the earlier work are replaced by the elongated figures and oily colours in the later version. In the same room, the anonymous *Last Supper* (previously attributed to El Greco), portrays a highly irreverent version of events, with a drunken apostle, dogs and cats eyeing up the food and Christ being virtually ignored by all those present.

The Early Baroque fascination with light and shade is brilliantly demonstrated by **Caravaggio**'s *St Catherine of Alexandria* (1597) and by **José Ribera**'s *Lamentation over the Body of Christ* (both room 12), in which the ghostly white body of Christ and the grieving faces are highlighted. The

Bernini sculpture of *St Sebastian* heralds the more exuberant later Baroque work exemplified by **Murillo**'s *Madonna and Child with St Rosalina of Palermo*. **Claude Lorrain**'s *Pastoral Landscape with the flight into Egypt* (1663) is a characteristic romantic twilight landscape, full of nostalgia for the classical world, while **Tiepolo**'s *Death of Hyacinthus* uses monumental figures and rich colours to capture the full drama of the event. Even more theatrical is **Luca Giordano**'s *Judgement of Solomon*, which portrays the moment when the Biblical king threatens to cut the baby in two in order to determine which of the two women is the genuine mother. Catering for the eighteenth-century interest in architectural scenes and the demand for souvenirs of the Grand Tour of Italy, **Canaletto** is represented by three flawless views of Venice (Room 17). The floor is completed with more classics, this time Flemish and Dutch. The richly coloured small oil of *Christ in the Storm on the Sea of Galilee* by **Jan Brueghel the Elder**, **Van Dyck**'s marvellous portrait of the disdainful *Jacques Le Roy* and **Ruben**'s luxurious *Toilet of Venus* are amongst the highlights.

AMERICANS, IMPRESSIONISTS AND EXPRESSIONISTS: FIRST FLOOR

The collections on the **first floor** were largely brought together by the late Hans Heinrich Thyssen, who began collecting, according to his own account, to fill the gaps in his father's collection, after it was split among his siblings. He, too, began with old masters, but in the 1960s branched out into German Expressionists, closely followed by Cubists, Futurists, Vorticists and also American art of the nineteenth century.

The floor begins with a comprehensive round of seventeenth-century **Dutch painting** of various genres:

still lifes, scenes from everyday life, landscapes and seascapes (rooms 22–28). Supreme technical skill and minute observation is demonstrated in still lifes such as **Willem Claesz Heda**'s *Rummer, Silver Tazza, Pie and Other Objects*, while **Frans Hals** introduces more lively subjects with his *Family Group in a Landscape* and his laughing *Fisherman Playing a Violin*. The characteristic Dutch landscape features in a number of pictures, including *View of Naarden* by **Jacob Isaacksz van Ruisdael**, where alternating patches of sunlight and shade are used to give the impression of depth. The British eighteenth-century painters **Thomas Gainsborough** and **Sir Joshua Reynolds** also get a look in with their contrasting portraits of English aristocrats.

In rooms 29 and 30 is displayed one of the largest and best collections of American painting outside the US. The theme of landscape seen to good effect in **Thomas Cole**'s *Expulsion, Moon and Firelight* predominates, reflecting the nineteenth-century vision of America as an idyllic virgin land awaiting the settlement of the pioneers. The native population only feature as nostalgic stereotypes in the later paintings, such as Frederick Remington's *Apache Fire Signal* and George Catlin's *Falls of Saint Anthony*. Works by James Whistler, Winslow Homer and John Singer Sargent are displayed, as is James Goodwyn Clonney's wonderful *Fishing Party on Long Island Sound*.

This is followed by a group of European **Romantics and Realists**, including Constable's *The Lock*, **Goya**'s *Asensio Julia* and his *El Tío Paquete* from his Black Paintings.

- -
For more on Goya and his Black Paintings, see p.76.
- -

Impressionism and **post-Impressionism** are also strong points of the collection, with eye-catching works by **Manet**, **Monet**, **Renoir**, **Gauguin**, **Degas**, **Lautrec** and **Cézanne** (Room 33). Monet and Pissarro indulge in some marvellous experimentation with light and reflections in their respective works, *The Thaw at Vétheuil* and *Saint-Honoré Street in the Afternoon. Effect of Rain*. The shimmering green dress of the *Swaying Dancer* and the pastel shades of the jockey's colours in *Race Horses – The Training*, both by Degas, are a real treat. The pioneering *Portrait of a Farmer* by Paul Cézanne foreshadows the Cubism of Braque and Picasso, seen on the ground floor, and marks him out as one of the most influential of this group of painters. The collection is especially strong on paintings by **Vincent van Gogh**, which includes the fiery *Stevedores at Arles* and one of his last and most gorgeous works, *Les Vessenots*. The influence of van Gogh is apparent in the work of the Fauvists, particularly *Waterloo Bridge* by André Derain and *Olive Trees* by Maurice Vlaminck.

The broad-ranging **Expressionist movement** (rooms 34–40), with its powerful emotions and equally powerful colours, is fully represented. The stunningly vivid paintings of **Ernst Ludwig Kirchner**, **Wassily Kandinsky**, **Emile Nolde** and **Franz Marc** are fascinating, as is the apocalyptic work, *Metropolis,* by **George Grosz**.

AVANT-GARDES: GROUND FLOOR

Works on the ground floor cover from the beginning of the twentieth century through to around 1970. The most interesting work in the "experimental avant-garde" sections is from the **Cubists**. There is an inspired, side-by-side hanging of parallel studies by **Picasso** (*Man with a Clarinet*), **Braque** (*Woman with a Mandolin*) and **Mondrian** (*Grey–Blue Composition*). Picasso's range is fully demonstrated by the inclusion of the classical *Harlequin with a Mirror* next to the more abstract *Bullfight*.

The **Synthesis of Modernity** section includes the minimalist work *Catalan Peasant with a Guitar* by **Joan Miró**, the chaotic *Brown and Silver* by **Jackson Pollock**, and the explosive *Picture with Three Spots* by **Wassily Kandinsky**. There are also some superbly vivid canvases by **Max Ernst** and **Marc Chagall**. Surrealism is, not surprisingly, represented by **Salvador Dalí** with his *Dream caused by the Flight of a Bee Around a Pomegranate a Second before Awakening*, in which the artist's wife is depicted sleeping naked in the centre of a fantastic landscape populated by dream images which include an elephant on stilts and a tiger-eating fish. Following on in the Surrealist tradition is **Francis Bacon**'s painfully distorted image *Portrait of George Dyer in a Mirror*. More down to earth are the stark *Hotel Room* by **Edward Hopper** and the cartoon iconography of **Roy Lichtenstein**'s *A Woman in A Bath*. Sharing the same room is a fascinating **Lucian Freud**, *Portrait of Baron Thyssen*, in which the baron is depicted standing in front of Watteau's *Pierrot*, hanging upstairs. To finish, there is a clever play on light and reflections in Richard Estes' *Telephone Booths*, while downstairs by the café is the series of five colourful canvases that make up *The Blinding Exile* cycle by Roberto Matta.

Centro de Arte Reina Sofía

Map 4, I5. Mon & Wed–Sat 10am–9pm, Sun 10am–2.30pm; €3.01, concessions €1.50, free Sat after 2.30pm & all day Sun. ⓦmuseoreinasofia.mcu.es. Metro Atocha.

The other essential stop on the Madrid art circuit is the **Centro de Arte Reina Sofía**, an immense exhibition space providing a permanent home for the Spanish collection of contemporary art, the twentieth-century works from the Prado, and the Miró and Picasso legacies including the jewel in the crown – **Guernica**.

The museum is housed in a vast building that was once the Hospital General de San Carlos. Constructed on the initiative of Carlos III in the second half of the eighteenth century and designed by Francesco Sabatini, the hospital was initially envisaged as a gargantuan complex of seven quadrangles, of which this was the only one ever actually completed. It ceased functioning as a hospital in 1965; twelve years later it was declared a monument of historical and artistic interest, and work began on transforming it into a museum of modern art. The initial conversion took until 1986, when Queen Sofía opened the space for staging temporary exhibitions. It was not until 1990 that the final renovation work was completed and it was opened as a museum with a permanent collection.

See p.72 for details on the Paseo del Arte ticket which gets you into all three art museums on the Paseo del Prado.

Although it's rather sombre-looking from the outside, inside, the light from the central courtyard, the white walls, vast galleries and high ceilings create a sensation of spaciousness ideally suited to the display of so many large-scale works. As well as its collection of twentieth-century art on the second and fourth floors, the museum has a **theatre, cinema**, excellent **shops**, a print, music and photographic **library**, a **restaurant**, **bar** and **café** in the basement and a peaceful inner courtyard garden. An informative catalogue is available from the shop, priced €8.01. At the entrance, there are audio-guides in English (€2.40), which give a good introduction to Spanish art.

THE SECOND FLOOR

The permanent collection traces the development of artistic movements in the twentieth century from the perspective of Spanish art, whilst providing an international context through the display of key works by foreign artists. Although the collection is a little erratic in its coverage, you can still appreciate how the artists interacted, cooperated, competed and responded to each other's work. The collection begins on the second floor with a selection of work entitled **A Change of Century**, examining the origins of modern Spanish art mainly through the two artistic nuclei that developed in Catalonia and the Basque Country at the end of the nineteenth century.

Among the early highlights are the luscious *Retrato de Sonia de Klamery* (*Portrait of Sonia de Klamery*, 1913) by Hermenegildo Anglada Camarasa and the vivid Expressionist work *La Comulgante* (*The Communicant*, 1914) by María Blanchard. Impressionist influences are clear in the work of the landscape artists Santiago Rusiñol and Joaquín Mir, while Francisco Iturrino's pleasant pastel *Jardin de Málaga* (*Málaga Garden*, 1916) owes much to Fauvism. There is a room dedicated to the Madrid painter, **José Gutiérrez Solana**, whose highly idiosyncratic work reflects his obsession with death. Works include the solemn *La Visita del Obispo* (*The Visit of the Bishop*, 1926), the melancholy *La Procesión de la Muerte* (*The Procession of Death*, 1930) and his famous portrayal of *La Tertulia del Café de Pombo* (*The Tertulia at the Café Pombo*, 1920), with a range of leading Spanish artistic and literary figures including Solana himself on the far right.

Like Madrid's two other great galleries, the Reina Sofía is undergoing an ambitious expansion programme, with French architect Jean Nouvel supervising a €68 million scheme to add a triangle-shaped extension and increase space by 55 percent.

Picasso's early work *Mujer en Azul* (*Woman in Blue*, 1901), a study of a bourgeois woman in all her finery, is another highlight, and is followed by strong sections on Cubism, including fine work by **Juan Gris**, notably his *Retrato de Josette* (*Portrait of Josette*, 1916). The early Cézanne-influenced *Paisaje de Cadaqués* (*Cadaqués Countryside*, 1923) by Salvador Dalí features amongst other works of the Paris School.

Sculpture is well represented, with the Cubist-influenced ironwork of Julio González and the innovative

THE SECOND FLOOR

studies by Pablo Gargallo, such as the mysterious *Máscara de Greta Garbo con Mechón* (*Mask of Greta Garbo with Lock of Hair*, 1930), the semi-religious semi-dictatorial figure of *El Gran Profeta* (*The Great Prophet*, 1933), and the plump-faced head of *Picasso* (1913).

Midway round the collection is the Reina Sofía's main draw – **Picasso's Guernica** (see box p.100). Superbly displayed and no longer protected by bullet-proof glass and steel girders, this icon of twentieth-century Spanish art and politics carries a shock that defies all familiarity. The sheer size of the monumental work at 3.5m high and over 7.5m long is the first thing that impresses. The preliminary studies, displayed around the room, deserve equal attention as they show how Picasso developed its symbols, making their incorporation into the painting all the more marvellous. Picasso's notorious reluctance to talk about the painting has led to decades of debate about its exact meaning. Common interpretations view the screaming horse as symbolizing the suffering of the people and the bull the overthrow of reason and the rise of animal passion. Whatever the arguments, this disturbing work certainly lives up to expectations.

The post-*Guernica* halls feature the artist's later work with the vividly colourful *Mujer Sentada Acodada* (*Seated Woman Leaning on her Elbows*, 1939), the slightly unsettling sculpture *Hombre del Cordero* (*Man with a Lamb*, 1943) and the series entitled *El Pintor y la Modelo* (*The Painter and the Model*, 1963). There are also rooms devoted to the heavyweights **Dalí** and **Miró**, as well as a host of lesser-known Spanish artists representing the main currents in Spanish art in the 1920s and 1930s. The development in Dalí's work and his variety of techniques are clearly displayed in the classic portrait of his sister gazing out of the window, *Muchacha en la Ventana* (*Girl at the Window*, 1925); the Cubist-influenced pieces entitled *Autorretrato* (*Self-portrait*, 1923), *Arlequín* (*Harlequin*, 1925); and finally his more famous Surrealist work such as *El Gran Masturbador* and *El Enigma de Hitler* replete with dream landscapes, sexual imagery, insects and symbols of putrefaction. A large range of Miró's impenetrable but pleasing canvases and sculptures are exhibited with their characteristic images of dots, spots and crescents symbolizing the stars, sun, moon, birds and people.

Among the work of the **lesser-known Spanish artists** is a fine series of contrasting nudes by Aurelino Arteta, José de Togores and Roberto Fernández Balbuena. Angeles Santos's portrayal of four women in languid conversation in *Tertulia* (1929) and Alfonso Ponce de León's semi-comic *Accidente* (1936) also stand out. The final room on the second floor is used for rotating exhibitions of work from the museum's holdings.

THE FOURTH FLOOR

The permanent collection continues on the fourth floor, although here it does not match the heavyweight attractions of the previous exhibits. This section covers Spain's postwar years up to the present day and includes Spanish and international examples of abstract and avant-garde movements such as **Pop Art**, **Constructivism** and **Minimalism**. Spanish artist José Guerrero adds a touch of Mediterranean colour to *Composición* (1956), a work which reflects his close connections with the leading figures of Abstract Expressionism, Rothko and Pollock. Antonio Saura's *Grito No. 7* (*Shout no. 7*, 1959) is an altogether more forbidding piece, with blacks, whites and greys combining to create a disturbing image of pain and desperation. There are some striking pieces by the Basque abstract sculptor, **Eduardo Chillida** and by Catalan Surrealist painter **Antoni Tàpies**. Spanish-style Pop Art is represented by the Valencian group Equipo Crónica, whose *Pintar es como golpear* (*Painting is like Hitting*, 1972) is one of their most memorable pieces.

THE STORY OF GUERNICA

When the Spanish Civil War broke out in July 1936, Picasso was living in France, continuing his hedonistic lifestyle detached from politics, although he did accept the honorary post of Director of the Prado in support of the Popular Front government. In January 1937, he accepted a commission to paint a mural for the Spanish Republic's pavilion at the World Fair in Paris on a subject of his own choosing. By April he had still not started work, but on April 26, 1937, the German Condor Legion, acting in concert with Franco's Nationalist forces, bombed and machine-gunned the Basque town of Guernica, home of Basque "liberties" and cultural traditions. Defenceless and without obvious military significance, the town was bombarded for three hours by German planes and almost completely destroyed, although the sacred oak before which Spanish monarchs had sworn to observe Basque rights since medieval times was miraculously preserved. Despite initial denials, the Nationalists later admitted responsibility, and Göring, head of the German Luftwaffe, revealed in a chilling statement shortly before his suicide that Germany had regarded Guernica as a testing ground for aerial bombing. Photojournalists captured the horror of the atrocity, which sent shockwaves around Europe, and for Picasso the time for sitting on the fence was over. He began working on the commission and, amid rumours that he was pro-Franco, issued the following statement: "The Spanish struggle is the fight of reaction against the people, against freedom. My whole life as an artist has been nothing more than a continuous struggle against reaction and the death of art. How could anyone think for a moment that I could be in agreement with reaction and death. In the panel on which I am working and which I shall call Guernica and in all my recent works of art I clearly express my abhorrence of the military caste which has sunk Spain in an ocean of pain and death".

The resulting canvas, produced in little over a month, relied on allegory and metaphor, combined with the legacy of Cubism to produce a general commentary on the barbarity and terror of war itself. The Right criticized the painting as the degenerate work of a madman, while many on the Left were disappointed because of its inaccessibility and its failure to make an explicit rallying call for the forces opposed to Fascism. However, it soon came to be recognized as a timeless masterpiece. Herbert Read commented when it was shown in London in 1938: "It is a monument to destruction, a cry of indignation and horror intensified by the spirit of genius. Not only Guernica, but Spain, not only Spain, but Europe are symbolized in this allegory." Shortly after, the work was "loaned" to the Museum of Modern Art in New York, until such time, as Picasso put it, Spain had regained its democratic liberty. The artist never lived to see that time, dying in 1973, two years before Franco, but in 1981, following the restoration of democracy and amid much controversy, the painting was moved to Madrid to hang (as Picasso had stipulated) in the Prado. Its transfer to the Reina Sofía in 1992 again prompted much soul-searching and protest, though for anyone who saw it in the old Prado annexe, it looks truly liberated in its present setting. More recently there have been calls to relocate the painting to the newly opened Guggenheim Museum in Bilbao, which is in the same province as the town of Guernica. However, after close examination by art experts it has been declared too delicate and too damaged by previous moves to be transferred once again:

THE STORY OF GUERNICA

The highlight of the international avant-garde work has to be **Francis Bacon**'s marvellous *Figura Tumbada* (*Reclining Figure*, 1966), featuring one of his characteristic angst-ridden figures reclining on a bed, while pieces by **Graham Sutherland** and **Henry Moore** provide further reference points.

If the avant-garde work all gets too much for you, there are also offerings from the Spanish Realists. Xavier Valls' simple pastel-shaded still lifes *Bodegón con Cerezas* (*Still Life with Cherries*, 1980) and *Melocotones y Jarro* (*Peaches and Jug*, 1974) are soothing offerings, while **Antonio Lopéz Garcia** contributes with his dusty dry Madrid landscape *Visto desde el Cerro del Tío Pío* (*Madrid from the Cerro del Tío Pío*, 1962–63). The collection ends with galleries dedicated to contemporary art, using manufactured products and industrial materials, and range from the dizzying experience of Jesús Rafael Soto's *Extensión amarilla y blanca* (*Yellow and white extension*), a floor full of yellow-tipped metal filaments, to the blinding display of fluorescent strip lighting by Dan Flavin.

The Retiro and around

I n addition to the heavyweight sites of the Prado, Thyssen-Bornemisza and Reina Sofía galleries, the area around the Paseo del Prado is home to a host of other minor attractions. These include the impressively renovated **Estación de Atocha**, the fascinating **Real Fábrica de Tapices** (Royal Tapestry Workshop), a number of the city's smaller museums, the startlingly peaceful **Jardines Botánicos** and the **Parque del Retiro**, a delightful mix of formal gardens and wider open spaces – the perfect place to escape the city bustle for a few hours.

The area covered by this chapter is
shown in detail on colour map 7.

PARQUE DEL RETIRO

Map 7. Metro Retiro/Atocha.

The origins of the **Parque del Retiro** go back to the early seventeenth century, when Felipe IV's royal adviser, the

Conde Duque de Olivares, produced a plan for a new palace and playground, the Buen Retiro (literally "Good Retreat"). Work began in 1630, and the architects Crescenzi, Gómez de Mora and Carbonell built a huge complex, of which only the ballroom (**Casón del Buen Retiro**, see p.85) and the Hall of Realms (**Museo del Ejército**, see p.106) survive. Gardens were laid out at the same time and included a zoo for the exhibition of savage animals, an aviary for exotic birds and a large lake where mock battles could be staged. Other elements were added over the years, such as a French-style parterre during the reign of Felipe V (1700–46), a royal porcelain factory constructed by Carlos III (1759–88) and an astronomical observatory by Carlos IV (1788–1808). During the Peninsular War, the gardens, used by the French as a fortified barracks, were badly damaged, but restored under Fernando VII, who opened most of the park to the public. After the 1868 Revolution, the park became municipal property.

For information on other parks and gardens, see "Kids' Madrid", p.261.

Although *Madrileños* jog, rollerblade, cycle, picnic and row on the lake (you can rent boats by the Monumento a Alfonso XII) in the park, their main activity here is to promenade. The busiest day is Sunday, when half of Madrid turns out for the **paseo**. Dressed for show, families stroll around, nodding at neighbours and building up an appetite for a long Sunday lunch. Strolling aside, there's almost always something going on in the park, including a good programme of concerts and *ferias* (fairs), the most popular of which is the **Feria del Libro** (Book Fair), held from the end of May into early June, when every publisher and bookshops set up stalls and offer a 25 percent discount on their wares. In the summer months, at weekends there are

PARQUE DEL RETIRO

puppet shows by the Puerta de Alcalá entrance (1pm, 7pm & 8pm), while on Sunday, you can often watch groups of Peruvian musicians or Catalans performing their traditional dance, the *sardana*.

In addition, travelling art exhibitions are frequently housed in the beautiful **Palacio de Velázquez** (map 7, F4; June–Sept Mon & Wed–Sat 11am–8pm, Sun 11am–4pm; Oct–May Mon & Wed–Sat 10am–6pm, Sun and hols 10am–4pm; free), close to the southern end of the main lake; the nearby **Palacio de Cristal** (map 7, F5; during exhibitions same hours as above; ☎915 746 614 for information); and **Casa de Vacas** (map 7, E2; daily 10.30am–2.30pm & 4–8pm; closed Aug except for puppet shows), at the opposite end of the lake. Look out, too, for *El Angel Caído* (Fallen Angel), the world's only public statue of Lucifer, in the south of the park. Alongside is the very fine rose garden designed by municipal head gardener Cecilio Rodríguez, who died in 1953. His service spanning 75 years is commemorated by the well-groomed formal gardens that bear his name on the east side of the park (daily 8am–3pm). In the northeast corner, remains of Fernando VII's private recreational zone can be clearly seen around the pink Casita del Pescador.

El Retiro has a safe reputation by day, but it's best not to wander alone in the late evening. Note also that east of La Chopera is a cruising ground for gay prostitutes.

PUERTA DE ALCALÁ TO LOS JARDINES BOTÁNICOS

Leaving the park at the northwest corner takes you into Plaza de la Independencia, in the centre of which is one of the two remaining gates of the old city walls. Built by Sabatini to commemorate Carlos III's first twenty years on the throne, the **Puerta de Alcalá** (map 7, B1) was the biggest city gate in Europe at that time, and, like the bear and bush, is now one of the city's emblems.

South from here, you pass the **Museo de Artes Decorativas** (map 7, B3; Tues–Fri 9.30am–3pm, Sat & Sun 10am–2pm; €2.40, concessions €1.20, free on Sun), a former nineteenth-century aristocratic residence, which has its entrance at c/Montalbán 12. The museum's highlight is its collection of *azulejos* and other decorative ceramics with a magnificent eighteenth-century tiled Valencian kitchen on the top floor. The rest of the exhibits include an interesting but unspectacular collection of furniture, a series of reconstructed rooms and *objets d'art* from all over Spain.

A couple of blocks west, in a corner of the Naval Ministry at Paseo del Prado 5 is the **Museo Naval** (map 7, A3; Tues–Sun 10am–2pm; closed Aug; free; Metro Banco de España). Beyond the security guards you'll find a well-presented array of exhibits, including the first map to show the New World drawn by Juan de la Cosa in 1500, cannons from the Spanish Armada, part of Cortés's standard used during the Conquest of Mexico, and the giant globes made by Coronelli in the late seventeenth century. The room dedicated to the *Nao San Diego*, which was sunk during a conflict with the Dutch off the Philippines in 1600, contains some fascinating items recovered during the salvage operation in the early 1990s.

The military theme continues with the **Museo del Ejército** (Army Museum; map 7, B4; Tues–Sun 10am–2pm; €0.60, concessions €0.30, free on Sat; Metro Retiro) just to the south, at c/Méndez Núñez 1. A gloomily eccentric timewarp of a museum, it's crammed full of often chaotically displayed military memorabilia and, seemingly unaware of the changes over the past twenty-five years, preserves a distinctly pro-Franco stance. The motley collection includes *La Tizona*, a sword purporting to belong to El Cid, a piece of shirt worn by Pizarro when he was assassinated, a death mask of Napoleon and part of a bomb thrown at a royal wedding procession in 1906 (see p.25), all accompanied by curious piped music ranging from *Doctor Zhivago* to the theme tune from *Shaft*. Of more interest perhaps are the beautiful ceilings of the building itself, fragments of Don Juan's flag from the Battle of Lepanto (1571) and a piece of the cross which Columbus carried to the New World.

The Museo del Ejercito is due to be moved to Toledo's Alcázar (see p.292) as the current building features in the Prado extension plans (see p.71) and a number of exhibits have already been removed.

South again, past the Prado's Cáson del Buen Retiro anncxe, is **San Jerónimo el Real** (map 7, A5; July–Sept Mon–Fri 8am–1.30pm & 6–8pm, Sat & Sun 9am–1.30pm & 6.30–8pm; Oct–June Mon–Fri 8am–1.30pm & 5–8pm, Sat & Sun 9am–1.30pm & 5.30–8pm). A monastery was founded on this site in the early sixteenth century by the Catholic monarchs, Fernando and Isabel, becoming an important destination for religious processions, site of the swearing in of the heirs to the throne (the Princes of Asturias) and setting for royal marriages and coronations (including that of King Juan Carlos in 1975). Despite significant remodelling and two Gothic towers added in the mid-nineteenth century, the old form of the church is still clearly visible. The seventeenth-century cloisters have fallen victim to the Prado extension plan (see p.71).

Opposite San Jerónimo is the **Real Academia Española de la Lengua** (Royal Language Academy; map 7, A4), established in 1714 by Felipe V to "cultivate and establish the purity and elegance of the Castilian language". Its job nowadays is to make sure that the Spanish language is not corrupted by foreign or otherwise unsuitable words. The results are entrusted to their official dictionary – a work that bears virtually no relation to the Spanish spoken on the streets.

A short distance to the west, on Paseo del Prado, is **Plaza de la Lealtad** (map 5, G4), an aristocratic semicircular plaza that contains a war memorial, the Monumento a los Caídos por España. Originally a memorial to the *Madrileños* who died in the 1808 rebellion (the urn at the base contains the ashes of those killed by the French), it was later altered to commemorate all those who have died fighting for Spain, and an eternal flame now burns here. On one side of the plaza stands the *Ritz Hotel* (map 5, G4), work of Charles Mewès, who was also the architect of the *Ritz* in Paris and London.

If your wallet can stretch to it and you feel suitably attired, a drink on the summer *terraza* at the *Ritz* is a real treat.

Opposite is the elegant **Bolsa de Comercio** (stock exchange; map 7, A3; Mon–Fri 10am–2pm) where you can watch the dealing from the first floor and visit the rather routine exhibition on the history of the place.

Los Jardines Botánicos

Map 7, A6–B7. Daily: March & Oct 10am–7pm; April & Sept 10am–8pm; May–Aug 10am–9pm; Nov–Feb 10am–6pm; €1.50. Metro Atocha.

Just below the Plaza de Murillo entrance to the Prado are the delightful, shaded **Jardines Botánicos**. Opened in 1781 by Carlos III, the aim was to collect and grow species from all over the Spanish Empire, develop a research centre and supply medicinal herbs and plants to Madrid's hospitals. The gardens were abandoned after the Peninsular War, and although they were renovated later in the nineteenth century and a zoo was installed, they soon fell into disrepair once more. The nineteenth-century writer and traveller, Richard Ford, reported that they became so neglected they were inhabited by a pair of escaped boa constrictors who survived on a diet of stray cats and dogs. The gardens were eventually restored in the 1980s, using the original eighteenth-century plans, and are now home to some thirty thousand species from around the globe.

On the southern side of the botanical gardens is the sloping **Cuesta de Claudio Moyano** (map 7, A7–B7), lined with little wooden bookstalls. You can buy anything here, from secondhand copies of Captain Marvel to Cervantes or Jackie Collins. There's always something of interest, such as old prints of Madrid and relics from the Franco era. Although the street's at its busiest on Sundays, some of the stalls are open every day.

At the end of the Cuesta de Claudio Moyano stands the grandiose **Ministry of Agriculture**, a building of epic proportions designed by Ricardo Velázquez Bosco in 1893. Its exterior features decorative tile work, monumental caryatids representing industry and agriculture, and a striking figure of Glory, flanked by winged horses.

ESTACIÓN DE ATOCHA AND BEYOND

Map 7, A8. Metro Atocha.

At the bottom of the Paseo del Prado stands the impressive **Estación de Atocha**, worth a look even if you're not travelling. It's actually two stations, old and new, the former a glorious 1880s glasshouse, revamped as a kind of tropical garden in 1992. It's a wonderful sight from the walkways above, as a constant spray of water rains down on the jungle of vegetation. On the platforms beyond sit the gleaming white high-speed AVE trains, built to ferry passengers to the 1992 Expo in Seville in two and a half hours and soon to be joined by a new fleet serving Barcelona.

Also in this area, at c/Alfonso XII, is the **Museo Nacional de Antropología/Etnología** (map 7, B8; Tues–Sat 10am–7.30pm, Sun 10am–2pm; €2.40, concessions €1.20, free Sat after 2.30pm & all day Sun), founded by the eccentric Dr Pedro González Velasco to house his collection. The unimaginatively displayed exhibits are designed to give an overview of different cultures of the world, in particular those linked to Spanish history; the ground floor focuses on the Philippines and Asian religions, the first floor Africa and the second the Americas. The most interesting exhibits are to be found in a side room on the ground floor – a macabre collection of deformed skulls, a Guanche mummy (the original inhabitants of the Canary Islands), shrivelled embryos, and the skeleton of a circus giant (2.35m tall) with whom Velasco had signed a deal to buy his skeleton after his death – payment in advance of course.

- -

It's said that Doctor Velasco embalmed his own daughter when she died and was regularly seen taking her out for meals and rides in his carriage.

- -

On the hill opposite, at the edge of the Retiro, the **Observatorio Astronómico** (map 7, C8; Mon–Fri 9am–2pm) was another ingredient of Carlos III's academic complex (see box on p.79), although not actually finished until 1845. The beautiful Neoclassical building, designed by Prado architect Juan Villanueva, houses a poorly displayed collection of telescopes, chronometers, sundials and sextants.

Real Fábrica de Tapices

Map 7, F9. Mon–Fri 10am–2pm; €2; closed Aug. Metro Atocha Renfe/Menéndez Pelayo.

Ten minutes' walk southeast of the station, the fascinating **Real Fábrica de Tapices** (Royal Tapestry Workshop) on c/Fuentarrabia runs tours every half an hour or so (guides usually speak English) and is well worth a visit. The original factory, situated in Plaza Santa Bárbara, was founded in 1721 by Felipe V, who wanted to emulate the Gobelins factory in Paris. The young Goya was employed to paint the cartoons – now in the Prado – for a series of tapestries depicting everyday *Madrileño* life. The factory was moved to its present site at the end of the nineteenth century, but the processes have not changed for hundreds of years, and the eighteenth-century vertical looms are still in use. The workers, now numbering only 42 compared to four hundred fifty years ago, can be seen coolly looping handfuls of bobbins around a myriad strings, sewing up worn-out masterpieces with exactly matching silk, and weaving together hundreds of different threads to produce different shades for a new tapestry. With progress being painfully slow – a square metre of tapestry every three and a half months – the astronomical price of €9000 per square metre soon becomes believable. One of the giant sixteenth-century Flemish tapestries on display took more than two generations to complete.

Just across the road from the factory is the **Panteón de Hombres Ilustres** (map 7, E9; April–Sept Mon–Sat 9am–7pm, Sun 9am–4pm; Oct–Mar Mon–Sat 9.30am–6pm, Sun 9am–3pm; free). Built adjacent to the Real Basílica de Atocha (see box) this late-eighteenth-century Byzantine-style building with its Neo-Gothic cloister was meant to serve as a mausoleum for the most important figures in Madrid's history. The full extent of the plans

ESTACIÓN DE ATOCHA AND BEYOND

was never realised and many of the bodies have since been removed. There are, however, some impressively elaborate marble tombs commemorating nineteenth-century politicians, many of whom were assassinated during this turbulent period in the city's history.

THE VIRGIN OF ATOCHA

The Real Basílica de Atocha is built near the site of one of Madrid's miraculous incidents, this time involving the Virgin of Atocha. During the eighth century Arab invasion, Gracián Ramírez, a local dignitary, found a figure of the Virgin hidden in the grass and built a chapel to commemorate the event. Before heading off to battle and probable death, and fearing his wife and daughters might be captured by the Arabs, Ramírez took the precaution of cutting their throats. To his surprise and dismay he survived and went to the chapel to beg for forgiveness, where he saw his wife and daughters still alive and praying at the Virgin's feet, the knife marks on their necks bearing witness to the miracle.

ESTACIÓN DE ATOCHA AND BEYOND

Gran Vía, Chueca and Malasaña

The **Gran Vía**, Madrid's great thoroughfare, runs from just above Plaza de la Cibeles to Plaza de España, effectively dividing the old city in the south from the newer northern parts. Permanently jammed with traffic and crowded with shoppers and sightseers, it's the commercial heart of the city and, if you spare the time to look up, quite a monument in its own right, with early twentieth-century, palace-like shops, offices and hotels.

C/Fuencarral heads north from the Gran Vía to the Glorieta de Bilbao, site of the *Café Comercial*, where many *tertulias* were held after the Civil War and still one of the most popular meeting places in Madrid. To either side of c/Fuencarral are two of Madrid's most characterful *barrios*: **Chueca** to the east, and **Malasaña** to the west, their chief appeal lying in their amazing concentration of bars, restaurants and, especially, nightlife. However, the **Museo Municipal**, **Museo Romántico** and a number of beautiful **churches** provide a more than adequate excuse to look around here by day, while further to the east is the elegant area of **Las Salesas**.

- -

**The area covered by this chapter is shown
in detail on colour map 6.**

- -

GRAN VÍA

The **Gran Vía** (Great Way) was built in three stages over
nearly half a century in order to link the two new districts
of Argüelles and Salamanca. Its construction involved the
destruction of fourteen streets, the alteration of fourteen
more, and the road itself became a symbol of the nation's
arrival in the twentieth century. Financed on the back of
the economic boom that Spain experienced as a result of its
neutrality in World War I, the Gran Vía is a showcase for a
whole gamut of architectural styles, from Modernist and
Art Deco to Neo-Rococo and Rationalist.

The finest section is the earliest, constructed between
1910 and 1924, stretching from c/Alcalá to the Telefónica
skyscraper. Two buildings at the junction with c/Alcalá
really stand out. The **Edificio Metrópolis** (map 6, I8),
built between 1905 and 1911 by the French architects Jules
and Raymond Février, with its cylindrical facade, paired
columns, white stone sculptures, zinc-tiled roof, gold garlands and winged statue, is wonderfully over-the-top; while
the **Grassy building** (1916–17) just above it, is equally
overblown, featuring curved balconies, colonnades and a
dome. Look out for the Art Deco **Museo Chicote** at no.
12 (map 6, H7), where you can sample a rather overpriced
cocktail in the bar founded in 1931 by Perico Chicote,
whose aim was to "mix drinks, lives and opinions" (see
p.191 for more on this bar). A bit further along, the vast
81-metre-high slab of the **Telefónica** building, with its
plain sand-coloured facade decorated with touches of
Spanish Baroque, was Spain's first skyscraper and prompted

King Alfonso XIII to declare that Spain had finally entered the modern world.

> The section of Gran Vía around Telefónica was known as "Shell Alley" during the Civil War, as the tall building was used as a reference point by Franco's forces to bomb the Gran Vía from their trenches in Casa de Campo.

The next stretch of the street down to Plaza de Callao is dominated by shops, cafés and cinemas with their massive old-fashioned hand-painted posters. The neon-lit Plaza de Callao is now the gateway to the shoppers' paradise of **c/Preciados**, home to the French store FNAC and to the ubiquitous department store El Corte Inglés. On the corner, just before the street begins to slope down towards Plaza de España (see p.130), you'll see the classic Art Deco **Capitol** building (1930–33; map 6, E7), its curved facade embellished with lurid neon signs.

CHUECA AND LAS SALESAS

The smaller streets immediately to the north of Gran Vía just opposite Plaza del Callao are shady hinterland areas home to all manner of vice-related activities and are notorious for petty crime, but this only becomes a problem at night. In the *barrio* of **Chueca**, east of c/Fuencarral, there's a strong neighbourhood feel, with kids and grannies on the streets during the day, and a lively **gay scene** around Plaza de Chueca at night. The area has experienced a rejuvenation in recent years, as boarded-up properties have reopened and new businesses have set up, taking advantage of the growing gay café/bar scene. The plaza (map 6, I6; Metro Chueca) is fronted by one of the best old-style *vermút* bars in the city, *Bodega Angel Sierra* on c/Gravina. To the south at c/Augusto Figueroa 35 is *La Tienda de Vinos* or

"*El Comunista*", so called because it acted as a meeting place for left-wing critics of the old Franco regime.

For details of the bars and nightlife venues in Chueca, see pp.189–191, 198–199 and 209–213.

From Plaza de Chueca east to **Paseo de Recoletos** (the beginning of the long Paseo de la Castellana) are some of the city's most enticing streets. Offbeat restaurants, small private art galleries and odd corner shops are to be found here in abundance, and **c/Almirante** has some of the city's most fashionable clothes shops, too. Head south down c/Barquillo to **Plaza del Rey** for a look at the **Casa de las Siete Chimeneas** (House of Seven Chimneys; map 6, I7), which is supposedly haunted by an illegitimate daughter of Felipe II who disappeared in mysterious circumstances. The sixteenth-century house has been heavily restored, but is still recognizable as the work of the architects of El Escorial, Juan Bautista de Toledo and Juan de Herrera. Charles I of England stayed here when he came to Madrid to press his unsuccessful suit for marriage to the Infanta María.

To the north up c/Barquillo is the stately **Plaza de las Salesas** (map 6, J5), dominated by the church and convent of Las Salesas Reales. The complex was founded in 1747 by Barbara of Bragança, Portuguese wife of Fernando VI, as somewhere she might go to escape from her mother-in-law, Isabella Farnese, should her husband die before she did (in the event, it was never needed, as Barbara was outlived by Fernando). The **church** (9am–1.30pm & 6–9pm; free), with its impressive white granite Baroque facade decorated with marble statues, is set behind a very fine forecourt containing a rose garden, palm trees and magnolias. Inside, there's a grotto-like chapel, impressive frescoes and stained-glass windows, an extravagant pulpit and striking green marble altar decoration. The elaborate tomb of Fernando VI lies in the main church, as does that of the military hero General O'Donnell, while Barbara's has been relegated to a side chapel. The convent behind the church now houses the Palacio de Justicia, the city's Law Courts, facing the elegant Plaza de la Villa de París.

West along c/Fernando VI, past the marvellous grocers and fishmongers, overflowing with fresh produce, are the Gaudíesque flowing lines of the cream-coloured **Sociedad de Autores** (Society of Authors; map 6, I4), its dripping decoration of flowers, faces and balconies giving the appearance of a melting candle. The only really significant *modernista* building in Madrid, it was designed in 1902 by the Catalan José Grasés Riera. Just beyond is Plaza de Santa Bárbara and Alonso Martínez, one of the main centres of student nightlife in Madrid, with the nearby streets packed with bars and nightclubs.

Museo Romántico

Map 6, H4. Tues–Sat 9am–3pm, Sun & public holidays 10am–2pm; closed Aug; €2.40, concessions €1.20, free on Sun.
ⓦwww.mcu.es/bbaa/index.html. Metro Tribunal.

Nearby at c/San Mateo 13, the **Museo Romántico** (currently closed and undergoing a refurbishment programme) was founded on donations by the Marqués de la Vega-Inclán in the early 1920s and aims to show the lifestyle and outlook of the late-Romantic era through the re-creation of a typical residence of the period (the building itself dates back to the late eighteenth century). It's a successful attempt, with its musty atmosphere, creaking floorboards, cracking walls crowded with canvases, and rooms overflowing with kitsch memorabilia and period furniture.

CHUECA AND LAS SALESAS

Museo Municipal

Map 6, G4. Tues–Fri 9.30am–8pm, Sat & Sun 10am–2pm; Aug: Tues–Sun 10am–2pm; €1.80, concessions €0.90, free Wed & Sun. ⓦwww.mcu.es/bbaa/index.html. Metro Tribunal.

Just around the corner from the Museo Romántico is the **Museo Municipal**, c/Fuencarral 78, opened on this site in 1929 in the former city almshouse, remodelled in the early eighteenth century by Pedro de Ribera. True to form, he created a fantastically decorated Baroque doorway placed on an otherwise plain red-brick facade. Inside, the museum contains a chronological collection of paintings, photos, models, sculptures and porcelain, all relating to the history and urban development of Madrid since 1561 (the date it was designated imperial capital by Felipe II) through to the twentieth century.

Exhibits on the early history of Madrid are in the Museo de San Isidro (see p.31).

The **ground floor** contains displays relating to Habsburg Madrid, including Pedro Texeira's fascinating plan dated 1656 and paintings of Plaza Mayor, the Retiro and other famous landmarks. Bourbon Madrid is the focus of most of the **first floor**, with some huge Bayeu canvases portraying *Madrileño* life, Goya's *Allegory of the City of Madrid* (see p.27), a great display of crude cartoons satirizing Napoleon and a supremely accurate model of the city in 1830, plus a fine collection of porcelain from the Real Fábrica del Buen Retiro.

Back on the ground floor, don't leave without visiting the recently renovated eighteenth-century chapel, which survives from the time de Ribera remodelled the building. Luca Giordano's dramatic canvas *San Fernando ante la Virgen* hangs above the altar. A very good selection of reasonably priced prints, posters and books is available in the museum shop.

MALASAÑA

To the west of c/Fuencarral is **Malasaña** district, named after the young orphan and seamstress, Manuela Malasaña, who became a heroine of the 1808 rebellion. One version of the story states that French troops searched her on her way home from work and found the scissors she used for cutting cloth. Since they had forbidden the carrying of any weapons, she was summarily executed. The area became extremely poor and run-down after the Civil War; there were even plans to bulldoze it. However, the availability of cheap accommodation brought an injection of life with the arrival of students and young people in the 1960s. More recently, the quarter was the focus of the *Movida Madrileña*, the "happening scene" of the late 1970s and early 1980s, when bars appeared behind every doorway, drugs were sold openly on the streets, and an extraordinary atmosphere of new-found freedom prevailed. Today, the threatened takeover by drug addicts has been largely halted and the area immediately around **Plaza Dos de Mayo** (map 6, F3) has been redeveloped, with an often eccentric selection of **bars**, **restaurants**, **clubs** and **cafés** springing up. The dark and narrow streets to the south of the square, however, are best avoided at night.

Bars and restaurants aside, the streets in Malasaña have some wonderful old shop signs and architectural details. Best of all is the old pharmacy on the corner of c/San Andrés and c/San Vicente Ferrer with its irresistible 1920s *azulejo* scenes depicting cures for diarrhoea, headaches and suchlike.

Finally, two notable churches are also to be found in the area. The **Convento de San Plácido** on c/San Roque (map 6, E6) is famous for the scandals that plagued it in the early seventeenth century. Rumours abounded about nuns possessed by devils, while their confessor dispensed sexual

THE BATTLE OF THE BOTELLON

In recent years, both Plaza Dos de Mayo and the corner of c/Barceló and c/Fuencarral became major centres of the *botellón* or the "Big Bottle" scene. On Friday and Saturday nights hundreds of under-age drinkers would come here with their *litronas* – litre bottles of soft drinks to mix with spirits – and *calimochos* – a mixture of cheap red wine and cola – to create impromptu open-air *terrazas*, leaving the area strewn with broken bottles, vomit and assorted rubbish. Distraught residents responded by mounting protests and calling for action, and Madrid council recently ordered police to enforce bylaws forbidding street drinking. The whole ritual has prompted a debate about the rising levels of alcoholism amongst teenagers and the provision of alternatives to keep kids off the streets. For the moment the clampdown appears to have forced the *botellón* scene out of the centre, but how long the authorities maintain the costly police presence, and whether or not it's gone for good, is debatable.

favours in exchange for forgiveness. The convent hit the headlines more recently with the discovery of a mummified body, claimed by some to be the painter Velázquez. Unfortunately, it's not usually open.

Round the corner on Corredera de San Pablo is one of the city's hidden treasures, the church of **San Antonio de los Alemanes** (daily 9am–1pm & 6–8pm). The building was designed in 1624 by the Jesuit architect Pedro Sánchez and Juan Gómez de Mora, but it's the recently restored decoration of the elliptical interior that makes this little church so special. Dizzying floor-to-ceiling pastel-coloured frescoes by Neapolitan artist Luca Giordano feature scenes from the life of St Anthony, and provide a spectacular backdrop for the services.

MALASAÑA

Salamanca

T he elegant tree-lined Paseo del Prado continues beyond Plaza de la Cibeles as the aristocratic and palatial Paseo de Recoletos, until it reaches the cascading fountains of Plaza de Colón where it metamorphoses into the Manhattan-style urban landscape of the **Paseo de la Castellana**. Bus 27 will take you the full distance – an architectural odyssey spanning the eighteenth to the late-twentieth centuries. Spreading out to the east of the Castellana is the exclusive **Barrio de Salamanca**, Madrid's designer shopping district, and there are also a scattering of other sights, museums and galleries to tempt you up here, in particular the **Museo de Lázaro Galdiano** and the **Museo Sorolla**, the pick of Madrid's smaller museums.

The area covered by this chapter is
shown in detail on colour map 8.

The grid-like *barrio* of **Salamanca** was developed in the second half of the nineteenth century as a new upmarket residential zone under the patronage of the Marquis of Salamanca. This flamboyant arch-capitalist became Minister of Finance at the age of 32, established the forerunner to the Bank of Spain, developed Madrid's first rail and tram lines and was the proud owner of the first flush toilets in the capital. A generous patron of the arts, renowned party host and master of insider dealing, he made and lost a fortune on three separate occasions, the last time as a result of his massive investment in the *Barrio de Salamanca*. Today the area is still a smart address for apartments and even more so for shops, with the streets populated by the fur-coat and

EXHIBITION SPACES

A number of businesses and financial institutions have exhibition spaces scattered across the city – mainly around the Castellana and Salamanca districts – staging high-quality exhibitions and cultural events. See press and the *Guía del Ocio* for details.

Fundación Arte y Tecnología c/Fuencarral 3 (Tues–Fri 10am–2pm & 5–8pm, Sat & Sun 10am–2pm; free; ®www.fundacion.telefonica.com; Metro Gran Vía). This exhibition space in the Telefónica building on Gran Vía displays selections from the twentieth-century Spanish art owned by the telecommunication giant, as well as hosting frequently appealing temporary shows.

Fundación BBVA Paseo de la Castellana 81 (Mon–Sat 11.30am–1.30pm & 5.30–8.30pm, Sun 11am–2.30pm; free; Metro Nuevos Ministerios). This fine exhibition space in the AZCA complex has hosted a variety of shows from Spain and abroad.

Fundación Banco Santander Central Hispano c/Marqués de Villamagna 3 (Tues–Sat 11am–2pm & 5–9pm, Sun 11am–2.30pm; free; ®www.fundacion.bsch.es; Metro Serrano). A permanent collection spanning the sixteenth to twentieth centuries, along with temporary exhibitions.

Fundación La Caixa c/Serrano 60 (Mon & Wed–Sat 11am–8pm, Sun 11am–2pm; free; Metro Serrano). Hosts a

sunglasses brigade, decked out in Gucci and plenty of gold. The *barrio* is also the haunt of *pijos* – universally denigrated rich kids – and the grid of streets between c/Goya and c/José Ortega y Gasset contains most of the city's **designer emporiums**. Unsurprisingly, the bars and restaurants in this area tend to be rather pricey, although the quality is high

variety of prestigious exhibitions, which recently included an original display of art from Tibetan monasteries.

Fundación Caja de Madrid Sala de las Alhajas, Plaza de San Martín 1 (Tues–Sat 11am–2.30pm & 5–8pm, Sun 11am–2.30pm; closed Aug; free; @www.fundacioncajamadrid.org; Metro Sol). In a beautiful old building, opposite the Monasterio de las Descalzas, this was being refurbished at the time of writing.

Fundación Cultural MAPFRE c/General Perón 40 (Mon–Sat 10am–9pm, Sun noon–8pm; free; Metro Santiago Bernabéu). A variety of enticing temporary shows by Spanish and international artists in this pleasant exhibition space opposite the Palacio de Congresos.

Fundación Juan March c/Castelló 77 (Jan–June & Sept–Dec Mon–Fri 10am–2pm & 5.30–9pm, Sat & Sun 10am–2pm; free; @www.march.es; Metro Núñez de Balboa). This outstanding cultural centre houses over 1300 works and is a venue for art exhibitions and classical concerts. It was founded in 1955 by a Catalan businessman seeking to make amends after spending time in prison for embezzlement.

Sala del Canal de Isabel II c/Santa Engracia 125 (Tues–Fri 11am–2pm & 5–9pm, Sun 11am–2pm; free; Metro Rios Rosas). This neo-*mudéjar* water tower has been turned into an exhibition space specializing in photographic displays.

(see pp.178–180, 194–195 and 200). The Salamanca area is also home to a number of excellent **exhibition spaces** (see box p.122) and in summer, the area between Plaza de Colón and the Glorieta Emilio Castelar transforms into "La Costa Castellana", littered with trendy *terrazas* that play host to the city's beautiful people (see p.204).

For a full rundown of Salamanca's best shops see p.248.

AROUND PLAZA DE COLÓN

Map 8, B9. Metro Colón.

The first point of interest you come to in the *barrio* of Salamanca after emerging from the metro is **Plaza de Colón**, marking the point where Paseo de Recoletos becomes Paseo de la Castellana. The square is dominated by a Neo-Gothic monument to Christopher Columbus (*Cristóbal Colón*), given as a wedding gift to Alfonso XII and identical to the one in Barcelona, and an enormous Spanish flag. Directly behind are the Jardínes del Descubrimiento (Discovery Gardens), a small park containing three huge stone blocks representing Columbus's three ships. Below the plaza, underneath the cascading wall of water facing the Castellana, is the 1970s **Centro Cultural de la Villa** (map 8, C9; Tues–Sat 10am–9pm, Sat & Sun 10am–2pm), a good place for film, theatre and occasional exhibitions. Across the plaza, at Paseo de Recoletos 41, you'll see the **Museo de Cera** (map 6, L4–5; Mon–Fri 10am–2.30pm & 4.30–8.30pm, Sat & Sun 10.30am–8.30pm; €7.20, children €4.20; Metro Colón), a pricey and pretty lamentable wax museum.

A better bet is the **Museo Arqueológico Nacional**, just off the plaza, entrance at c/Serrano 13 (map 2, J3;

Tues–Sat 9.30am–8.30pm, closes 6.30pm in summer; Sun 9.30am–2.30pm; €3, concessions €1.50, free Sat after 2.30pm and all day Sun; ⓦwww.mcu.es/bbaa/index.html; Metro Colón). The collections trace the evolution of human cultures from prehistory, and most exhibits are from Spain, including some impressive Celto-Iberian busts known as *La Dama de Elche* and *La Dama de Baza*, and a wonderfully rich hoard of Visigothic treasures found at Toledo. Good coverage is also given to Roman, Egyptian, Greek and Islamic finds, but rooms are often closed for rearrangement, sometimes at very short notice. In the gardens, downstairs to the left of the main entrance, is a reconstruction of the prehistoric cave paintings discovered at Altamira in Cantabria. Given that the caves themselves are now closed to the public, this is the nearest you'll get to the real thing.

In the same complex, but with entry from the Castellana, are the **Biblioteca Nacional** and **Museo del Libro** (National Library and Book Museum; map 2, J3; Tues–Sat 10am–9pm, Sun & hols 10am–2pm; free; ⓦwww.mcu.es/bbaa/index.html), housed in a grand Neoclassical pile built in the late nineteenth century. The *biblioteca* contains over three million volumes, including every work published in Spain since 1716, while the museum displays a selection of the library's treasures, including Arab, Hebrew and Greek manuscripts and an interesting interactive exhibition on the development of written communication (in Spanish only).

North of Plaza de Colón, several modern buildings stand out along the Castellana, including the green-capped Torres Heron completed in 1976; La Pirámide at no. 31; the shiny black, late 1960s La Unión y el Fénix (no. 33); and further north, the 1987 Catalana Occidente, with its impressive opaque-glass finish. Look out, too, for the **Museo de Escultura al Aire Libre** (map 8, D3; Metro Rubén Darío; free), an innovative use of the space underneath the

Juan Bravo flyover, with its haphazard collection of sculptures, including a huge six-tonne suspended block titled *The Meeting* by Eduardo Chillida, and assorted cubes, walls, fountains and optical trickery that appears most appreciated by the city's skateboard community.

MUSEO SOROLLA

Map 8, A2. Tues–Sat 10am–2.30pm, Sun 10am–2pm; €2.40, concessions €1.20, free Sun. ⓦwww.mcu.es/nmuseos/sorolla. Metro Iglesia–Ruben Dario.

To the west of the Glorieta de Emilio Castelar, Paseo del General Martínez Campos leads to one of the hidden treasures of Madrid. Part museum and part art gallery, the **Museo Sorolla** gets little of the publicity of the mammoth collections in the Prado and the Thyssen-Bornemisza, but this tribute to a single artist's life and work is in many ways just as rewarding. The museum, which has recently undergone a €700,000 refurbishment programme, is situated in Joaquín Sorolla's former home, built in 1910 and donated to the nation by his widow after his death in 1923. It's a delight to stumble upon this oasis of peace and tranquillity, its cool and shady Andalusian-style courtyard and gardens decked out with statues, fountains, assorted plants and fruit trees.

Sorolla was born in Valencia in 1863 and studied in Rome and Paris. Enormously successful during his lifetime and famous throughout Europe and the USA, he was dubbed the "Spanish Impressionist" and received countless prizes for his paintings, including first prize at the Paris Universal Exhibition of 1900. However, his work experienced a decline in popularity after his death and soon went out of fashion, and it's only more recently that it has experienced a revival. A video on the artist's life and work is shown Tuesday to Friday at 11am and noon. The ground floor has been kept largely intact, re-creating the authentic atmosphere of the artist's living and working areas. These rooms contain his **collection of popular jewellery**, including religious icons and charms, hair combs and earrings, garnered during his travels around the Iberian peninsula. The **studio** itself is bathed in the powerful Madrid sunlight from massive skylights and, amongst the artist's clutter, you'll see the *cama a la turca*, a small bed lined on three sides by cases of books, where Sorolla used to take his afternoon siesta.

The upstairs rooms, originally the sleeping quarters of the house, have been turned into a **gallery**, with works arranged chronologically from the far end. The development from his first darker, more sombre paintings such as *Trata de Blanca* (*White Slave Trade*, 1894) and *An Investigation* (1897) to brighter, more optimistic works such as the lush, green, dreamlike *Siesta* (1911) and the vivid red *Puerto de Valencia* (*Valencia Port*, 1907) is striking. Powerful sunlight, sea, intense colours, women and children dominate his rather romantic paintings. On your way out, you'll see a small, tastefully displayed collection of his sketches and gouaches.

MUSEO LÁZARO GALDIANO

Map 8, E1. Tues–Sun 10am–2pm (July & Sept also open Thurs 7–11pm for guided tours); €3, €4.50 guided tour, concessions €1.50; free Sat. ⓦwww.flg.es. Metro Nuñez de Balboa.

Just east of the Glorieta de Emilio Castelar at c/Serrano 122 is the **Museo Lázaro Galdiano**, the private collection of publisher and businessman José Lázaro Galdiano, given to the state after his death in 1947. Spread over the four floors of his former home, it's a vast treasure trove of paintings and *objets d'art*.

The museum provides informative leaflets
in both Spanish and English.

The **collection** contains some outstanding archeological pieces, beautifully decorated thirteenth-century Limoges enamels, and a magnificent late sixteenth-century rock crystal and bejewelled drinking cup belonging to Emperor Rudolf II, the mad cousin of Felipe II. In the room on Renaissance sculpture is a superb little picture of *The Saviour* from the late-fifteenth-century Lombard School, formerly claimed by the museum to be by Leonardo da Vinci. The museum also has an excellent collection of European paintings from the fifteenth to nineteenth centuries, including Bosch, Rembrandt, Turner and Constable, plus Spanish artists including Zurbarán, Velázquez, El Greco and Goya.

PASEO DE LA CASTELLANA

A little to the north just off the Paseo de la Castellana on c/José Gutiérrez Abascal is the **Museo de Ciencias Naturales** (Natural History Museum; Tues–Fri 10am–6pm, Sat 10am–8pm, Sun 10am–2.30pm; €2.40; Metro Nuevos Ministerios), one of the most interactive of the traditional museums in the city centre, with audio-visual displays on the evolution of life on earth and plenty of dinosaur exhibits (see "Kids' Madrid" p.261). Farther north along the Paseo de la Castellana, you reach the vast monolithic complex of government buildings known as **Nuevos Ministerios**, whose construction was initiated during the Second Republic, but completed under Franco. The conspicuously modern business quarter **Zona Azca** (Metro Nuevos Ministerios/Santiago Bernabéu) follows, and is home to the city's tallest skyscraper – the 43-storey Torre

Picasso (designed by Minori Yamasaki, who was also responsible for the former Twin Towers in New York). Just beyond it, and easily the most famous sight up here, is the magnificent **Santiago Bernabéu** football stadium, home of Real Madrid.

For details on football in Madrid, see p.237.

The remainder of the Castellana is a relatively uninspiring strip of anonymous grey concrete offices and apartment blocks, ending with a flourish at the dramatic leaning towers known as the **Puerta de Europa** on Plaza Castilla. Construction of the smoked-glass office blocks was initiated with finance from the Kuwait Investment Office (KIO), but following the collapse of its Spanish subsidiary in one of the country's biggest ever bankruptcies, the towers stood unfinished for several years until the powerful local bank Caja Madrid came to the rescue. All-in-all they provide a pretty fitting testimony to the uncontrolled property speculation of the 1980s.

Over the next 20 years the plan is to **extend** the Castellana another three and a half kilometres northwards as part of the local authority's ambitious plan to convert the area into one of Europe's major business centres. As well as a forest of high-rise office blocks, a futuristic new terminal for high-speed trains, a new metro line and bus station are also to be constructed. The authority has pledged to set aside some space for parks and recreation facilities, with a state-of-the-art Olympic-standard sports stadium as the centrepiece.

PASEO DE LA CASTELLANA

Plaza de España
and beyond

The northwest corner of the city, beyond **Plaza de España** and its monumental skyscrapers, is a mixture of aristocratic suburbia, university campus and parkland, distinguished by the green swathes of **Parque del Oeste** and **Casa de Campo**. Sights include the downbeat **Museo Cerralbo**, the fascinating **Museo de América**, the **Ermita de San Antonio de la Florida**, with its stunning Goya frescoes and, further out, the pleasant royal residence of **El Pardo**, while the spacious **terrazas** along Paseo del Pintor Rosales provide ample opportunity for refreshment.

PLAZA DE ESPAÑA AND AROUND

Map 6, B5–6. Metro Plaza de España.

The **Plaza de España**, at the west end of Gran Vía, is a product of Franco's conscious attempt in the 1950s to portray Spain as a dynamic, modern country. Dominated by two of what used to be the city's tallest buildings, the square has a certain American feel to it. The grandiose apartment complex of the **Edificio de España** which heads the square, looking as though it has been transplanted from 1920s New York, was in fact completed in 1953. Four years later, the neighbouring 32-storey **Torre de Madrid**, which like its neighbour was designed by Joaquín and José María Otamendi, took over as the tallest building in Spain. Together they tower over an elaborate monument to Cervantes in the middle of the square, in which the seated author gazes intently into the distance while the bewildered bronze figures of Don Quixote and Sancho Panza stand below. The plaza itself can be a little seedy at night, although it does play host to occasional festivities and an interesting **craft fair** during the fiesta of San Isidro (on or around May 15); while behind the Edificio de España, on c/San Leonardo and c/San Bernardino, you'll find a host of international restaurants ranging from Mexican and Peruvian to Egyptian, Thai and Indian.

To the northwest, **c/Martín de los Heros** is a lively place, day and night, with three of the city's best original-language-version cinemas, and behind them the **Centro Princesa**, a complex of shops, clubs, bars and a 24-hour branch of the ubiquitous VIPS multi-purpose store (see p.249).

Museo Cerralbo

Map 6, A5. Tues–Sat 9.30am–2.30pm (July 10am–2pm), Sun 10am–2pm, closed Aug; €2.40, concessions €1.20, free Wed & Sun. @www.mcu.es/bbaa/index.html. Metro Ventura Rodríguez.

Just to the west of Plaza de España is the **Museo Cerralbo**, c/Ventura Rodríguez 17, an elegant nineteenth-century mansion endowed by the seventeenth Marqués de Cerralbo, a reactionary politician, poet, traveller and archeologist, who still had time to build up a substantial collection of paintings, furniture, armour and artefacts. He bequeathed his home and its eclectic contents to the state, although it didn't open as a museum until 1962. The cluttered nature of the exhibits is partly explained by the fact that his will stipulated that the collection should be displayed exactly as he arranged it. Among the chaos of objects and ornaments is a dark and moody *Francis of Assisi* by El Greco; work by José de Ribera, Zurbarán, Van Dyck and Tintoretto; a fascinating collection of clocks, pocket watches and mini sundials; and some outrageously gaudy icing-sugar chandeliers. The highlight is a fabulous over-the-top mirrored ballroom with a Tiepolo-inspired fresco, golden stucco work and marbled decoration.

ARGÜELLES AND MONCLOA

C/Princesa stretches northwest from Plaza de España into the *barrios* of Argüelles and Moncloa, the former home to some elegant apartment blocks, the latter a centre of student life. Up the steps opposite the Centro Princesa is **c/Conde Duque**, dominated by the massive former barracks of the royal guard constructed in the early eighteenth century by Pedro de Ribera. The barracks have been turned into a dynamic **cultural centre**, known as Centro Cultural Conde Duque, which stages concerts, plays and dance as part of the Veranos de la Villa season (see p.214). It's home to the city's collection of **contemporary art** (Tues–Fri 9.30am–8pm, Sat & Sun 10am–2pm; Aug Tues–Sun 10am–2pm; €1.80, free Wed & Sun; Metro San Bernardo/Ventura Rodríguez) and also hosts a variety of temporary exhibitions. Just to the east of this, the **Plaza de las Comendadoras**, a tranquil space bordered by a variety of interesting craft shops, bars and cafés, is named after the convent that occupies one side of the square. The nuns are from the military order of Santiago and the attached church is decked out with banners celebrating the victories of the order's knights. A large painting of their patron, St James the Moor-slayer, by Luca Giordano, hangs over the high altar.

About 400m from Plaza de España along c/Princesa, obscured by trees, stands the **Palacio de Liria**, the residence of one of the wealthiest and most important aristocratic families in Spain, the dukes of Alba. Housed within is a vast private collection of artistic treasures, but visitors are only allowed entry once a week, after a written request, and the current waiting list is well over a year. The far end of Princesa is dominated by the **Ministerio del Aire** (Air Ministry), another product of the post-Civil War Francoist building boom. Work on the mammoth edifice began in 1942, and even the Third Reich's architect, Albert Speer, was consulted. However, with the defeat of the Nazis, plans were soon changed and a Habsburg-style structure was built instead, inspired by the work of Juan Gómez de Mora and nicknamed the "Monasterio" del Aire because of its similarity to El Escorial. Franco also constructed the neighbouring **Arco de la Victoria** in 1956 to commemorate the Nationalist military triumph in the Civil War. During term time, the stretch of parkland by the arch often becomes the scene of one big student party, with picnickers from the nearby Complutense University drinking and chatting under the trees and leaving a trail of debris across the grass.

The **Mirador del Faro** (Tues–Sun: June–Aug 11am–1.45pm & 5.30–8.45pm; Sept–May 10am–2pm & 5–8pm; €1, concessions €0.50; Metro Moncloa), the futuristic 92-metre-high viewing tower just past the Arco de la Victoria, was opened in 1992 and provides stunning views over the city and to the mountains beyond, though there are no explanation panels to identify what you're seeing. Alongside, with its main entrance at Avenida de los Reyes Católicos 6, is the **Museo de América** (Tues–Sat 10am–3pm, Sun 10am–2.30pm; €3.01, concessions €1.50, free Sun). This fabulous collection of pre-Columbian

American art and artefacts includes objects brought back at the time of the Spanish conquest, as well as more recent acquisitions and donations. The layout is thematic, with sections on ideas and myths about America, geography and history, social organization, religion and communication. Each of the imaginatively displayed exhibits is introduced by a short video presentation in Spanish, but the lack of chronological development can be rather disconcerting. The Aztec, Mayan and Inca civilizations are well represented and exhibits include the Madrid Codex (one of only three surviving hieroglyphic manuscripts depicting scenes from everyday Mayan life); the Tudela Codex, including indigenous paintings describing the events of the Spanish conquest; and the Quimbayas Treasure, a breathtaking collection of gold objects from a funeral treasure of the Colombian Quimbaya culture, dated 900–600 BC.

Beyond the museum lies the campus of the **Ciudad Universitaria**, rebuilt after the Civil War when it was completely devastated in some of the fiercest fighting, lying as it did along the front line between the defending Republican forces and the besieging Nationalists. Alongside the campus, by the side of the road, is the **Palacio de la Moncloa**, the official residence of the Spanish prime minister since 1977.

THE PARQUE DEL OESTE

Map 2, A1–B3. Metro Argüelles.

To the west of Plaza de España, the **Parque del Oeste** follows the railway tracks up to the suburbs of Moncloa and Ciudad Universitaria. Originally laid out by municipal gardener Cecilio Rodríguez at the beginning of the twentieth century, the park was devastated by the Civil War and had to be completely redesigned. It features a pleasant stream, assorted statues and shady walks, and in summer there are numerous *terrazas* overlooking the park on Paseo del Pintor Rosales. Also here is the **Teleférico** (April–Sept daily 11am–2.30pm & 4.30pm–dusk; Oct–March Sat, Sun & public holidays noon–2.30pm & 4.30–8pm; €2.60 one-way, €3.60 return), a cable car which shuttles its passengers high over the river to a restaurant/bar in the middle of Casa de Campo (see p.137). The round trip is nothing spectacular, but there are some fine views of the park itself, the Palacio Real, the Almudena Cathedral and the city skyline.

Below the Teleférico is the beautiful Rosaleda, a vast rose garden, at its best in May and June.

Down the hill, past a ceramic school and towards the railway line, is a small cemetery where the 43 Spaniards executed by the occupying French troops on May 3, 1808 – and immortalised by Goya in his famous painting that hangs in the Prado – lie buried (see p.78). At the southeastern tip of the park is the **Templo de Debod** (map 2, B3; April–Sept Tues–Fri 10am–2pm & 6–8pm; Oct–March Tues–Fri 9.45am–1.45pm & 4.15–6.25pm, Sat & Sun 10am–2pm; €1.80, free Wed & Sun), a fourth-century BC Egyptian temple dedicated to the gods of Amon and Isis and given to Spain in 1968 in recognition of the work done by Spanish engineers in salvaging the archeological sites threatened by the construction of the Aswan High Dam. Reconstructed here stone by stone, it seems comically incongruous. Inside is a new multimedia exhibition on the culture of Ancient Egypt.

For information on other parks and gardens, see "Kids' Madrid", p.266.

THE PARQUE DEL OESTE

135

The Ermita de San Antonio de la Florida

Tues–Fri 10am–2pm & 4–8pm, Sat & Sun 10am–2pm (from 13th to 23th July daily only 10am–2pm); €1.80, concessions €0.90, free Wed & Sun. Metro Príncipe Pío.

Rail lines from commuter towns to the north of Madrid terminate at the recently renovated **Estación del Norte**, a quietly spectacular construction of white enamel, steel and glass which enjoyed a starring role in Warren Beatty's film *Reds*, and is set to house a shopping and leisure complex. About 500m from the station along the Paseo de la Florida stands the **Ermita de San Antonio de la Florida** at Glorieta de la Florida 5. This little church on a Greek cross plan was built by an Italian, Felipe Fontana, between 1792 and 1798 and decorated by **Goya**, whose **frescoes**, which took him only 120 days to complete, provided Carlos IV with enough evidence to appoint him court painter. The recently-restored frescoes in the dome depict Saint Anthony of Padua, while around it, heavenly bodies of angels and cherubs hold back curtains to reveal the main scene – a group of villagers watching the saint resurrect a dead man whose father had been unjustly accused of his murder. Beyond this central group, Goya created a gallery of highly realistic characters, modelled on court and society figures, while for a lesser fresco of the angels adorning the Trinity in the apse, he took prostitutes as his models. The church also houses the artist's remains. The mirror-image chapel on the other side of the Glorieta was built in 1925 for parish services so that the original could become a museum.

On St Anthony's Day (June 13) girls queue at the church to ask the saint for a boyfriend; if pins dropped into the holy water stick to their hands, their wish will be granted.

THE PARQUE DEL OESTE

CASA DE CAMPO

Metro Batán/Lago. Bus #33 from Príncipe Pío goes to the zoo and Parque de Atracciones or you can get here by cable car from Paseo del Pintor Rosales (see p.135) or on foot from the Estación del Norte via the Puente del Rey.

The **Casa de Campo**, an enormous expanse of heath and scrub, is in parts surprisingly wild for a place so easily accessible from the city. Founded by Felipe II in the mid-sixteenth century as a royal hunting estate, it was only opened to the public in 1931 and it later acted as a base for Franco's forces from which they shelled much of the city. Large sections have been tamed for conventional pastimes and there are picnic tables and café/bars throughout the park, the ones by the lake providing fine views of the city. There are also mountain-bike trails, a jogging track, open-air swimming pool (mid-June–Sept 10.30am–8pm; €3; Metro Lago), tennis courts, and rowing boats for rent on the lake (again near Metro Lago). During the summer, open-air films are shown in the conference area. Other attractions include a popular, well-laid-out **Zoo** and a sprawling **Parque de Atracciones** (see "Kids' Madrid", p.261 for information on both). Be warned that many of the main access roads through the park have been taken over by prostitutes, both day and night (the council has supposedly banished them from the city) and can become crowded with kerb-crawlers – not particularly pleasant for picnics or excursions with the kids.

EL PARDO

Map 1, E5. April–Sept Mon–Sat 10.30am–6pm, Sun 9.30am–1.30pm; Oct–March Mon–Sat 10.30am–5pm, Sun 9.30am–1.30pm; €3, concessions €1.50, free Wed for EU citizens. Sometimes closed for official events. Bus from Moncloa (services daily every 10–15min, 6.30am–midnight; 25min).

Nine kilometres northwest of central Madrid is Franco's former principal residence at **El Pardo**. A garrison still remains at the town, where most of the Generalíssimo's staff were based, but the stigma has lessened over the years, and this is now a popular excursion for *Madrileños*, who come here for long lunches in the excellent *terraza* restaurants along Avenida de la Guardia, or to play tennis and swim at one of the nearby country clubs. The tourist focus is the **Palacio del Pardo**, rebuilt by the Bourbons on the site of the hunting lodge of Carlos I and still used by visiting heads of state. The present building is largely the work of Francesco Sabatini, although traces of the old palace by Juan Gómez de Mora are still evident. The interior is pleasant enough and houses the chapel, where Franco prayed, and the theatre where the Caudillo used to censor films. On display are a number of mementos of Franco, including his desk, a portrait of Isabel la Católica by her court painter, Juan de Flandes, and an excellent collection of tapestries. Tickets to the palace are valid also for the neighbouring pavilion, the **Casita del Príncipe** (currently being refurbished, scheduled to re-open early in 2003).

LISTINGS

Accommodation

Madrid has lots of **accommodation**, most of it pretty central and, on the whole, pretty functional. Few places, in any price range, have great character, and you're basically paying for location and facilities. At the lower end of the range, there are bargains to be had, with double rooms for as little as €30 a night – and less if you're looking for an extended stay. Move upmarket a little and you can find plenty of places at €50–70 a night, offering comfortable rooms with a private bath or, more often, shower. The upper-range hotels regularly offer special deals, so it's worth checking these even if your budget is limited.

Although it's advisable to make **reservations** at all times of the year, especially during Spanish fiestas (see p.232), you'll always be able to find something if you look around. Alternatively, you could use an **accommodation service** – you'll find outlets at the airport, the Estación Sur de Autobuses and the train stations. Brújula (℡915 599 705) is particularly helpful, with offices at Atocha and Chamartín train stations, Colón bus terminal and on the sixth floor of the Torre de Madrid in Plaza de España (see p.130).

Much of the cheapest accommodation in Madrid is to be found in the wedge-shaped zone between **c/Atocha** and **Paseo del Prado** and in the *barrios* of **Chueca** and

Malasaña. Similarly, the huge old buildings on **Gran Vía** harbour a vast array of hotels and *hostales* at every price, often with a delightfully decayed elegance. After dark, however, the area can feel somewhat seedy.

In the very heart of the city – **Sol**, **Ópera** and **Plaza Mayor** – there is a surprising number of reasonably priced options, and if you want to be right in the thick of Madrid's nightlife, you'll find plenty of good choices around **Plaza de Santa Ana**.

North of Gran Vía, a number of *hostales* cluster on and around **c/Fuencarral**, although the streets near the southern end form a red-light district, so take care after dark. Further north towards Bilbao is another nightlife centre; the pleasantest options here are around **Plaza Santa Bárbara**.

The city's most expensive hotels are grouped around **Paseo del Prado**, **Recoletos** and in **Salamanca**, although even in these upmarket districts you'll find several more modest options.

ACCOMMODATION PRICES

Throughout this guide, accommodation is graded on a scale from ① to ⑨. These categories show the cost of the cheapest double room in each establishment. In Madrid there is no high or low season; however, many upper-range hotels offer good deals at weekends and during July and August. It's also worth enquiring about the *bonos* (hotel vouchers) on sale in all travel agents which often give substantial reductions on the more upmarket options.

① Under €30	⑤ €90–110
② €30–50	⑥ €110–130
③ €50–70	⑦ €130–160
④ €70–90	⑧ €160–200
	⑨ Over €200		

Calling Madrid from abroad, dial your international access code, then 34, followed by the subscriber's number, which will nearly always start with 91.

HOTELS

Noise from the street can be a problem in the city centre, so it's a good idea to ask for a room on one of the higher floors or facing away from the street. In summer, air conditioning is advisable – all **hotels** in the ⑤ category and above will have it, while our reviews will say if it's available in the cheaper options. Swimming pools are a rarity, but you'll always be within striking distance of one of the public pools scattered around the city (see p.244). If you're arriving by **car**, a hotel with a garage is a must, given the city's parking and security problems. **Breakfast** is often not included in the price of a room, but it's usually much better value and more fun to go to a local café or bar.

ATOCHA AND PASEO DEL PRADO

Hotel Mediodía
Map 4, I5. Plaza Emperador Carlos V 8 ☎915 273 060, ℻915 307 008. Metro Atocha. Huge hotel right by the Reina Sofía and Estación de Atocha. Simple, standard rooms, with bathroom and TV in all are a good bargain. Directly below, the *El*

Brillante café does a nice cup of coffee and some decent tapas. ❸

Hotel Mercator
Map 4, I4. C/Atocha 123 ☎914 290 500, ✉mercator@husa.es. Metro Atocha. Slightly faded, but decent value hotel, popular with tour groups. Rooms have TVs and all the doubles have air conditioning, but they can be noisy at weekends because of

a huge disco next door. Car park costs €11 a day. ④

Hotel Mora

Map 4, I2. Paseo del Prado 32 ℡914 201 569, 🖷914 200 564. Metro Atocha.

Friendly and very good-value hotel. All rooms have air conditioning, and some have views of the Paseo del Prado (double-glazing helps block out the traffic noise). Some rooms on the fifth floor have a small lounge area. Perfectly positioned for all the galleries on the Paseo del Arte. ③

Hotel Nacional

Map 4, I3. Paseo del Prado 48 ℡914 296 629, 🖷www.nh-hoteles.es. Metro Atocha.

Large, plush hotel, part of the high-quality NH chain, attractively situated just opposite the Jardines Botánicos. Not that pricey, given the excellent facilities and luxurious surroundings. Special offers can reduce the price substantially. ⑧

Hotel Palace

Map 5, F4. Plaza de las Cortes 7 ℡913 608 000, 🖷www.

palacemadrid.com. Metro Banco de España.

Colossal, sumptuous hotel belonging to the Sheraton chain, with every facility, including a beauty salon, conference rooms and business services – but none of the snootiness of the *Ritz* across the road. Doubles start at €400. ⑨

SOL AND SANTA ANA

Hotel Asturias

Map 5, C3. C/Sevilla 2 ℡914 296 676, 🖷www.chh.es. Metro Sevilla.

Comfortable, well-appointed hotel housed in a beautiful building only a stone's throw from Puerta del Sol. Service is very courteous and rooms are en suite and quite large. ④–⑤

Hotel Carlos V

Map 3, H6. C/Maestro Vitoria 5 ℡915 314 100, 🖷www.hotel carlosv.com. Metro Sol.

Large, early twentieth-century hotel, just off c/Preciados. Some of the air-conditioned rooms on the fifth floor have balconies (at extra cost), though there isn't much of a view. There's an elegant lounge and café, and the hotel has a deal with a nearby car park which guests can use at reduced rates. ⑥

Hotel Ópera

Map 3, E5. C/Cuesta de Santo Domingo 2 ⓣ915 412 800, ⓦwww.hotelopera.com. Metro Ópera.
Located close to the Plaza de Oriente, this hotel has good facilities at a reasonable price. Rooms are comfortable and large, while, appropriately enough, the waiters in the café downstairs entertain diners with arias from operas and *zarzuelas*. ⑤

Hotel Paris

Map 5, B3. C/Alcalá 2 ⓣ915 216 496, ⓕ915 310 188. Metro Sol.
Friendly, old-fashioned hotel, right on Puerta del Sol with spacious, pleasantly decorated rooms. There's a nice interior patio and a laundry. It's seen better days, but is very good value given its central position. Breakfast included. ④

Hotel Regina

Map 5, D2. C/Alcalá 19 ⓣ915 214 725, ⓦwww.hotelregina madrid.com. Metro Sevilla.
Plush, well-located place between Sol and Cibeles. Good for tourists, with English-speaking staff, plenty of sightseeing information and its own cafeteria and bar; popular with organized tour groups. Make sure you ask for one of the refurbished rooms. Triples available for €136. ⑥

Gran Hotel Reina Victoria

Map 5, C5. Plaza de Santa Ana 14 ⓣ915 314 500, ⓦwww.solmelia.com. Metro Sol.
A giant cream cake of a hotel, perfectly placed, although it has lost a little of its character since it became part of the Tryp chain. A favourite of bullfighters, it has a taurine bar where *tertulias* are still held during the San Isidro Festival, and a rather grand foyer. It comes with all the services you'd expect, including currency exchange and a car park. ⑨

HOTELS

●

Hotel Santander

Map 5, D4. C/Echegaray 1 ⓣ914 296 644, ⓕ913 691 078. Metro Sevilla.

Spacious, well-decorated and spotless rooms with large bathrooms and many with a small seating area, along with classy old-fashioned decor and very friendly staff. Air conditioning is planned. Perfectly located for the bars and restaurants in the Santa Ana/Huertas area. ❸

PLAZA DE ESPAÑA, GRAN VÍA, CHUECA AND SANTA BÁRBARA

- - - - - - - - - - - - - - - - - - - -

Hotel Arosa

Map 5, B1. C/Salud 21 ⓣ915 321 600, ⓔarosa@hotelarosa. com. Metro Gran Vía/Sol.

Friendly, well-equipped hotel, right in the heart of town, just south off Gran Vía. Spacious, air-conditioned rooms in attractive pastel shades, all with modern bathrooms and a safe. Some of the surrounding streets are a little down-at-heel, but don't let this put you off. ❽

Casón del Tormes

Map 6, B6. C/del Río 7 ⓣ915 419 746, ⓦwww.bestwestern. es/casondeltormes. Metro Plaza de España.

Pleasant hotel in a surprisingly quiet street off Plaza de España. The en-suite rooms are very comfortable and have air conditioning. There's also a bar and breakfast room (not included in price). The staff speak English and are very helpful. Parking is available for €11 per night. A very good option in this price range. ❻

Hotel Emperador

Map 6, D6. Gran Vía 53 ⓣ915 472 800, ⓦwww.emperador hotel.com. Metro Santo Domingo/Plaza de España.

The only real reason to come here is the superb rooftop swimming pool with its magnificent views, while the hotel itself is geared up for the organized tour market and is rather impersonal, though the rooms are large and nicely decorated. ❽

HOTELS

Hotel Santo Domingo

Map 6, D7. Plaza Santo Domingo. ℡915 479 800, Ⓦwww.hotelsearch.com/madrid/santodomingo. Metro Santo Domingo.

Comfortable hotel with modern, attractively decorated rooms and very helpful staff. Some of the more expensive rooms have small terraces; all have air conditioning, satellite TV, minibars and a safe. There are reductions at the weekend. ❼

RECOLETOS, SALAMANCA AND CHAMBERÍ

Hotel Alcalá

Map 7, G1. C/Alcalá 66 ℡914 351 060, Ⓦwww.nh-hotels.es. Metro Príncipe de Vergara/Retiro.

Large, classy hotel with very friendly staff, just to the north of the Retiro, with smart rooms (some decorated in the garish colours of designer Agatha Ruiz de la Prada), laundry facilities and a car park. Expensive, but good deals available during the summer and at weekends.

Residencia Don Diego

Map 8, F8. C/Velázquez 45, 5° ℡914 350 760, Ⓟ914 314 263. Metro Velázquez.

This is a comfortable, friendly, medium-sized hotel in an upmarket area of town. The quiet rooms have full facilities, including newly-equipped bathrooms, air conditioning and satellite TV. Recommended. ❹

Galiano Residencia

Map 8, B8. C/Alcalá Galiano 6 ℡913 192 000, Ⓦwww.hotelgaliano.com. Metro Colón.

Hidden away in a quiet street behind the Heron building on the Castellana, this small hotel has a sophisticated air. There's a pleasant, well-furnished salon off the entrance lobby, staff are polite and the excellent rooms are air-conditioned. Breakfast included. Car parking available. ❻

Residencia El Viso

C/Nervión 8. ℡915 640 370, Ⓦwww.residenciadelviso.com.

HOTELS

147

Metro Republica Argentina/ Cruz del Rayo.
Charming, peaceful hotel in the leafy northern *barrio* of El Viso. Each of the tastefully decorated rooms has air conditioning, satellite TV and a safe, and there's a very pleasant patio with adjoining restaurant, serving quality but pricey food. A little out of the way for the main sites, but very convenient for the new metro link to the airport. ❻

Hotel Santo Mauro

Map 6, K1. C/Zurbano 36 ⓣ913 196 900, ⓦwww.ac-hotels.com. Metro Rubén Darío.
A palace in the nineteenth century, then an embassy and now a small luxurious hotel in the quiet Chamberí area. The rooms have tasteful modern decor while the communal areas are more traditional, and the excellent facilities include an indoor swimming pool, gym, sauna, car park and a babysitting service. Doubles start at a wallet-busting €298 per night. ❾

PENSIONES, HOSTALES AND HOSTELS

Pensiones and **hostales** are small, no-nonsense, frequently family-run establishments, sometimes with shared bathrooms and fewer facilities than a hotel. They are housed in large, centrally located apartment blocks and, in the more popular areas, you'll find two or three separate establishments, each on their own floor, in the same building. **Floors** (*pisos*) are written as 1° (first floor), 2°, etc, and often specify *izquierda* (*izqda*) or *derecha* (*dcha*), meaning to the left or right of the staircase respectively.

Some *hostales* in larger buildings – on Gran Vía, for example – don't always have an entryphone or doorbell at street level, making them inaccessible at night, unless you've got a key. If you book a room and intend to arrive after, say, 9pm, check you'll be able to get in.

APARTMENTS

An alternative, and often cheaper, accommodation option for families or groups is to rent an apartment. The most centrally-located of the tourist apartment blocks is *Apartamentos Turísticos* (Map 5, C4. C/Príncipe 11. ☎914 294 470, ⓦwww.atprincipe11.com. Metro Sevilla). The 36 apartments range from small studios to family suites for up to six. All are air-conditioned, have kitchenettes and are cleaned daily. Prices per apartment range from €92 for a four-person to €139 for a family one.

Though Madrid's two official **youth hostels** are not particularly convenient for the centre, there is one good option in a great location, *Los Amigos* (see p.150).

ATOCHA AND PASEO DEL PRADO

- -

Hostal Armesto
Map 5, E5. C/San Agustín 6, 1° dcha ☎914 290 940 or 914 299 031. Metro Antón Martín. A small standard six-room *hostal*. All rooms have bathrooms and TV and the best ones overlook the delightful little garden in the Casa de Lope de Vega next door. Very well-positioned for the Huertas/Santa Ana area. ❷

Hostal Barrera
Map 4, H3. C/Atocha 96 2° ☎915 275 381, ⓦwww.hostal barrera.com. Metro Antón Martín. Friendly, good-value 14-room *hostal*, with an English-speaking owner. Bathrooms have recently been re-equipped and air conditioning installed. Internet access available. One of the best in this part of town. ❷

Hostal Gonzalo
Map 5, E5. C/Cervantes 34, 3° ☎914 292 714, ⓕ914 202 007.

PENSIONES, HOSTALES AND HOSTELS

Metro Antón Martín.
Spotless 15-room *hostal*; all rooms have bathroom, TV and fan. The charming owner, Antonio, and his brother Javier run a very smart place at an excellent price. Highly recommended. ❷

SOL AND SANTA ANA

- - - - - - - - - - - - - - - - - - -

Hostal Aguilar

Map 5, D4. Carrera de San Jerónimo 32, 2° ☎91 429 59 26 or 91 429 36 61, ⒲www.hostal aguilar.com. Metro Sevilla.
Large *hostal*, with airy rooms all with bath, TV and air conditioning. Specializes in multi-bed rooms offering very good prices for quadruples (€69), making it an ideal budget place for families. ❷

Hostal Alfonso

Map 3, H7. Plaza Celenque 1, 2° ☎915 319 840, ⒻÐ915 329 225. Metro Sol/Ópera.
Nicely located just off c/Arenal, this clean, friendly *hostal* has fourteen small double rooms, two triples and a handful of singles at a very competitive price, all with bathrooms and TV. ❷

Hostal Astoria

Map 5, D4. Carrera de San Jerónimo 30, 5° ☎914 291 188, ⒲hostalastoria.com.
Metro Sevilla.
Friendly 26-room option in a building full of *hostales*. Decor is basic, but all of the bright, clean rooms have a bathroom, air conditioning and satellite TV. ❸

Hostal La Macarena

Map 3, F9. C/Cava de San Miguel 8, 2° ☎913 659 221, ⒻÐ913 642 757. Metro Sol.
Fine, family-run *hostal* in a pedestrianized characterful alley just off the Plaza Mayor. Rooms are quite small, but all have bathrooms, satellite TV and fans. ❸

Los Amigos Backpackers' Hostel

Map 3, E6. C/Campomanes 6, 4° izda. ☎ & ⒻÐ915 471 707, ⒲www.losamigoshostel.com.
Metro Ópera.
In a quiet street right by the opera house and just five

minutes from Sol, *Los Amigos* is a great option for backpackers on a tight budget. Dormitories cater for 4–6 people, and there are a couple of communal rooms, plus access to the internet. Friendly staff all speak English. Bed linen and use of the kitchen are included in the €17 price. ❶

Hostal Madrid

Map 3, H8. C/Esparteros 6, 2º ☎915 220 60, Ⓦwww.hostal-madrid.com. Metro Sol.
The owners of this very convenient *hostal* have gone to a lot of trouble to make their guests feel at home. Well-kept rooms all have air conditioning and TVs. Four good-value apartments also available for €84–102. ❸

Hostal Persal

Map 5, B5. Plaza del Angel 12 ☎913 694 643, Ⓦwww.hostal persal.com. Metro Sol.
Eighty-room hostal which is closer to a hotel in terms of services and facilities. Nearly all rooms have air conditioning, bathrooms are a little old-fashioned, but the rooms are surprisingly quiet given the central location. Breakfast included. ❹

Hostal Plaza D'Ort

Map 5, B5. Plaza del Angel 13, 1º ☎914 299 041, Ⓦwww.plaza dort.com. Metro Sol.
Smallish rooms in a very clean *hostal*, all with a shower or bath, TV, telephone and air conditioning. There are also several self-catering apartments, sleeping four to eight people for between €115–150 a night, making it a good family or group option. Internet connection available in all rooms. ❷

Hostal Rifer

Map 3, H8. C/Mayor 5, 4º ☎915 323 197. Metro Sol.
Spotless, bright rooms, all with en-suite facilities, in the highest – and therefore quietest – of three options in this block. The friendly owner is anxious to please and has plans to upgrade the rooms. ❷

Hostal Tijcal

Map 3, H9. C/Zaragoza 6 ☎913 655 910,

PENSIONES, HOSTALES AND HOSTELS

Ⓦwww.hostaltijcal.com.
Metro Sol.
Between Plaza Santa Cruz and Plaza Mayor, this recently remodelled and very helpful *hostal* offers salmon pink rooms with air conditioning, bathroom, TV and very comfortable beds. Triples and quadruples also available. ❸

Hostal Villar
Map 5, C5. C/Príncipe 18, 1º
Ⓣ915 316 600 or 915 316 609,
Ⓦwww.villar.arrakis.es.
Metro Sevilla.
Large *hostal* on four floors of a centrally situated building. Most of the standard rooms have small bathrooms, some have air conditioning, and all have satellite TV and telephone. ❷

GRAN VÍA, CHUECA AND SANTA BÁRBARA

- -

Hostal Asunción
Map 6, J3. Plaza Santa Bárbara 8 Ⓣ913 082 348,
Ⓔhotelasuncion@hotmail.com.
Metro Alonso Martínez.
In a pretty location

overlooking the square, this *hostal* offers small but well-furnished rooms with bath, TV and mini-bar; two have air conditioning. Free use of internet for guests. ❷

Hostal Buenos Aires
Map 6, C6. Gran Vía 61, 2º
Ⓣ915 420 102 or 915 422 250,
Ⓕ915 422 869.
Metro Plaza de España.
This recently refurbished thirty-room *hostal* at the Plaza de España end of Gran Vía is a cut above the rest. Pleasantly decorated rooms have air conditioning, satellite TV and new en-suite bathrooms. Double glazing keeps out most of the noise from the Gran Vía. Triples available at €68. ❸

Hostal Kryse
Map 6, G7. C/Fuencarral 25, 1º izqda Ⓣ915 311 512 or 915 228 153, Ⓕ915 228 153.
Metro Gran Vía.
Compact twenty-room *hostal* at the busy Gran Vía end of Fuencarral; all rooms have verandas and those above the street have double glazing. Small bathrooms, TV,

PENSIONES, HOSTALES AND HOSTELS

telephone and ceiling fans in all rooms. ❷

Hostal Medieval
Map 6, G5. C/Fuencarral 46, 2° izqda ⌒915 222 549.
Metro Chueca.
Small, well-run and functional family *hostal*. One of the airy rooms has a full bathroom, the rest have showers, but toilets are shared. Well-maintained building with attractive plants trailing from the verandas. Triples for €44 and quadruples for €50. ❷

Hostal Santa Bárbara
Map 6, I3. Plaza Santa Bárbara 4 ⌒914 457 334, ⌒914 462 345.
Metro Alonso Martínez.
Rather upmarket *hostal* in a good location. The nice rooms all have bathrooms and there's a great Art Deco TV salon. Some rooms have air conditioning. English spoken. ❷–❸

Hostal Sil/Serrano
Map 6, G3. C/Fuencarral 95, 3° ⌒914 488 972 or 915 930 993, ⌒914 474 829.
Metro Tribunal/Bilbao.
Two *hostales* run by a friendly owner on the quieter end of Fuencarral, up by the pleasant Glorieta de Bilbao. All rooms have air conditioning, new bathrooms and satellite TV. ❸

Hostal Zamora
Map 6, H7. Plaza Vázquez de Mella 1, 4° izqda ⌒915 217 031. Metro Gran Vía.
Simple rooms in an agreeable family-run *hostal*, most of which overlook the spruced-up plaza. Some rooms have air conditioning, and all have modern bathrooms and TV. There are good-value family rooms for €80. If you can't get in here, there are three other similar *hostales* in the same block. ❷

PENSIONES, HOSTALES AND HOSTELS

153

Eating

Eating out in Madrid is one of the highlights of any visit to the city. There's plenty to suit every pocket, from budget backstreet bars to high-class designer restaurants, and a bewildering range of cuisines encompassing tapas, traditional *Madrileño* and Spanish regional dishes, as well as international cooking.

Breakfast (*el desayuno*) is a pretty light affair, usually a cup of coffee and a *tostada* (toast and marmalade), but the traditional *Madrileño* breakfast of *chocolate con churros* – a glutinous dark chocolate with deep-fried hoops of batter – is sometimes preferred, especially after a night out on the tiles (see p.195). A mid-morning snack of a *bocadillo* (a French bread sandwich) or a *sandwich mixto* (a toasted ham and cheese sandwich) should keep hunger at bay until *aperitivos* and a few tapas at any time from 1pm onwards. **Lunch** (*la comida*) is taken very late, with few *Madrileños* starting before 2pm, and is often a long, drawn-out affair. **Dinner** (*la cena*), which again may be preceded by some tapas, will usually begin around 10pm, though many restaurants will not admit customers much later than 10.30pm. There are quite a number of **late-night options**, however, and the listings magazines all have sections for restaurants open past midnight (*después de medianoche/de madrugada* – see box on p.173).

Opening hours are given in all our listings, but note that bars often open and close according to how busy they are or the mood of the staff working that night. Many restaurants close on Sunday and/or Monday and for all or part of August.

The streets around **Puerta del Sol** are packed with places to eat and drink. You should spend at least one evening sampling the historic, tiled bars of **Santa Ana/Huertas**, while to the south, in the tiny streets of **La Latina** and **Lavapiés** there's an appealing neighbourhood feel to the bars and restaurants. On **Gran Vía**, burger bars fill most of the gaps between shops and cinemas, but head a few blocks north and there's plenty on offer, including a good cluster of ethnic restaurants on c/San Bernardino (north of the Plaza de España). **Chueca**, **Santa Bárbara** and **Malasaña**, further north, have some superb traditional old bars and bright new restaurants, serving some of the most creative food in the city, while the smarter districts of **Recoletos and Salamanca** contain few bars of note, but some extremely good (and extremely expensive) restaurants.

The recommendations given here include *bares*, *cafés*, *cervecerías* (beer halls), *marisquerías* (seafood specialists) and *restaurantes*, but have been divided simply into "Tapas bars" and "Restaurants", depending on whether they concentrate more on bar food or sit-down meals; many will actually have a bar area where you can get tapas, and also a more formal *comedor* (canteen) or *restaurante* out the back or upstairs.

Children are nearly always welcome and most places will make special arrangements for them. Restaurants are full to the brim at weekends, so it's vital to **book** at least a day ahead; even during the week it's advisable to reserve to avoid having to wait.

EATING

TAPAS GLOSSARY

Pincho Mouthful
Tapa Saucerful
Ración Small plateful
Adobado Marinated
Al ajillo With olive oil and garlic
A la marinera Seafood cooked with garlic, onions and white wine
A la parilla Charcoal-grilled
A la plancha Grilled on a hot plate
A la romana Fried in batter
Asado Roast

Standard tapas and raciones

Aceitunas Olives
Ahumados Smoked fish
Albóndigas Meatballs
Almejas Clams
Anchoas Anchovies
Bacalao Cod (often salted)
Berberechos Cockles
Berenjena Aubergine/ eggplant

Boquerones Small, anchovy-like fish, usually served in vinegar
Calamares Squid
Callos Tripe, often served in a spicy tomato sauce
Cangrejos de río Freshwater crayfish
Carabineiros Large red prawns
Caracoles Snails
Champiñones Mushrooms, usually fried in garlic
Chistorra Sausage with paprika
Chorizo Spicy sausage
Cocido Meat and chickpea stew (a *Madrileño* speciality)
Croquetas Croquettes, usually with bits of ham in
Empanada Slices of fish/meat pie
Ensaladilla Russian salad (diced vegetables in mayonnaise) often with tuna thrown in

TAPAS

Madrid is renowned for its **tapas** (usually three or four chunks of fish or meat, or a dollop of salad), which traditionally were served up free with a drink on a small plate to

Gambas Prawns
Hígado Liver
Jamón serrano Cured ham
Jamón de York Regular ham
Lacón Gammon
Langostinos Langoustines
Mejillones Mussels
Mollejas Sweetbreads
Morcilla Black pudding
Navajas Razor clams
Nécora Fiddler crab
Orejas Pigs' ears
Ostras Oysters
Patatas alioli Potatoes in garlic mayonnaise
Patatas bravas Fried potatoes in a spicy tomato sauce
Patatas a lo pobre Slices of fried potato mixed with egg (and sometimes *chorizo*)
Pimientos Peppers
Pimientos de Padrón Small peppers, with the odd hot one

Pincho moruno Kebab
Pisto Assortment of cooked vegetables, similar to ratatouille
Pulpo Octopus
Ques Cheese, the most common is the tasty Manchego made from ewe's milk
Riñones al Jerez Kidneys in sherry
Salchicha Sausage
Sepia Cuttlefish
Sesos Brains
Setas Oyster mushrooms
Tortilla española Potato omelette
Tortilla frances Plain omelette
Trigueros Green asparagus
Zarajo Grilled sheep's intestine wound around a stick, poached in brandy and wine and fried in olive oil

cover (or "tapar") the glasses and stop flies dropping in. These days, you have to pay for anything more than a few olives (where you do get free food now, it will often be called a *pincho*), but a single helping rarely costs more than €2–4 unless you're somewhere very flash. The procession

TAPAS

157

from one bar to the next, sampling its speciality, has evolved into a culinary ritual in the city. Fortunately, many of the best tapas bars are clustered together, particularly in the streets between **Puerta del Sol** and **Plaza de Santa Ana**, **La Latina** and **Lavapiés**. One of the main advantages of tapas is that you can experiment, and in many places food is laid out in glass display cases, so you can eat whatever takes your fancy even if you don't know what it's called.

Madrid's own speciality tapas include *patatas bravas*, *orejas* and *callos* (see "Glossary", p.156).

Raciones are simply bigger plates of the same, and can be a light meal in themselves. When ordering, make sure you specify whether you want a *ración* or just a *tapa*. The more people you're with the better; half a dozen *tapas* or *pinchos* and three *raciones* can make a varied and quite filling meal for three or four people. In recent years, the range of what's on offer has broadened significantly with new-wave tapas bars popping up all over the city, specialising in creative dishes that go beyond the traditional *tortilla*, *jamón* and *patatas bravas*.

SOL, PLAZA MAYOR AND ÓPERA

As de los Vinos
Map 5, A4. C/Paz 4. Metro Sol. Mon–Thurs & Sun 9.30am–4pm & 6.30–11.30pm, Fri & Sat 9.30am–4pm & 6pm–midnight. Closed Aug. Excellent wines and, for the sweet-toothed, the *torrijas* (deep-fried bread doused in wine and sprinkled with sugar and spices) are a must. A host of other tapas is available, including fine *callos* and *albóndigas*.

Las Bravas
Map 5, C5 & B5. C/Alvarez Gato 3, other branches at c/Espoz y Mina 13 and Pasaje Mathéu 5. Metro Sol.

TAPAS

Daily noon–4pm & 7pm–midnight.

Standing-room only at these three bars and, as the name suggests, *patatas bravas* is the thing to try; in fact, *Las Bravas* has patented its own version of the spicy sauce. The *tortilla*, *pulpo* and *callos* are tasty, too.

Casa del Abuelo

Map 5, C4. C/Victoria 12. Metro Sol. Daily 11.30am–3.30pm & 6.30–11.30pm. Tiny, highly atmospheric bar serving sweet, rich red house wine and cooked prawns – try them *al ajillo* (in garlic) or *a la plancha* (grilled). Use your free wine voucher to get a drink at the bar's sister *El Abuelo*, nearby.

Casa Labra

Map 5, A3. C/Tetuán 12 ℡915 310 081. Metro Sol. Mon–Sat 11am–3.30pm & 5.30–11pm. A great, traditional place dating from 1869 and retaining much of its original interior. This is where the Spanish Socialist Party was founded in 1879. Order a drink at the bar and a *ración* of cod fried in batter (*bacalao*) and some of the best *croquetas* in town at the counter to the right of the door. There's also a restaurant serving classic *Madrileño* food.

Mejillonera El Rocío

Map 5, B4. Pasaje Matheu. Metro Sol. Daily except Tues noon–midnight. Mussels (*mejillones*) served in every way imaginable in a bar-packed, pedestrian-only alleyway.

Museo del Jamón

Map 5, B3. Carrera de San Jerónimo 6. Metro Sol. Mon–Sat 9am–midnight, Sun 10am–midnight. The largest branch of this Madrid chain, from the ceilings of which are suspended hundreds of *jamones* (hams). The best – and they're not cheap – are the *jabugos* from the Sierra Morena, though a ham croissant won't set you back more than €2.

La Oreja de Oro

Map 5, C4. C/Victoria. Metro Sol. May–July & Sept Mon–Sat

TAPAS

1–4pm & 8pm–1am; Oct–April Tues–Sun 1–4pm & 8pm–1am. Closed Aug.

Standing room only in this bar, serving excellent *pulpo a la Gallega* (sliced octopus on a bed of potatoes fried in olive oil and seasoned with cayenne pepper), washed down with Ribeiro wine. Plenty of other seafood tapas on offer too.

El Oso y El Madroño

Map 5, A5. C/Bolsa 4. Metro Sol. Mon–Sat 10am–midnight. Closed last two weeks in July.

A tiny *castizo* bar where you can have a drink to the accompaniment of the *Madrileño chotis* and chat to the traditionally attired barmen who appear to have been here forever. Speciality *cocido*, snails, sangría and Jerez.

La Zapatería

Map 5, C4. C/Victoria 8. Daily 7pm–2am. **Metro**l Sol.

A relative newcomer on the scene which has carved out a niche of its own with its excellent *patatas a lo pobre* mixed with either *chorizo* or *morcilla*. Does a nice line in *caracoles* (snails) too.

SANTA ANA AND HUERTAS

Casa Alberto

Map 5, C6. C/Huertas 18 ☎914 299 356. Metro Antón Martín. Tues–Thurs noon–1am, Fri & Sat noon–2am, Sun noon–4pm.

Traditional *tasca* with a zinc and marble bar which has resisted the passage of time since it was founded back in 1827. Good *caracoles*, *gambas* and a great anchovy canapé, ideally accompanied by a glass of house vermouth. There's a small dining room at the back.

La Costa de Vejer

Map 5, C5. Corner of c/Núñez de Arce and c/Alvarez del Gato. Metro Sol. Tues–Sun noon–midnight.

The speciality here is prawns, grilled with garlic – an absolute must. Service is friendly and there's plenty of room to sit down at the back if you want to linger and try some of the other tapas.

TAPAS

El Lacón

Map 5, D5. C/Manuel Fernández y González 8 ☎914 293 698. Metro Sol. Daily noon–4pm & 8pm–midnight, Fri–Sun till 1.30am. Closed Aug. Large Galician bar/restaurant, with plenty of seats upstairs. Great *pulpo*, *caldo gallego* (meat and vegetable broth) and *empanadas* (pastry slices filled with tuna and vegetables).

Prada A Tope

Map 5, C5. C/Principe 11 ☎914 295 921. Metro Sevilla. 1.30–4.30pm & 8pm–midnight. Closed Tues & Aug. Excellent-quality produce from León. The *pimientos asados*, *morcilla* and *tortilla* are extremely tasty, while the smooth house wine provides the ideal accompaniment. Branch at Cuesta de San Vicente 32 (map 3, A4) just west of the Palacio Real.

Viña P

Map 5, C5. Plaza de Santa Ana 3. Metro Sol. Daily 1–4pm & 8pm–12.30am. Very friendly staff serving a great range of tapas in a bar decked out with bullfighting mementos and posters. Try the asparagus, stuffed mussels and the mouthwatering *almejas a la marinera* (clams in a garlic and white wine sauce).

LA LATINA AND LAVAPIÉS

Almendro 13

Map 3, E11. C/Almendro 13. Metro La Latina. Tues 1–5pm, Wed–Sun 1–5pm & 8pm–midnight. Fashionable wooden panelled bar that serves great *fino* from chilled black bottles. Help yourself to the glasses from the racks on the wall and tuck into original tapas of *huevos rotos* (fried eggs on a bed of crisps) and *roscas rellenas* (rings of bread stuffed with various meats).

El Almendro

Map 3, E12. C/Almendro 27. Metro La Latina. Daily except Tues, 1–4.30pm & 8.30pm–midnight. On the corner of Plaza de San Andrés, this is just the place for tasty and highly original

TAPAS

tapas. Fill in a card ticking your orders and choose from, among other dishes, an excellent asparagus in avocado sauce, wafer-thin chips and *chorizo*, three-cheese salad and *tortilla de bacalao*.

Los Caracoles

Map 4, A5. C/Toledo 106. Metro Puerta de Toledo. Tues–Sat 9am–10.30pm, Sun 9am–4pm. Closed July.

A continual supply of snails in spicy sauce is issued from the sizzling pan in this rough and ready local bar, all washed down with the local *vermút del grifo*.

La Chata

Map 3, F11. C/Cava Baja 24. Metro La Latina. Daily 12.30–4.30pm & 8.30pm–12.30am. Closed Sun eve.

One of the most traditional and popular tiled tapas bars in Madrid, with hams hanging from the ceiling, and taurine and football memorabilia on the walls. Serves a good selection of *raciones*, including *cebolla rellena* and *pimientos del piquillo rellenos* (stuffed onions and peppers).

Melo's

Map 4, F4. C/Avemaría 44. Metro Lavapiés. Tues–Sat 9am–2am. Closed Aug.

Standing room only at this very popular Galician bar serving huge *zapatillas* (hunks of Galician country bread filled with *lacón* and *queso*), great *pimientos de Padrón* and some fine *croquetas*.

La Taberna Angosta

Map 3, C12. C/Mancebos 6. Metro La Latina. Mon–Thurs 6pm–2.30am, Fri–Sun noon–3.30am.

Fantastic homemade patés – the *paté de ave al vino blanco* (white wine-flavoured paté) is especially good – accompanied by great wines in this friendly bar in the heart of old Moorish Madrid. Also serves some mean *boquerones angosta*. There's a small *terraza* on the pavement opposite in the summer.

Taberna de Antonio Sánchez

Map 3, H13. C/Mesón de Paredes 13. Metro Tirso de Molina. Mon–Sat noon–4pm & 8pm–midnight.

TAPAS

Said to be the oldest *taberna* in Madrid, this seventeenth-century bar has a stuffed bull's head (to commemorate Antonio Sánchez, the son of the founder, who was killed by a bull) and a wooden interior. Lots of *finos* on offer, plus *jamón* and *queso* tapas or *tortilla de San Isidro* (omelette with salted cod) and *callos*.

La Taberna de los Cien Vinos
Map 3, 4 E4. C/Nuncio 16. Metro La Latina. Tues–Sun 1–3.45pm & 8–11.45pm.
A vast array of Spanish wines (every month they sell a different selection of whites and reds) plus plenty of tapas to choose from, including excellent leek pie, smoked salmon and *pinchos* of roast beef. Not suitable for the indecisive.

La Taberna de Zapatero
Map 3, E12. C/Almendro 22. Metro La Latina. Tues–Sat 1–4pm & 8pm–midnight, Sun 1–4pm.
Excellent Ribera del Duero wine and original tapas in this friendly local haunt in a great bar-filled street. Try the downstairs cellar if you want a table.

La Tasca de Jesús
Map 3, E12. C/Cava Alta 32. Metro La Latina. Tues–Sun noon–5pm & 8pm–1am.
The staff ply you with a variety of excellent tapas while you wait at the minuscule bar for a table. When you do make it to the small brick-lined dining room the waiter is happy to recommend dishes – specialities include mini-steaks, grilled asparagus, shellfish and *patatas a lo pobre*.

GRAN VÍA, CHUECA AND SANTA BÁRBARA

El Bocaito
Map 6, I7. C/Libertad 4–6. Metro Chueca. Mon–Sat 1–4pm & 8.30pm–midnight. Closed Sat lunch and for two weeks in Aug.
You can watch the busy staff prepare the food in the kitchen/bar as you munch away on a variety of delicious

TAPAS

tapas, washed down by cold beer. Watch out for the *Luisito*, the hottest canapé your taste buds are ever likely to encounter.

Santander

Map 6, H6. C/Augusto Figueroa 25. Metro Chueca. Mon–Sat 10.45am–4pm & 7.30–11pm. Closed Aug. This bar in the heart of Chueca is famous for its vast range of tapas, including *empanadas*, *tortillas* and quiche lorraine, as well as a huge variety of fresh homemade canapés at very reasonable prices.

Stop Madrid

Map 6, G7. C/Hortaleza 11. Metro Gran Vía. Mon–Sat noon–4pm & 7pm–midnight. An old-time spit-and-sawdust bar specializing in dishes from Extremadura, accompanied by Belgian, Mexican and German beers as well as *vermút* on tap. Tapas consist largely of *jamón* and *chorizo*, with the *Canapé Stop* of ham and tomato doused in olive oil well worth a try.

Taberna de Sarmiento

Map 6, H6. C/Hortaleza 28. Metro Chueca. Mon–Sat noon–4pm & 8pm–midnight (Fri & Sat 1am). Closed Sat lunch. One of the new wave of tapas bars, specializing in artistically presented sit-down tapas. Try the spinach croquettes, or the fantastically refreshing melon salad served with prawns. The selection of canapés should not be missed, especially the paté with orange sauce, and there is an excellent selection of wines available from all over Spain.

MALASAÑA AND BILBAO

- -

Albur

Map 6, F2. C/Manuela Malasaña 15. Metro Bilbao. Sun–Wed noon–midnight, Thurs–Sat noon–1.30am. Wooden tables and rustic decor combine to make you feel that you're in a farm kitchen. The food is excellent, although service can be a little slow. The *champiñones en salsa verde* and the *patatas albur* (potatoes

TAPAS

fried with herbs and spices) are worth sampling, and the good wines are the ideal accompaniment.

La Camocha
Map 6, G1. C/Fuencarral 15. Metro Bilbao. Daily 7am–2am. Asturian-cider bar serving splendid *pulpo* and *almejas a la sidra*. You can use the special cider-pouring instruments stuck to the wall to make sure the cider is properly aerated.

Chipén
Map 6, G1. C/Cardenal Cisneros 39. Metro Bilbao. Daily noon–4pm & 7.30pm–midnight/ 1am.
A *castizo* bar, with tiles portraying famous city sights and serving a range of tapas from a menu written in *Madrileño* slang. Specialities include *chipén* (smoked-salmon canapé) and *fetén* (blue cheese canapé). Also serves frog's legs and draught vermouth.

RECOLETOS AND SALAMANCA

Hevia
Map 8, E2. C/Serrano 118. Metro Núñez de Balboa. Mon–Sat 9am–1.30am.
Plush venue and clientele for pricey but excellent tapas and canapés – the hot Camembert is a must and the *surtido de ahumados* (selection of smoked fish) is also worth a try.

José Luis
Map 8, E1. C/Serrano 89. Metro Núñez de Balboa. Mon–Sat 9am–1am, Sun noon–11pm.
The best of this chain of smart bar/restaurants, established by a Basque in the late 1950s. An unstoppable success, with branches in Seville, Valencia, Barcelona and Montréal, it serves dainty and delicious sandwiches, together with canapés of *cangrejo* (crab), *morcilla* (black pudding) and steak, but the bill quickly mounts up if you're not careful.

TAPAS

RESTAURANTS

Madrid's restaurants offer every regional style of **Spanish cooking**: Castilian for roasts (*horno de asar* is a wood-burning oven) and stews, *Gallego* for seafood, *Andaluz* for fried fish, Levantine (Valencia/Alicante) for paella and other rice-based (*arroz*) dishes, Asturian for cheeses and winter stews such as *fabada* and Basque for the ultimate gastronomy (and high prices).

Over the last few years, dozens of **foreign cuisines** have also appeared. There are some good Peruvian, Argentinian and Italian places and a scattering of enjoyable Indonesian and Japanese restaurants. With a few exceptions, Indian and Chinese restaurants are fairly dire, as, too, are most of the Mexican and Brazilian ones.

Traditional **Madrileño food** consists of robust mixed stews (such as the meat and chickpea *cocido*) and offal dishes,

RESTAURANT PRICES

Restaurants have been graded as inexpensive (under €15 a head for a three-course meal and wine), moderate (€15–20), expensive (€20–40) and very expensive (over €40). You can of course pay very different amounts at any restaurant depending on what you order and when. Fish and seafood generally boost the bill, while a set menú del día is often amazingly cheap (from as little as €6 for three courses and house wine), although it's usually only available weekday lunchtimes. If service is not included, a tip of somewhere between five and ten percent is sufficient, but never more than €4–5 in total.

Most – but by no means all – of the restaurants listed as "moderate" or above will accept credit/charge cards (*tarjetas*). If in doubt, phone ahead to check.

but the capital is also renowned for its quality seafood despite its distance from the sea – the best produce from Galicia is packed straight onto the train for Madrid each day.

SOL, PLAZA MAYOR AND ÓPERA

El Botín

Map 3, F9. C/Cuchilleros 17 ☎913 664 217. Metro Sol/Tirso de Molina. Daily 1–4pm & 8pm–midnight. **Expensive.**
Established in 1725, and highly picturesque, with its tiled and wooden panels, *El Botín* is cited in the *Guinness Book of Records* as Europe's oldest restaurant. Favoured by Hemingway, among others, it's inevitably a tourist haunt, but not such a bad one. Highlights are the Castilian roasts – especially *cochinillo* (suckling pig) and *cordero lechal* (lamb). Good house wine. The *menú del día* is around €27, but you could eat for less.

La Bola

Map 3, E5. C/Bola 5 ☎915 476 930. Metro Santo Domingo. Mon–Sat 1–4pm & 9pm– midnight, Sun 1–4pm. **Moderate.**
Established back in 1870, this is the place to go for *cocido madrileño* cooked in the traditional way over a wood fire (only served at lunchtime). Try the delicious *buñuelos de manzana* (battered apples) for pudding, and don't plan on doing anything energetic afterwards. No cards.

Casa Ciriaco

Map 3, C9. C/Mayor 84 ☎915 485 066. Metro Ópera. Daily except Wed 1.30–4pm & 8.30–11.30pm. Closed Aug. **Moderate.**
Attractive, old-style *taberna*, long reputed for its traditional Castilian dishes – trout *en escabeche* (marinated in vinegar and garlic), chicken *en pepitoria* (in almond sauce) and *cocido*. The *menú* is €17; main *carta* dishes a bit less. You can also sample some of the excellent wine in the front bar.

RESTAURANTS

167

Casa Gallega

Map 3, G7. C/Bordadores 11
☎915 419 055; also Plaza San
Miguel 8 ☎915 473 055. Both
Metro Ópera/Sol. Daily 1–4pm
& 8pm–midnight. Expensive.
An airy and welcoming
marisquería, with a branch at
Plaza San Miguel (map 3,
F9), that has been importing
seafood on overnight trains
from Galicia since it opened
in 1915. Costs vary greatly
according to the rarity of the
fish or shellfish that you
order. Gallego staples such as
pulpo (octopus) and *pimientos
de Padrón* are brilliantly done
and inexpensive, but the
more exotic seasonal delights
will raise a bill for two to
around the €60 mark.

Casa Paco

Map 3, F10. Plaza Puerta
Cerrada 11. ☎913 663 166.
Metro Sol La Latina. Mon–Sat
1.30–4.30pm & 8.30pm–
midnight. Moderate.
A great old-style eating house
with aluminium bar and small
comedor at the back,
specializing in simple but
tasty meat dishes.

La Finca de Susana

Map 5, D3. C/Arlabán. Metro
Sevilla. Daily 1–4.30pm &
8.30–11.45pm. Inexpensive.
One of two great-value
restaurants set up by a group
of Catalan friends (the other
is *La Gloria de Montera* just off
Gran Vía, see p.175). Great
menú del día for around €7,
consisting of simple dishes
served with imagination.
Stylish decor and quick,
efficient service, but arrive
early to avoid queuing.

Lhardy

Map 5, C3. Carrera de San
Jerónimo 8 ☎915 213 385.
Metro Sol. Shop: Mon–Sat
9.30am–3pm & 5–9.30pm, Sun
9am–2.30pm. Restaurant:
Mon–Sat 1–3.30pm &
9–11.30pm, Sun 1–3.30pm.
Very expensive.
Once the haunt of royalty,
this is one of Madrid's most
beautiful and famous
restaurants, but it's greatly
overpriced – expect to pay
over €45 per head for a
three-course meal. On the
ground floor, however, there's
a wonderful bar/shop where
you can snack on canapés,

RESTAURANTS

fino and *consommé*, without breaking the bank.

SANTA ANA AND HUERTAS

- - - - - - - - - - - - - - - - - - -

Anonimatto
Map 5, B5. Pasaje Alvarez Gato 4. ☏915 225 745. Metro Sol. Daily 1–5pm & 8pm–2am (3.30am on Fri & Sat). Inexpensive.
Ultra-modern decor and some creative budget cuisine in this café/restaurant just off Plaza Santa Ana. The *menú* is a good-value €7.21. Service can be a little on the slow side and you may have to wait for a table, but the atmosphere is friendly and relaxed, and there's a resident DJ in the evening.

Asia Society
Map 5, F6. C/Lope de Vega 4. ☏914 299 292. Metro Antón Martín. Mon–Sat 9pm–12.30am. Expensive.
One of the best places in the city for oriental-style food. New York chef Jamie Downing produces a great selection of Thai, Chinese, Japanese and Vietnamese-influenced dishes such as curried duck. Service is friendly but slow. Extensive wine list from Spain and abroad.

El Cenador del Prado
Map 5, D5. C/Prado 4 ☏914 291 561. Metro Antón Martín/Sevilla. Mon–Fri 1.30–4pm & 9pm–midnight, Sat 9pm–midnight. Closed Aug. Expensive.
Set in a relaxing and stylish mauve-coloured room, with imaginative cuisine combining Spanish, Mediterranean and Far Eastern influences. There's a *menú de degustación* (gourmet menu) at €21 and some spectacular desserts.

Champagnería Gala
Map 5, E7. C/Moratín 22 ☏914 292 562. Metro Antón Martín. Daily 1.30–4.30pm & 9pm–1.30am, Fri & Sat eve bar only. Inexpensive–moderate.
Fantastic-value restaurant run by a group of women, specializing in paellas and *fideuás* (like paella, only made with noodles instead of rice)

RESTAURANTS

●

and with excellent *pan tumaca* (toasted bread with tomato and garlic). Book ahead and try to get a table in the indoor patio at the back, but avoid weekends when the crowds mean the paellas and service aren't quite up to standard. No cards accepted.

Domine Cabra

Map 5, E6. C/Huertas 54 ☏914 294 365. Metro Antón Martín. Mon–Sat 2–4pm & 9–11.30pm, Sun 2–4pm. Closed Sat lunch & Sun in Aug and first half of Sept. Moderate.

Interesting mix of traditional and modern, with *Madrileño* standards given the *nueva cocina* treatment. Good sauces – a rarity in Spain – and look out for the *entrecot con crema de cabrales* (steak with blue-cheese sauce), the *vieiras gratinadas al vino Albariño* (roasted scallops in white wine) and the *berenjenas al horno* (roasted aubergines).

Donzoko

Map 5, D4. C/Echegaray 3 ☏914 295 720. Metro Sevilla. Mon–Sat 1.30–3.30pm & 8.30–11.30pm. Moderate.

One of the first Japanese restaurants in Madrid, and still very reasonable value with helpful service, decent sushi and delicious tempura. If you're in a group the *sukiyaki* (strips of meat and vegetables fried in a wok on the table) is a good bet.

El Inti de Oro

Map 5, D4. C/Ventura de la Vega 12. ☏914 296 703. Metro Sevilla. Daily 1.30–4pm & 8.30pm–midnight. Moderate.

The friendly staff at this Peruvian restaurant are more than ready to provide suggestions and give advice on those new to the cuisine. The *Pisco Sour*, a cocktail of Peruvian liquor, lemon juice, egg white and sugar is a recommended starter to clean the palate, while the *cebiche de merluza* (raw fish marinated in lemon juice) is a wonderful experience. Main courses include *papas rellenas* (potatoes stuffed with meat, olives and raisins) and chicken in a nut sauce.

La Sanabresa

Map 4, G2. C/Amor de Dios 12 ☎914 290 338. Metro Antón Martín. Mon–Sat 1–4pm & 8–11.30pm, Fri & Sat till midnight. Closed Aug. Inexpensive.

A real local place, with a TV in one corner and an endless supply of customers who come for its excellent and reasonably priced dishes. Don't miss the aubergines (*berenjenas a la plancha*).

La Vaca Verónica

Map 5, E7. C/Moratín 38 ☎914 297 827. Metro Antón Martín. Mon–Sat 2–4pm & 9pm– midnight. Closed Sat lunch & Sun. Moderate–expensive.

Something to suit all tastes in this amiable, well-run little restaurant. Excellent Argentinian-style meat, really good fresh pasta in imaginative sauces, quality fish dishes and tasty vegetables. Try the *Filet Verónica* and the *carabinero con pasta*. The *menú del día* is a very good €11.50.

LA LATINA AND LAVAPIÉS

Bar Salamanca

Map 3, F12. C/Cava Baja 31. Metro La Latina. Wed–Sat 1–4.30pm & 9pm–midnight. Cosy, family-run bar serving up good value home-made cooking with some of the best *croquetas* and *albóndigas* in the city. Often crowded at lunchtimes so best to arrive early if you want to grab one of the tables in the tiny *comedor*.

La Burbuja que Ríe

Map 3, C14. C/Angel 16 ☎913 665 167. Metro Puerta de Toledo/La Latina. Tues 1–5pm, Wed–Sun 1–5pm & 8pm–midnight. Moderate.

Very popular noisy Asturian restaurant, with a young clientele. Huge servings of mussels, an excellent selection of Asturian cheeses and very tasty *mero a la crema de anchoas* (grouper in anchovy sauce) and *merluza a la sidra* (hake in cider sauce). Get here early for a table.

RESTAURANTS

Casa Lastra Sidrería

Map 4, E2. C/Olivar 3 ☎913 690 837. Metro Antón Martín/Tirso de Molina. Mon, Tues & Thurs–Sat 1–5pm & 8pm–midnight, Sun 1–5pm. Closed July. **Moderate.**
Very popular restaurant serving huge portions of classic Asturian fare: *chorizo a la sidra* (*chorizo* in cider), *entrecot al cabrales* (steak in a strong blue-cheese sauce) and *fabada* (a stew of beans, *chorizo* and *morcilla*) washed down with, of course, *sidra natural* (cider).

Casa Lucio

Map 3, F12. C/Cava Baja 35 ☎913 653 252. Metro La Latina. Mon–Fri & Sun 1–4pm & 9–11.30pm, Sat 9–11.30pm. Closed Aug. **Expensive.**
Madrileños come here for Castilian dishes such as *cocido*, *callos* and roasts, cooked to perfection. It's where Queen Sofía took George Bush's wife. Booking essential.

Soidermersol aka El Económico

Map 4, F5. C/Argumosa 9. Metro Lavaplés.

Daily except Sat 1–5pm & 9pm–midnight. Closed mid-Aug to mid-Sept. **Inexpensive.**
Traditional family-run workmen's *comedor* in what looks like the front room of a house. Prices start at just over €2 a dish and there is an unbeatable €5 lunchtime *menú* offering a surprisingly large choice. Friendly service, very tasty food and, as the nickname suggests, superb value.

Viuda de Vacas

Map 3, I2. C/Cava Alta 23 ☎913 665 847. Metro La Latina. Daily except Thurs 1.30–4.30pm & 9pm–midnight. Closed Sun eve and early Aug. **Inexpensive–moderate.**
Highly traditional family-run restaurant established back in 1913. The place looks rather down-at-heel, but the good-quality Castilian fare certainly isn't. Try the *merluza al horno* (baked hake), the *callos* and the *rabo de toro* (oxtail).

AFTER MIDNIGHT

If you're desperate for that late-night stomach-filler to keep you going into the early hours, the following places are strategically situated in the key nighttime areas of the city.

La Carreta Map 6, I7. C/Barbieri 10 ☏915 327 042; Metro Chueca. The latest-opening of all – you can order up till 4.30am – and you get a show thrown in too. Live music, friendly service and quality grilled meats South American-style should satisfy even the most serious insomniac reveller. Daily 1–5pm & 9pm–5am. Moderate.

La Farfala Map 5, E7. C/Santa María 17 ☏913 694 691; Metro Antón Martín. The place to go for late-night food and a lively party atmosphere in the Huertas area. Good range of tasty pizzas and Argentinian-style meat. Daily 9pm–3am; Fri & Sat till 4am. Inexpensive.

Palacio de Anglona Map 3, D11. C/Segovia 13 ☏913 663 753; Metro La Latina. Italian-style dishes served up in this trendy joint situated in the cellars of an old palace. Daily 8.30pm–2am. Moderate.

GRAN VÍA, CHUECA AND SANTA BÁRBARA

El 26 de Libertad
Map 6, I6. C/Libertad 26 ☏915 222 522. Metro Chueca. Daily 1–4pm & 9pm–midnight. Closed Sun eve in July & Aug. Moderate.
Imaginative cuisine served up in an attentive, but unfussy manner in this brightly decorated restaurant, popular with the Chueca locals. Peppers stuffed with seafood, mushrooms in blue cheese and ostrich steaks in raspberry are some of the highlights. A good-value *menú del día* for €8.

RESTAURANTS

●

La Barraca

Map 6, H7. C/Reina 29 ☎915
327 154. Metro Gran Vía/Banco
de España. Daily 1–4pm &
8.30pm–midnight. Expensive.
Step off the dingy street into
this little slice of Valencia for
some of the best *paella* in
town. Service is attentive, the
starters are excellent and
there's a great lemon sorbet
for dessert. A three-course
meal with wine will set you
back around €30 a head.

El Buey

Map 6, B7. Plaza de la Marina
Española 1 ☎915 413 041.
Metro Santo Domingo;
c/General Díaz Polier 9 ☎915
753 128. Metro Goya. Mon–Sat
1–4pm & 9pm–midnight.
Moderate.
A meat-eaters' paradise,
specializing in superb steak
which you fry up yourself on
a hotplate. Very good side
dishes, too, including a great
leek-and-seafood pie and
excellent homemade desserts.
Help yourself to wine and
cheese in the tiny bar while
you wait to be seated.

Carmencita

Map 6, I7. C/Libertad 16 ☎915
316 612. Metro Chueca.
Mon–Fri 1–4pm & 9pm–
midnight, Sat 9pm–midnight.
Inexpensive–moderate.
Beautiful old restaurant,
dating back to 1830, with
panelling, plenty of brass,
marble tables, Valencian tiles
– and a new Basque-
influenced chef. Popular with
politicians and the literary
crowd. The lunch *menú* is a
bargain at €8.50, with the
speciality being the *cocido*,
served on Thursdays. If you
choose to eat *à la carte* the
prices rise considerably.

El Comunista
(Tienda de Vinos)

Map 6, I6. C/Augusto Figueroa
35 ☎915 217 012. Metro
Chueca. Mon–Sat 1–4.30pm &
9.30–11.45pm, Sun 9.30–
11.45pm. Closed mid-Aug to
mid-Sept. Inexpensive.
Long-established, popular
comedor that has changed little
since it was given its unofficial
(but always used) name as a
student haunt under Franco.
The *sopa de ajo* (garlic soup) is
particularly recommended.

RESTAURANTS

La Gloria de Montera

Map 6, G8. C/Caballero de Gracia 10. Metro Gran Vía. Daily 1–4.30pm & 8.30–11.45pm. Inexpensive.

Sister restaurant to *La Finca de Susana* (see p.165) with the same successful formula. Excellent value *menú* with imaginative, well-presented dishes on offer in a cool and airy setting just off Gran Vía. No reservations accepted.

Momo

Map 6, I6. C/Augusto Figueroa 41 ℡915 327 162. Metro Chueca. Daily 1–4pm & 9pm–midnight. Inexpensive.

Now a well-established feature on the Chueca scene, this is the place to go for a *menú del día* with a little bit extra. For €8 you get three well-presented courses, with some imaginative sauces, drinks and coffee, all served in outrageously kitsch decor. Very popular.

Nova Galicia

Map 6, C4. C/Conde Duque 3 ℡915 594 260. Metro Plaza de España. Mon–Sat 7am–midnight, Sun 7am–4pm. Closed second half of Aug. Moderate.

Excellent-value Galician restaurant, specializing in seafood tapas and *arroz con bogavante* (rice with lobster). Pass through the ordinary-looking front bar and into the dining room hidden behind. For large parties they'll do a special *queimada* (flaming Galician liquor served in small terracotta bowls).

Salvador

Map 6, I7. C/Barbieri 12 ℡915 214 524. Metro Chueca. Mon–Sat 1.30–5pm & 9pm–midnight. Closed Aug. Expensive.

Bullfighting decor and traditional specialities such as *rabo de toro* (oxtail), *gallina en pepitoria* (chicken fricassee), fried *merluza* (hake) and *arroz con leche* (rice pudding).

La Tasca Suprema

Map 6, J4. C/Argensola 7 ℡913 080 347. Metro Alonso Martínez. Mon–Sat 1.30–4pm. Closed Aug. Inexpensive.

Very popular family-run local, only open at lunchtimes and worth

RESTAURANTS

booking ahead for. Perfect Castilian home cooking, including *callos*, and on Monday and Thursday, *cocido*.

MALASAÑA AND BILBAO

- - - - - - - - - - - - - - - - - -

Annapurna
Map 6, K2. C/Zurbano 5 ☎913 198 716. Metro Alonso Martínez. Mon–Fri 1.30–4pm & 9pm–midnight, Sat 9pm–midnight. Closed Sat lunch & Sun. Moderate–Expensive

To say this is the best Indian restaurant in Madrid is faint praise, but *Annapurna* could hold its own in London, especially if you go for the

---

MADRID'S VEGETARIAN RESTAURANTS

Madrid can be an intimidating city for vegetarians, given the mass of pigs, fish and seafood on display in restaurant windows and on counters. However, you can order vegetables separately at just about any restaurant in the city – though make sure you specify that you do not want stray pieces of ham included – and there is good pizza and pasta to be had at a number of Italian places. You can even find the odd vegetarian paella. As for tapas, *champiñones*, *patatas bravas*, *patatas alioli*, *pimientos de Padrón* and *tortilla* are probably the best bets.

Fortunately, the capital now has some decent and inexpensive vegetarian restaurants around the centre. These include:

Artemisa Map 5, D4. C/Ventura de la Vega 4 ☎914 295 092; Metro Sevilla and **Map 5, B1**. C/Tres Cruces 4 ☎915 218 721; Metro Gran Vía. A popular place, best known for its veggie pizzas, stuffed aubergines and an imaginative range of salads. No smoking. Mon–Sat 1.30–4pm & 9pm–midnight, Sun 1.30–4pm. Moderate.

tandoori dishes or *thali*. Elegant surroundings and attentive service.

Balear

C/Sagunto 18 ℡914 479 115. Metro Iglesia. Mon & Tues–Sat 1.30–4pm & 8.30pm–midnight, Sun 1.30–4pm. Moderate. This relaxed Levantine restaurant serves only rice-based dishes – fifteen different types of paella – but they're superb. There's an inexpensive *cava* and you can turn up any time before midnight.

La Giralda

Map 6, G1. C/Hartzenbush 12 ℡914 457 779. Metro Bilbao. Mon–Sat 1–4.30pm &

Elqui Map 5, F4. C/Buenavista 18 ℡914 680 462; Metro Lavapiés/Antón Martín. Excellent vegetarian venue in the heart of Lavapiés. Light and tasty main courses, imaginative soups and some great fruit-based drinks. There's a self-service lunchtime *menú* for €6.60. No smoking. Open Tues–Fri for lunch, Fri and Sat evenings for dinner.

El Estragón Map 3, D11. Plaza de La Paja 10 ℡913 658 982; Metro La Latina. Cosy atmosphere and a fine setting on the edge of this ancient plaza. Serves good vegetarian tapas, and a varied *menú del día* for €6 (weekends €9). The sort of place that non-veggies will also enjoy. Daily 1–4.30pm & 8.30pm–midnight; closed Sun evening. Inexpensive–moderate.

La Granja Map 6, F3. C/San Andrés 11 ℡915 328 793; Metro Bilbao/Tribunal. The good-value set menu at €6 changes daily, offering a choice of soup, salad, a main dish of vegetables, rice and fruits topped with sauce, dessert and drinks. Mon–Wed 1.30–4.30pm & 9pm–midnight, Thurs–Sun 1.30–4.30pm. Inexpensive.

RESTAURANTS

8pm–midnight.
Moderate–expensive.
A little slice of Andalucía
serving fish and seafood of
very high quality. Perfectly
cooked *chipirones* (small squid
fried in batter), *calamares* and
all the standards, plus
wonderful *mero* (grouper). A
second branch, across the
road at no.15, does a similarly
accomplished job on *pescados
fritos*.

La Glorieta
Map 6, E2. C/Manuela
Malasaña 37 ☎914 484 016.
Metro Bilbao. Mon–Sat
1.30–5pm & 9pm–midnight.
Closed Aug 10–25. **Moderate.**
Imaginative and tasty modern
Spanish cooking, with Basque
and French influences. Very
good-value *menú del día* at
€7.50, which includes a
better-than-average bottle of
wine, zesty lemon
cheesecake, coffee and a *copita*
of high-powered Galician
orujo (strong schnapps-like
drink).

Ribeira Do Miño
Map 6, H5. C/Santa Brígida 1
☎915 219 854. Metro Tribunal.

Daily 1–5pm & 8pm–1am.
Closed Mon. **Moderate.**
Great-value *marisquería* near
the Museo Municipal, serving
a *mariscada* (shellfish platter)
for two at only €21; go for
the slightly more expensive
Galician white wine, *Albariño*,
to accompany it. Efficient and
friendly service.

RECOLETOS AND SALAMANCA

El Amparo
Map 2, K3. Callejón Puigcerdá
8 ☎914 316 456. Metro
Serrano. Mon–Fri 1.30–3.30pm
& 9–11.30pm, Sat 9–11.30pm.
Expensive.
Critics rate this designer
restaurant among the top five
in Madrid, and you need to
book a couple of weeks ahead
for a table. Faultless Basque
cooking by Carmen Guasp,
with main dishes around the
€20 mark, and a bill of at
least €35 a head.

Casa Portal
Map 7, G1. C/Dr Castelo 26
☎915 742 026. Metro
Retiro/Ibiza. Mon–Sat 1.30–4pm

& 8.30–11.30pm. Closed Aug.
Expensive.
Superlative Asturian cooking – go for the *fabada* (beans, *chorizo* and *morcilla* stew) or *besugo* (bream), washed down with some cider. The shellfish is excellent too.

Paradis Madrid

Map 5, F3. C/Marqués de Cubas 14 ☎914 297 303. Metro Banco de España. Mon–Fri 1.30–4pm & 9pm–midnight, Sat 9pm–midnight. Closed Easter & Aug. Expensive.
Part of a chain of restaurants run by a Catalan duo, with branches in Barcelona and New York. Designerish details include a menu for olive oils. The cooking is light, Mediterranean and tasty; try the wonderful *arroz negro* (rice cooked in squid ink) with seafood.

Suntory

Map 8, D4. Paseo de la Castellana 36–38 ☎915 773 733. Metro Rubén Darío. Mon–Sat 1.30–3.30pm & 8.30–11.30pm. Closed Sun & holidays. Expensive.
Authentic and upmarket Japanese restaurant with showy service and great presentation. A mixed sushi will set you back around €25. The best bet is to go for the lunchtime set menu at €24, but if you feel like really splashing out you could try the *menú de degustación* at €42.

Viridiana

Map 5, H3. C/Juan de Mena 14 ☎91 523 44 78 or 915 315 222. Metro Retiro. Mon–Sat 1.30–4pm & 9pm–midnight. Closed Easter & Aug. Very expensive.
Bizarre temple of Madrid *nueva cocina*, offering mouthwatering creations like *solomillo* (sirloin) with black truffles and *mero* (grouper) with *crepes*, while also conducting pyrotechnic experiments – dishes often arrive decorated with small incendiary devices. Superb selection of wine. Main courses are around €16.

Zalacaín

Just off Map 8, C1. C/Alvarez de Baena 4 ☎915 614 840. Metro Gregorio Marañon.

RESTAURANTS

Mon–Fri 1.15–4pm & 9pm–midnight, Sat 9pm–midnight. Closed Aug. **Very expensive.** Luxurious setting for the best restaurant in town and the only one with three Michelin stars. As you'd expect, the Basque-style cooking of master chef Benjamín Urdaín is top-notch and the wines are superb. You pay heavily for the pleasure, however, with a meal setting you back around €70 per person.

ARGÜELLES

Casa Mingo
Off Map 2, A3. Paseo de la Florida 2 ☎915 477 918. Metro Príncipe Pío. Daily 11am–midnight. Closed Aug. **Inexpensive.**
Next to the Ermita de Antonio de la Florida, this is a great-value, noisy and crowded Asturian chicken and cider house. Tables are like gold dust, so loiter with your bottle of *sidra* in hand. The spit-roast chicken is the practically compulsory main course, while *chorizo* cooked in cider and *cabrales* (blue cheese) is also very good. They do takeaways for a picnic in the Casa de Campo, too.

La Vaca Argentina
Map 2, A1. Paseo del Pintor Rosales 52 ☎915 596 605. Metro Argüelles. Daily 1–5pm & 9pm–midnight. **Moderate.** Good views (its terrace is very pleasant in summer) and great grilled steaks (*churrasco*) at this Argentinian restaurant overlooking the Parque del Oeste. There's another branch on c/Ribera de Manzanares 123 (☎915 593 780) with a fine riverside terrrace.

Drinking

With over 12,000 **bars** in the city, it's clear that the bar – and its close cousins, the café and *terraza* – is a central feature of *Madrileño* life. There's a bewildering variety to choose from: *cervecerías* (beer specialists), *coctelerías* (cocktail bars), *champagnerías* (champagne bars), *tabernas* (old-style taverns), *bares de copas* (bars mainly serving spirits) and, of course, a host of Irish pubs. You'll also find *discobares* and *pubs*, where music is the primary attraction; these are covered in "Nightlife", see p.195.

Hanging out in bars is one of the best, and most pleasant, ways to get the feel of the city and its people, although you'll need to adopt *Madrileño* bar **customs** as quickly as possible. Don't be perturbed if the barman or waiter appears to ignore you; just give a firm shout of "*oiga*", which, although it sounds rude to English-speaking ears, is the polite way of calling someone's attention. Once you've ordered don't be in a hurry to thrust your euros into the barman's hand; instead, wait until you're ready to go, and then ask for "*la cuenta*" (the bill). Leave a few small coins as a **tip** if you wish, and remember that you normally pay a little more for sitting at a table with waiter service than for standing at the bar. You won't often find bins for your bar detritus of olive stones, paper napkins, toothpicks, etc – it's usual to throw them on the floor.

Most cafés and bars serve some sort of **food**, but if this is their primary attraction we have listed them under "Tapas bars" in the "Eating" chapter (see p.156). There is, however, no absolute dividing line, and you often find excellent snacks in the places listed below. Many bars, and especially nightclubs, set up outdoor *terrazas* in summer. For details of these, see pp.204–205.

SOL AND SANTA ANA

Aloque

Map 4, F3. C/Torrecilla del Real 20. Metro Antón Martín. Daily 7.30pm–1am. Closed Aug. Relaxed wine bar where you can try top-quality wines by the glass. Its owner, Paco Parejo, is a science professor and expert on viticulture. Regular wine-tasting sessions and a wine connoisseurs' *tertulia* (Tues) are held here. The tapas, served up from the tiny kitchen at the back, are original and very tasty.

El Anciano

Map 3, C8. C/Bailén 19. Metro Ópera. Daily except Wed 10am–3pm & 5.30–11pm, Fri & Sat till 12.30am. Closed Aug. Stylish old bar across the road from the Palacio Real, and just the place to refresh yourself after some hard work on the tourist trail. Tasty beer and a good range of wines in an old-fashioned establishment, dating back to 1907.

Begin the Beguine

Map 5, E7. C/Moratín 27. Metro Antón Martín. Daily 8pm–2.30am. Dimly-lit corner bar that sells a vast range of huge cocktails. The ideal place for a late-evening chill-out after a tough bar crawl.

Café de Oriente

Map 3, D7. Plaza de Oriente 2. Metro Ópera. Daily 8.30am–1.30am, Fri & Sat till 2.30am. Elegant, traditional-style café, founded a decade or so ago by priest Luis Lezama, to finance a charity rehab programme for ex-convicts. Plenty of mirrors, marble tabletops and candlesticks with occasional accompaniment from the pianist. A popular *terraza* in summer looks out onto Plaza de Oriente.

Cervecería Alemana
Map 5, C5. Plaza de Santa Ana 6. Metro Sol. Daily except Tues 10am–12.30am, Fri & Sat till 2am.
Stylish old beer house, founded in 1904, with dark wooden panels, white marble tables and a packed bar. Frequented in times past by Hemingway and, these days, seemingly every other American tourist. Order a *caña* and go easy on the tapas, as the bill can mount up fast.

Cervecería Santa Ana
Map 5, C5. Plaza de Santa Ana 10. Metro Sol. Daily 11am–1.30am, Fri & Sat till 2.30am.
Cheaper than the *Alemana*, with tables outside, but few inside. Good beer, friendly

service and a fine selection of tapas. Always packed at night.

La Fidula
Map 5, E6. C/Huertas 57. Metro Antón Martín. Daily 8pm–3am.
A fine bar where you can sip *fino* to the accompaniment of classical tunes, performed from the tiny stage. Concerts scheduled for most nights of the week from June to September.

Los Gabrieles
Map 5, D5. C/Echegaray 17. Metro Sol. Daily 2.30pm–2.30am.
This impressively tiled bar, which includes scenes from *Don Quixote* and a version of Velázquez's *Los Borrachos*, is a Madrid monument and it's worth going earlier than is cool to appreciate the fabulous tableaux, created by sherry companies in the 1880s. Drinks are reasonable, considering the venue. Live flamenco on Tuesdays. Very crowded after 10pm.

SOL AND SANTA ANA

DRINKING – THE ESSENTIALS

Drinking out needn't be expensive, especially if you stick to the more down-to-earth local bars and, even better, get to know the barman. If you venture into cocktail bars and *bares de copas* you'll pay a lot more for both beers and spirits, although measures are very generous indeed and it's usually up to you to tell the barman to stop pouring. It's worth remembering that imported beers and spirits (*importación*) are always a good deal more expensive than the Spanish equivalents (*nacional*).

Beer

Cerveza, lager-type beer, is generally of very good quality. It comes bottled in *tercios* (a third of a litre) or smaller *botellines*, and on draught (*de barril*), in *cañas* (small glasses), *dobles* (larger glasses), *jarras* (jugs) or even *pintas* (pints). Non-alcoholic beers (*cerveza sin alcohol*) are available by the bottle in all bars. The most popular local brand is Mahou, although practically every major international brand is now available in Madrid.

Wine and liqueurs

Wines (*tinto* – red, *blanco* – white and *rosado* – rosé) are a very cheap option and many bars have a fine selection, so ask for it by name, as you tend to get the cheapest if you don't specify. In addition to the internationally renowned Rioja, it's worth trying the red wines from Ribera del Duero, with their smooth blackcurrant flavour; 1989, 1995, 1996 and 1999 are particularly good years. Fine reds are also to be found from Navarra, Valdepeñas and Penedès. As for white wines, those from Rueda are recognized for their quality, while the Galician whites of Ribeiro and Albariño are refreshing and make an excellent accompaniment to seafood. The light white, Barbadillo, from near Cádiz, is an excellent summer option. A non-alcoholic alternative to wine is the sweet white *mosto*, which is available in most bars.

Sherries are also worth trying, especially the chilled dry *fino* or fuller bodied *palo cortado* served in many Andaluz bars, as is *vermút de barril* (draught vermouth), all of which make an ideal apéritif. Catalan champagne-like sparkling wine, cava, is good value and can be ordered at specialist wine bars and *champagnerías*. Sangría, a deceptively strong but refreshing punch-like mixture of red wine, fruit and lemonade, is common in summer. A variety of after-dinner drinks and liqueurs are available, including locally produced *anís* (aniseed), *pacharán* (another more fruity aniseed drink from Navarra) and *orujo* (a powerful schnapps-type drink).

Soft drinks

As you'd expect, all the major brand-name soft drinks are available, but also worth trying are the specifically Spanish soft drinks such as *horchata* (a milky drink made from tiger nuts) and *granizado* (crushed ice with lemon, orange or coffee). When ordering water specify if you want it still (*sin gas*), sparkling (*con gas*) or from the tap (*del grifo*).

Coffee and tea

Coffee is usually of excellent quality and generally served black in a small cup (*café solo*). If you want a larger, more dilute black coffee ask for an *americano*; with a drop of milk it's *café cortado*; and white with lots of hot milk it's *café con leche*. For decaffeinated ask for *descafeinado*. Tea (*té*) is usually poor, and ordering it with milk will often get you a glass of milk with a tea bag floating on top, so it's best to order the two separately.

Naturbier

Map 5, C5. Plaza de Santa Ana 9. Metro Sol. Daily 8pm–3am.

Just up from the *Santa Ana*, the *Naturbier* brews its own tasty, cloudy beer and serves a variety of German sausages to accompany it. There's usually room to sit in the cellar down below if the top bar is too crowded.

Repórter

Map 4, H3. C/Fúcar 6. Metro Antón Martín. Tues–Sun noon–2.30am.

The cool terrace garden at the rear of this bar makes a great place for a relaxing cocktail. Also does tapas and a good-value *menú del día* during the day.

Salón del Prado

Map 5, D5. C/Prado 4. Metro Sol. Daily 2pm–2am.

Elegant Parisian-style café/bar serving great coffee and hosting classical music concerts on Thursday nights at 11pm. Turn up early if you want a table.

La Taberna de Dolores

Map 5, F6. Plaza de Jesús 4. Metro Antón Martín. Daily 11am–midnight.

Splendid canapés at this popular and friendly tiled bar, decorated with beer bottles from around the world. The beer is really good, and the food specialities include roquefort and anchovy, and smoked-salmon canapés.

La Venencia

Map 5, D4. C/Echegaray 7. Metro Sol/Sevilla. Daily 7pm–1.30am. Closed Aug.

This rather dilapidated, wooden-panelled bar covered in yellowing advertising posters is great for sherry sampling. The whole range is here, served from wooden barrels, and accompanied by delicious olives and *mojama* (dry salted tuna). Atmospheric and authentic.

Viva Madrid

Map 6, D5. C/Manuel Fernández y González 7. Metro Antón Martín. Daily noon–2am, Fri & Sat till 3am.

Another fabulous tiled bar both outside and in – offering

wines and sherry, plus basic tapas. Get here early if you want to see the tiles in their full glory, as it gets very crowded. Quite pricey, but certainly worth a stop.

LA LATINA AND LAVAPIÉS

El 21
Map 3, G10. C/Toledo 21. Metro La Latina. Daily 11am–3.30pm & 7–11pm. Closed Aug.
Seedy-looking, but excellent *chupito* (a thimbleful of spirits) bar, serving a vast range of mini-cocktails (including non-alcoholic), with evocative names such as *Erótico*, *Medias de seda* (Silk Stockings), *Terremoto* (Earthquake) and *Volcán* (Volcano). The cheap and cheerful alternative to a full-scale cocktail bar; all drinks are €1–€1.50.

Alquezar
Map 4, E4. C/Lavapiés 53. Metro Lavapiés. Daily 1pm–1am, Fri & Sat till 3am.
An Arabian atmosphere is

created with walls adorned with camels and mosques, background music and sweet-smelling tea served from silver-plated teapots. If you get peckish try the Arab pastries.

Café del Nuncio
Map 3, E11. C/Segovia 9. Metro La Latina. Daily 12.30pm–2.30am.
A great place for cocktails, alcoholic coffees and the house speciality, *Agua de Valencia* (a sort of bucks fizz). Good cakes and biscuits, too, and a very pleasant *terraza* in summer.

El Madroño
Map 3, F10. Plaza Puerta Cerrada 7. Metro Sol/La Latina. Inexpensive. Daily 11am–2am.
Once a liquor shop that also sold cakes and pastries, but now a friendly bar that also does a varied *menú del día* costing €7.80. You can, however, still buy a bottle of Madrid's own local liqueur made from the berries of the madroño tree for €6.50.

LA LATINA AND LAVAPIÉS

187

LAS TERTULIAS

People everywhere meet to chat and argue, but only in Spain – a country where conversation is considered to be one of the fine arts – has this simple custom been converted into an established ritual. To earn the name tertulia, a regular time and place must be fixed – usually in a café or bar – and participants must come prepared to speak, interrupt, contradict and generally intensify the discussion. Subjects can range from politics, philosophy and literature to bullfighting and flamenco.

The first *tertulias* began with the eighteenth-century Enlightenment and were largely political, with liberals and absolutists – supporters and opponents of the French Revolution – arguing out their differences. In the late nineteenth and early twentieth centuries, with the rise of the literary groups, the "Generation of '98" and subsequent "Generation of '27", they became a forum for intellectual and artistic ideas, with participants including the poet Federico García Lorca and painter José Gutiérrez de Solana (whose famous painting of the *tertulia* at the *Café del Pombo* hangs in the Centro de Arte Reina Sofía). Not all writers, however, enjoyed these literary gatherings: Hemingway, for one, hated them and regarded the people who attended them as "a load of show-offs".

Cafés such as *Gijón*, *El Lion* and *El Parnasillo* built their reputations on the standard of their *tertulias*, and as one old *contertulio* said, "In life there are only three fundamental choices: marital state, profession and café." However, many were silenced during the Civil War and afterwards under Franco, when meetings of more than five people were seen as suspect. They reappeared in the late 1940s, with the emergence of Juventud Creadora, a group of young writers who met in *Café Gijón*, headed by Nobel Prize-winner Camilo José Cela, and to this day, although they have declined in importance and may not reach the intellectual heights of the past, they are still alive and well in a number of the city's old cafés and bars.

María Panadora

Map 3, B12. Plaza Gabriel Miró 1. Metro La Latina.
Tues–Thurs 6pm–2am, Fri & Sat 6pm–3am, Sun 1pm–2am. Closed second half of Aug.
An incongruous mixture of *champagnería* and library, where quality *cava* can be enjoyed with the perfect accompaniment of chocolates and mellow jazz – a decadent and highly enjoyable outing.

Montes

Map 4, E3. C/Lavapiés 40. Metro Lavapiés/Tirso de Molina.
Tues–Sat noon–4pm & 7.30pm–midnight; closed Aug.
A Lavapiés favourite for those in search of a decent glass of wine and a very tasty canapé. Ask owner César for advice and he'll help you find the ones to suit. A great place to start the evening.

Nuevo Café Barbieri

Map 4, F4. C/Avemaría 45. Metro Lavapiés. Daily 3pm–2am, Fri & Sat till 3am.
Slightly seedy, well-known café with a vaguely intellectual reputation, situated just off the Plaza de Lavapiés. It's a relaxed place, with unobtrusive music, lots of wooden tables, old-style decor, newspapers and a wide selection of coffees.

El Tempranillo

Map 3, E12. C/Cava Baja 38. Metro La Latina. Daily noon–4pm & 9pm–2am.
Excellent little wine bar serving a vast range of Spanish wines by the glass. Although a relative newcomer, it feels as though it's been here for years and has already established a faithful clientele. A great place to discover your favourite Spanish wine, and the tapas are very tasty too.

GRAN VÍA AND CHUECA

- - - - - - - - - - - - - - - - - - - -

Café Moderno

Map 6, D3. Plaza de las Comendadoras 1. Metro Noviciado. Daily 3pm–2am, Fri & Sat till 3am; June–Sept from noon.
Hidden away in a quiet, hippyish square alongside the Convento de las

GRAN VÍA AND CHUECA

Comendadoras is this mock Art Deco café. Activities include musical recitals, tarot readings, theatrical performances and Arabian dancing. Plenty of coffees and herbal teas.

Carpe Diem

Map 6, D5. Plaza Conde de Toreno 2. Metro Plaza de España/Noviciado. Tues–Sat 9pm–3am.

Part of the takings here goes towards oversea projects and it often stages markets in aid of developing countries. The single-roomed bar is decorated with Pop Art, while noticeboards keep the clientele informed of upcoming events. Happy hour goes on until midnight, with a variety of Spanish pop and salsa played.

Círculo de Bellas Artes

Map 5, E2. C/Alcalá 42. Metro Banco de España. Daily 8am–2am, Fri & Sat till 3am.
You pay €1 for day membership to the Círculo, which gives access to the exhibitions (see p.67) and to a luxurious bar, complete with reclining nude sculpture, chandeliers and sofas. From May to October there's a comfortable *terraza* on the pavement outside.

El Cock

Map 6, H7. C/Reina 16, behind Museo Chicote. Metro Gran Vía. Daily 7pm–3am.
Formerly connected to the *Museo Chicote* (see opposite) by a secret corridor, this is now a smart and very *moda* bar, styled like a gentlemen's club, and you have to knock to get in. Attracts an arty crowd late at night, and the music is good. *Cañas* or wine cost around €4, cocktails €6.

Del Diego

Map 6, H7. C/Reina 12. Metro Gran Vía. Mon–Sat 9pm–3am. Closed Aug.
Another smart New York-style cocktail bar set up by a former *Chicote* waiter who personally mixes all the excellent cocktails. Friendly, unhurried atmosphere and open until the early hours. The house special, vodka-based *Del Diego,* is the one to go for.

Museo Chicote

Map 6, H7. Gran Vía 12. Metro
Gran Vía. Mon–Thurs
7pm–3am, Fri & Sat 7pm–4am.
The place to go to wallow in
nostalgia. Opened in 1931 by
Perico Chicote, ex-barman at
the *Ritz*, and still full of Art
Deco lines and pistachio-
coloured booths. At the back,
Perico set up a museum to
house his collection of over
ten thousand special bottles,
including original Napoleon
brandy, Chinese
chrysanthemum liquor and
vodka from the Tsar. Sophia
Loren, Frank Sinatra, Ava
Gardner, Luis Buñuel, Orson
Welles and the ubiquitous
Hemingway have all passed
through its doors. The
collection has, alas, long
gone, sold by Perico's
descendants and then
auctioned off bottle by bottle
in 1984. Nowadays, they'll
mix you any (expensive)
cocktail while you savour the
memories. Busiest after
midnight.

Taberna Angel Sierra

Map 6, I6. C/Gravina 11, on
Plaza Chueca. Metro Chueca.
Daily noon–1am.
One of the great bars in
Madrid, where everyone
drinks *vermút,* which is on tap
and delicious, accompanied
by free, exquisite *boquerones en
vinagre* tapas. *Raciones* are also
available, though they're quite
expensive.

MALASAÑA AND BILBAO

- - - - - - - - - - - - - - - - - - - -

La Ardosa

Map 6, G5. C/Colón 13. Metro
Tribunal. Daily noon–3pm &
6.30pm–midnight.
A great selection of beers on
offer in this classic *cervecería*,
decorated with Goya
reproductions. Over a
century old and serving
Guinness years before the
boom in Irish bars, *La Ardosa*
also serves great *tortilla* and a
very tasty *salmorejo de Córdoba*
(a substantial gazpacho with
pieces of ham).

MALASAÑA AND BILBAO

IRISH PUBS

Although pints of the "black stuff" have long been available in Madrid, specialist Irish pubs sprang up all over the city in the 1990s and the Celtic music scene took off in a big way. Prices are high compared to most Spanish bars, but they're still popular with the city's ex-pat community, and young *Madrileños*.

La Fontana de Oro Map 5, C4. c/Victoria 1; Metro Sol/Sevilla. It's a heresy to have turned this ancient bar (dating back over two hundred years) into an Irish pub, but it's an attractive and lively venue with some swinging Celtic sounds. Daily 11am–late.

Finnegans Map 6, J5. Plaza de las Salesas 9; Metro Colón. Large bar with several rooms, and fittings and floors brought from Ireland. English-speaking staff and TV sports. Mon–Thurs & Sun 12.30pm–2am, Fri & Sat 1pm–3am.

The Irish Rover Avda. Brasil 7; Metro Lima. Behind the Azca centre, off the Castellana. Inside it's modelled on an Irish street, but the clientele is more Spanish than most of the Irish pubs. Daily 11am–late.

Moore's Map 6, H3. C/Barceló 1; Metro Tribunal. One of the most popular Irish pubs with TV sports and a pub quiz on Mondays. Daily 10am–2am.

The Quiet Man Map 6, G5. C/Valverde 44; Metro Tribunal. One of the first on the scene, designed in the style of an early twentieth-century Dublin pub and full of authentic fittings. Pub quiz on Thursdays. Mon–Thurs 5.30pm–2am, Fri–Sun 1pm–3.30am.

The Triskel Tavern Map 6, G4. C/San Vicente Ferrer 3, Metro Tribunal. Quiz on Mondays, jazz on Tuesdays, open mic session on Thursdays and, to complete a typical pub night out, they even do curries. Daily 8pm–2am.

Café Comercial

Map 6, G2. Glorieta de Bilbao
7. Metro Bilbao. Daily
8am–1am, Fri & Sat till 2am.
A *Madrileño* institution and
one of the city's most popular
meeting points. This is a
lovely traditional café full of
mirrors, substantial tables and
the whole cross-section of
Madrid society. Settle in,
relax and listen to the pianist
on Friday and Saturday
nights. Regular *tertulias* on
Monday at 6pm and
bimonthly meetings for
English writers on Saturday
evening, there's also a
cybercafé upstairs.

Café del Foro

Map 6, F3. C/San Andrés 38.
Metro Tribunal. Daily 7pm–3am,
Fri & Sat till 4am.
Expensive but enjoyable bar,
with live music or some form
of entertainment most nights.
Attracts a slightly older, fairly
smart crowd. The decor,
intended to look like a town
square, is designed by Costus,
Almodóvar's sidekick.

Café de Ruiz

Map 6, F2. C/Ruiz 11. Metro
Bilbao. Daily 2pm–2am.
Classic old-fashioned café in
the midst of Malasaña – a
great place to while away an
afternoon reading the paper.
Discreet background music
and good cakes and biscuits.

Medina Magerit

Map 6, F3. C/Divino Pastor 21.
Metro Bilbao. Daily 7pm–2am.
Original bar with a friendly
and enthusiastic owner
serving an interesting
selection of drinks, including
Tisana India con zumos (fruit
juices with herbs and seeds),
Agua de Cebada (a crushed ice
and barley concoction) and
delicious *mojito cubanos* (rum
cocktails). A selection of
board games is available to
pass the time, and downstairs
there's a very small, but
atmospheric, cellar, where
traditional flamenco is
sometimes performed.

MALASAÑA AND BILBAO

RECOLETOS

- - - - - - - - - - - - - - - -

Café el Espejo

Map 6, L6. Paseo de Recoletos 31. Metro Colón. Daily 10am–2am, Fri & Sat till 3am.

Opened in 1978, but you wouldn't guess it from the antiquated decor. Mirrors, gilt and a wonderful, extravagant glass pavilion, plus a leafy outside *terraza*. Just the place to buy a coffee and watch the world go by.

Café Gijón

Map 6, K6. Paseo de Recoletos 21. Metro Banco de España. Daily 8am–1.30am. Famous literary café dating from 1888, decked out in Cuban mahogany and mirrors. A centre of the intellectual/arty *Movida* in the 1980s. Best for morning or late afternoon coffee, as tables are turned over for the set menu at lunchtime. There's also a cellar restaurant and a very pleasant summer *terraza*. Regular artistic *tertulias* are still held here (see box, p.188).

El Gato Persa

Map 6, K5. C/Bárbara de Braganza 10. Metro Colón. Daily 10am–1am. Closed second half of Aug.

This tearoom, set in a small library with comfortable seats, soft lighting and Baroque music (jazz at night), makes a very relaxing escape from the bustle of the city. A wide range of fruit and floral teas is on offer, including *mil y una noches*, a combination of black tea and wild flowers.

Nightlife

Madrid's renowned **late-night scene** really took off with **La Movida Madrileña** in the late 1970s, when the end of the Franco era produced an explosion of artistic creativity combined with a long-suppressed desire to indulge in pure hedonistic enjoyment. Although the true *Movida* has passed, and **opening hours** have been somewhat curtailed by the local authorities who are attempting to close bars by 3am, there are still plenty of opportunities to dance the night away. This is the only city in Europe where you can get caught in traffic jams at 4am, when clubbers are either going home or moving on to the dance-past-dawn discos. In *discobares* and *discotecas*, *bakalao*, a Spanish (originally Ibizan) version of house music, is still horribly popular.

As with everything *Madrileño*, there is a bewildering variety of types of nightlife. The mainstays of the Madrid scene are the **discobares** – bars of all musical and sexual persuasions, whose unifying feature is background (occasionally live) rock, dance or salsa music and usually a small dance floor. These don't generally charge admission, but drinks are more expensive than in other bars; they get going around 11pm and stay open till 2 or 3am. **Discotecas** are rarely worth investigating until around 1 or 2am, although queues often build up quickly after this time. They aren't always that different from *discobares*, though they tend to be bigger and flashier, with a lot of attention to lights, sound system and decor, and they stay open very late – most until 4am, some till 6am.

Although the whole dance scene is refreshingly unpretentious, for really serious clubbers there are a number of cutting-edge venues with top-notch guest DJs and a number of **"after hours" venues**, which open at between 5 and 6am and keep going until late morning (some even through until the afternoon), when you can grab some *chocolate con churros* (see box, p.202) before finally heading home to bed.

Venues with regular live music – rock, jazz, flamenco, salsa and classical – are covered in the "Live Music" chapter; see p.214.

In summer, many of the trendier clubs suspend operations and set up all-night outdoor **terrazas**, which are effectively open-air discos. Like many of the "after hours" venues, they're often unlicensed and change location from year to year.

DISCOBARES

Discobares are scattered all over the city, but each area has its own very particular identity. The magnet for the teenage crowd is **Alonso Martínez**, while **Argüelles** and **Moncloa** are student hangouts, and **Salamanca** is the place for chic bars and high prices. If you want to be at the cutting edge of trendiness, head for **Malasaña** and **Chueca**, while you'll find a more eclectic mix in the streets around **Sol** and **Santa Ana**.

SOL, ÓPERA AND SANTA ANA

La Comedia
Map 5, C4. C/Príncipe 16.
Metro Sol. Sun–Thurs
9pm–4am, Fri & Sat 9pm–5am.
Modern, relaxing bar for a
quiet drink by day, getting
livelier as the night progresses.
Good selection of varied and
danceable music, and it's a
favourite haunt of staff from
earlier-closing bars, as it's
open until 5am at the
weekends. €6 entry at night.

No se lo digas a nadie
Map 5, D4. C/Ventura de la
Vega 7. Metro Sol. Mon–Thurs
9pm–3am, Fri & Sat 9pm–5am.
Founded – and still run – by
a women's co-op, though this
bar has mellowed a bit in
recent years (the toilets no
longer proclaim *nosotras* and
ellos – "us" and "them").
Nonetheless, it retains a
political edge, hosting benefit
events from time to time.
There's no door policy or
dress code and drinks are
reasonably priced. Upstairs
you'll find six pool tables and

plenty of places to sit;
downstairs there's a disco
playing mainly dance music.

Villa Rosa
Map 5, C5. Plaza de Santa
Ana 15. Metro Sol. Mon–Sat
11pm–5am.
This dance bar was formerly a
famous flamenco club which
later featured in Pedro
Almodóvar's *High Heels*. The
exterior is adorned with
beautiful *azulejos* of famous
Spanish cities, and the
interior is straight out of the
Alhambra, with its *Mudéjar*
arches and ceilings. Monday
and Tuesday are salsa,
Wednesday flamenco, the rest
of the week mainstream
disco.

LA LATINA AND LAVAPIÉS

Kappa
Map 4, F3. C/Olmo 26. Metro
Antón Martín. Tues–Thurs and
Sun 8.30pm–2am, Fri & Sat
8.30pm–3.30am.
Relaxing chill-out bar, with
comfy seats, good music and
a mixed gay and straight

DISCOBARES

197

clientele. Midweek it's a good place for a chat, while the party gets going with DJs at the weekend.

El Viajero
Map 3, E13. Plaza de la Cebada 11. Metro La Latina. Tues–Sun 2pm–2.30am.
A fashionable La Latina nightspot spread over a number of floors. The summer *terraza* on the top floor affords great views of San Francisco El Grande. Also has a restaurant serving good pizzas and pastas.

GRAN VÍA, CHUECA AND SANTA BÁRBARA

Big Bamboo
Map 6, J7. C/Barquillo 42. Metro Alonso Martínez. Daily 10.30pm–5am, Fri & Sat till 6am.
Reggae music and great cocktails, including a margarita poured directly down the throat – mixing takes place by vigorous shaking of the head before you swallow. Plenty of room for dancing.

Impacto
Map 6, J3. C/Campoamor 3. Metro Alonso Martínez. Daily 11pm–3am.
A mini-labyrinth of a place, with little rooms and bars around every corner. A fairly trendy, slightly older crowd, reasonably priced drinks and a good variety of music, despite the lack of a dance floor. Door policy of sorts.

Kingston's
Map 6, J5. C/Barquillo 29. Metro Chueca/Alonso Martínez. Daily 11pm–5am.
Relaxed multicultural *discobar*, with colourful ethnic designs. Music ranges from soul and funk to reggae and rap. At the weekend, professional dancers get things going.

El Morocco
Map 6, D6. C/Marqués de Leganés 7. Metro Santo Domingo. Thurs midnight–3am, Fri & Sat 9pm–5.30am.
Originally started up by rock singer Alaska, long-time mover of the *Movida* and mate of Pedro Almodóvar. Leopardskin furnishings, varied music selection, the odd (and odd is

DISCOBARES

the word) band, and a pulsing dance floor. Occasional entrance charge.

MALASAÑA AND BILBAO

Al Lab'Oratorio
Map 6, G5. C/Colón 14. Metro Tribunal. Tues–Thurs 9pm–3am, Fri & Sat 9pm–6am.
Famous 1980s bar with very loud rock music and frequent live gigs for up-and-coming groups. Young studenty clientele.

Taboo
Map 6, F4. C/San Vicente Ferrer 23. Metro Tribunal. Daily 11pm–6am. Entry fee for concerts and guest DJs around €9 with drink.
Despite frequent changes of name and ownership this *discobar* remains a fixture on the Malasaña scene. With plenty of room to dance, varied music and reasonably priced drinks, it's a recipe for a good night out. Live music on Mondays and Wednesdays and regular sessions from guest DJs.

Tupperware
Map 6, G4. C/Corredera Alta de San Pablo 26. Metro Tribunal. Fri & Sat 8pm–3.30am. *The* place to go for the latest on the indie scene, with a mixture of grunge, Britpop and old classics from the punk era.

La Vaca Austera
Map 6, F3. C/Palma 20. Metro Tribunal. Mon–Thurs 10pm–3.30am, Fri & Sat till 4.30am.
American-style rock bar playing punk/indie classics, with pool tables, mixed clientele and friendly atmosphere.

Vía Lactea
Map 6, F3. C/Velarde 18. Metro Tribunal. Daily 8pm–3am.
Call in here to see where the *Movida* began. A Malasaña classic, *Vía Lactea* was a key meeting place for Spain's designers, directors, pop stars and painters in the 1980s, and it retains its original decor from the time, billiard tables included.

DISCOBARES

Warhol's Club

Map 6, H1. C/Luchana 20.
Metro Bilbao. Wed & Thurs
7pm–1am, Fri & Sat
7pm–10am.

Very popular *discobar* spread over two floors, with lots of chrome, glass, video screens and ultraviolet lighting. Attracts an early-20s crowd.

SALAMANCA

Teatriz

Map 8, E9. C/Hermosilla 15.
Metro Serrano. Mon–Sat café noon–3pm, bars 9pm–3am.

Closed Sat lunch & Aug.
This former theatre, redesigned by the Catalan, Mariscal together with Philippe Starck, is as elegant a venue as any in Europe. There are bars on the main theatre levels, overlooked by a restaurant in the circle which serves tapas and pasta dishes. Down in the basement there's a library-like area and small disco; look out too for the futuristic toilets. Drinks are pricey (around €10 for spirits), but there's no entrance charge.

DISCOTECAS

Discotecas are usually the last stop on a *Madrileño* night out, visited long after the metro has closed, so public transport can be a problem. Fortunately, most are situated in the central areas, so the best bet is to hop into a taxi or go on foot. Although **dress codes** are not, in general, particularly strict, some of the more upmarket joints are fairly selective about who they let in and you may at times need to ingratiate yourself with the doorman. Being foreign, oddly enough, seems to make it easier to get in. Long queues are also frequent, so it may be worth arriving slightly earlier than is cool. **Entry charges** are quite common and pretty hefty (€5–€20), but usually include the first drink. You might, however, be able to pick up a free entry pass from the public relations staff who often hang around the entrance. Be aware that many *discotecas* in Spain are fairly ephemeral institutions and frequently only last a season before opening up somewhere else under a different name, so it's a good idea to consult *La Guía del Ocio* (see p.7) for the very latest information.

SOL, ÓPERA AND SANTA ANA

Joy Madrid
Map 3, G7. C/Arenal 11. ⓦwww.joy-eslava.com. Metro Sol. Daily 11.30pm–5.30am, Fri–Sun till 6am. €12–15 including first drink.
This big-name disco is frequented by musicians, models, media folk and footballers. Home to the thirty-something yuppie crowd rather than serious clubbers. If you can't get in, console yourself at the *Chocolatería San Ginés* (see box, p.202).

Kapital
Map 4, I4. C/Atocha 125. Metro Atocha. Thurs–Sat midnight–5.30am. €15.
Seven-floor macroclub catering for practically every taste. Three dance floors,

complete with lasers and go-go dancers, a cinema and a top-floor *terraza*. Varied musical menu of disco, merengue, salsa, *sevillanas* and even some karaoke. Has its own "after hours" session, known as *Sundance*, at noon on a Sunday.

Palacio de Gaviria
Map 3, H7. C/Arenal 9. Metro Ópera/Sol. Daily 11pm–late. Mon–Thurs €10, Fri–Sun €12 including first drink.
Nineteenth-century palace where you can wander through extravagant Baroque salons, listen to a chamber concert in the ballroom, watch a live show or simply dance the night away. It hosts regular "International Parties", has dance classes and is a fantastic setting for a late drink. A frequent stopping-off point before *Joy Madrid*. Around €10 a drink.

DISCOTECAS

The Room/ Mondo at Stella

Map 5, D3. C/Arlabán 7. Metro Sevilla. Thurs–Sat 1–6am. €9–11 including first drink. Now unrecognisable from its days as a *Movida* classic, *Stella* has undergone a complete make-over to become a cool modern disco with transparent dance floor, but it remains a big favourite with the city's serious party goers.

Torero

Map 5, C4. C/Cruz 26. Metro Sevilla/Sol. Tues–Sat 11pm-5.30am (4.30am Wed). Very popular and highly enjoyable two-floored disco right in the heart of the Santa Ana area. No entry fee, but bouncers are pretty strict and you have to be reasonably smart to get in.

GRAN VÍA

Arena

Map 6, B5. C/Princesa 1. Metro Plaza de España. Thurs–Sun midnight–6am. €10–15 including first drink. Crowds of teenagers queue for the early evening session

---

CHOCOLATE BEFORE BED

If you stay up through a Madrid night, then you must try one of the city's great institutions, the Chocolatería San Ginés on Pasadizo de San Ginés, off c/Arenal between the Puerta del Sol and Teatro Real. Established in 1894, this *chocolatería* serves *chocolate con churros* (hot chocolate with deep-fried hoops of batter) to perfection – just the thing after a night's excess. There's an almost mythical *Madrileño* custom of winding up at San Ginés after the clubs close (not that they all do any longer), before heading home for a shower and then off to work.

San Ginés is open Tues–Sun 1am–7.30am, also Fri–Sun 7–10pm for weekend shoppers when the *chocolate* is half-price.

DISCOTECAS

that finishes at 11pm, and then a very slightly older clientele takes over after midnight at this club housed in a converted cinema. Reggae and funk progresses to house music during the night, and there are occasional live concerts too – Paul Weller, Asian Dub Foundation and the Dead Kennedys have performed here in recent years.

El Calentito

Map 6, D7. C/Jacometrezo 15. Metro Callao. Daily 11pm–5am. A fine place to experience wild, abandoned Madrid. It's tiny and cramped with strictly South American sounds: be prepared to dance with anyone. The entrance is easily missed, however – look out for the painted window. Drinks are modestly priced.

For gay bars and clubs listings, see "Gay Madrid", pp.209–213.

Ohm/
Bash Line/Weekend

Map 6, E7. Plaza Callao 4. Metro Callao. Wed midnight–6am, Fri & Sat midnight–6am, Sun midnight–5am. €10.
One of the major venues on the Madrid club scene. *Ohm* is the main techno-house session on Friday and Saturday nights and is very popular with the gay crowd; *Bash Line* is for those who need a midweek hip-hop and soul fix; and *Weekend* is the Sunday session for those who don't like Mondays.

Davai

Map 6, C6. C/Flor Baja 1, corner Gran Vía 59. Metro Santo Domingo/Plaza de España. Wed–Sat 11pm–5am, Sun 9am–2pm & midnight–6am. €6 including first drink.
A multi-club operating under several different names during the week and catering for a wide range of musical tastes with everything from house to 70s disco.

El Sol

Map 6, G8. C/Jardines 3. Metro Gran Vía. Tues–Thurs 12.30am–5am, Fri & Sat till

TERRAZAS AND CHIRINGUITOS

Madrid is a different city during summer: temperatures soar, and life moves outside and becomes even more late-night. In July and August, those *Madrileños* who haven't headed for the coast meet up with each other from 10pm onwards at one or other of the city's immensely popular terrazas. These can range from a few tables set up outside a café, or alongside a chiringuito (a makeshift bar) in one of the squares, to extremely trendy, and very expensive, designer bars, which form the summer annexe of a club or *discoteca*.

Paseo de Recoletos and Paseo la Castellana

The biggest concentration of *terrazas* is to be found along the grass strip in the middle of the Paseo de Recoletos and its continuation, Paseo de la Castellana. On the nearer reaches of Paseo de Recoletos are *terrazas* of the old-style cafés *Gran* (no.8), *Gijón* (no.21) and *Espejo* (no.31), all popular meeting points.

Past Plaza de Colón – in the region known as "La Costa Castellana" – the trendier *terrazas* such as *Boulevard* (no.37) begin. Most pump out music, and some offer entertainment, especially midweek, when they need to attract custom. They are extremely posey places, where clubbers dress up for a night's cruise along the length – an expensive operation, with cocktails at €7 a shot, and even a *caña* costing €4. The rooftop terrace in the ABC Serrano shopping centre (no.34) has a mixed clientele and some great views of the Castellana below.

Elsewhere in Madrid

Jardines de Conde Duque
Map 6, C3. Corner of c/Conde Duque 11 and c/Santa Cruz del Marcenado.
Metro Ventura Rodríguez.

Close to the Centro Cultural where the Veranos de Villa concerts are based in the summer months.

Jardines de las Vistillas Map 3, B11. C/Bailén, on the south side of the viaduct. Metro La Latina. This area has a number of *terrazas* and *chiringuitos*. It's named for the "little views" to be enjoyed in the direction of the Guadarrama Mountains to the northwest.

Paseo del Pintor Rosales Map 2, A2. Metro Argüelles. There's a clutch of late-night *terrazas* at the base of the Teleférico, with views over the river to the Casa de Campo.

Plaza de las Comendadoras Map 6, D3. Metro San Bernardo. One of the city's nicest squares, this has a couple of *terrazas* attached to the *Café Moderno* and a Mexican restaurant.

Plaza Dos de Mayo Map 6, F3. Metro Tribunal. The *chiringuito* on Malasaña's main square is always diverting.

Plaza de Olavide Off map 6, H1. Metro Quevedo. An attractive neighbourhood square, with more or less

year-round *terrazas* attached to four or five cafés and tapas bars.

Plaza de Oriente Map 3, D7. Metro Ópera. The *Café de Oriente terraza* is a popular café on the Madrid nightlife scene.

Plaza San Andrés/Plaza Humilladero Map 3, D12–E13. Metro La Latina. In the heart of old Madrid, this square is particularly lively during the summer *verbenas*.

Plaza de Santa Ana Map 5, C5. Metro Sol. Several of the *cervecerías* here have seats outside and there's a *chiringuito* in the middle of the square from June to September.

La Vieja Estación Map 7, A8. Avda Ciudad de Barcelona. Metro Atocha. A massive multi-*terraza* just behind Estación de Atocha, this attracts a glamorous clientele ranging from football stars to TV personalities. If you don't fancy people-watching, there are concerts, talent contests and exhibitions.

TERRAZAS AND CHIRINGUITOS

5.30am. €6–12.

Around twenty live concerts a month, followed by (usually at about 1.30am) a disco with passable house, soul and acid jazz. Very good acoustics and well ventilated.

CHUECA, MALASAÑA AND SANTA BÁRBARA

- - - - - - - - - - - - - - - - - - - -

Nasti Club

Map 6, F4. C/San Vicente Ferrer 35. Metro Tribunal. Thurs–Sat 11pm–6am.
Regular and guest DJs playing a diet of mainly electronic sounds in this popular Chueca venue. Occasional live acts.

Pachá

Map 6, H3. C/Barceló 11. ⓦwww.pacha-madrid.es. Metro Tribunal. Thurs–Sat 11.30am–5am. €12 including first drink.
An eternal survivor on the Madrid disco scene. Once a theatre, and retaining the Art Deco facade of the original building, it's exceptionally cool during the week, less so

at the weekend when the out-of-towners take over. Good if you like techno.

Speakeasy

Map 6, I4. C/Fernando VI 6. Metro Alonso Martínez. Mon–Wed 8pm–1am, Thurs–Sat 8pm–5am. Free or €6 including first drink.
Good-value, friendly disco that holds "International Parties" for foreigners new to the city. Good resident DJ.

OUT OF THE CENTRE

- - - - - - - - - - - - - - - - - - - -

Cocoon

C/Abdón Terradas 5. Metro Moncloa. Fri and Sat 1am-6am. €10–12.
Keeping track of the lastest dance sounds with a string of top notch DJs, this club has now moved to bigger premises in Moncloa. Chill-out upstairs or brave the hard-techno below.

Divino Aqualung

Paseo de la Ermita 48. Metro Puerta del Angel. Fri & Sat 11pm–6am, Sun 5pm–midnight.

DISCOTECAS

€9 including first drink.
Giant club, west of the river opposite the Atletico Madrid football stadium, which promises to "bring the spirit of Ibiza back to Madrid". Six bars, light shows, go-go dancers and a capacity for 2500 people.

Galileo Galilei
C/Galileo 100. Metro Ríos Rosas. Daily 6pm–4.30am.
Bar, concert venue and disco all rolled into one. Check the *Guía del Ocio* to find out whether it's the night for cabaret, salsa or a singer-songwriter.

Macumba Clubbing
Estación de Chamartín. Metro Chamartín. Sat midnight–6am. *Space of Sound* Sun 9am–6pm.
€15 including first drink.
Information ☎902 499 994.
Guest DJs from the Ministry of Sound in London come for the Saturday night *Elite Noche* session at this club on top of the Chamartín train station. If you've still got energy left, the *Space of Sound* "after hours" club will allow you to strut your stuff all morning – if you can take the constant bombardment of *bakalao*, lasers and smoke, that is.

DISCOTECAS

Gay Madrid

Recent years have witnessed a significant expansion in the **gay scene** in the capital. The area around Plaza Chueca remains at the heart of the action, but gay clubs are beginning to open up in other areas too. The **lesbian scene** has experienced a similar expansion and shares many of the places listed with gay men. There are, however, a few exclusively lesbian clubs listed separately on p.000. Madrid nightlife in general has a strong gay presence and most of the clubs and bars listed in the "Nightlife" chapter have a very mixed crowd.

Plaza **Chueca** and the surrounding streets, especially c/Pelayo, are the centre of the so-called **zona gay**. The barrio has been rejuvenated over the last few years with the opening of new restaurants, bars and cafés, largely gay-run but enjoying a mixed clientele. During *Carnaval* (the week before Lent), Chueca is especially lively, with fancy dress parades and general over-indulgence, while Gay Pride Day at the end of June is the signal for a week-long party throughout the *barrio*.

Despite the high level of integration in Madrid's nightlife and social scene, there has been a remarkably reactionary attitude from many quarters of Spanish society towards homosexuality. As a result, the gay community has become more organized and groups such as **Coordinadora Gay de Madrid** are actively involved in pushing for gay rights.

INFORMATION SERVICES

Berkana Map 6, I6.
C/Hortaleza 64; Metro Gran
Vía. Gay and lesbian bookshop. One of the best places
to find out what's happening
on the gay scene. Mon–Sat
10.30am–9pm; Sun noon–
2pm & 5–9pm.

**Centro de La Mujer Map 6,
J5**. C/Barquillo 44, 1° izq,
☏913 193 689; Metro Alonso
Martínez. Feminist and
lesbian groups all share this
centre, and it's the best stop
for information to do with the
lesbian community.

**Coordinadora Gay de
Madrid Map 6, G6**.
C/Fuencarral 37, ☏915 224
517; Metro Chueca. The main
gay organization in Madrid,
giving information on health,
leisure and gay rights. Mon–
Fri 5–9pm; Aug from 7pm.

Publications include the monthly magazine *Zero* (€3)
with plenty of news, features and interviews related to the
gay scene, while the free newspapers *Shangay Express* and
Odisea are available in most gay clubs and bars. The
Coordinadora also produces its own free monthly newsletter
which is available from their office. The **website**
Ⓦwww.chueca.com also includes its own gay listings section.

CAFÉS AND RESTAURANTS

A Brasileira
Map 6, H6. C/Pelayo 49 ☏913
083 625. Metro Chueca.
Mon–Sat 1–4pm & 8.30pm–
midnight, Sat & Sun till 2am.
Small Brazilian restaurant
offering a very tasty selection
of South American dishes.
Expect to pay around €18
per person.

Café Acuarela
Map 6, I6. C/Gravina 10. Metro
Chueca.

Daily 3pm–3am, Fri & Sat till 4am.

Very comfortable café, with over-the-top Baroque decor – the perfect place for a quiet drink.

Café Figueroa

Map 6, I6. C/Augusto Figueroa 17. Metro Chueca. Daily 2.30pm–1am, Fri & Sat till 2.30am. Sun opens at 4pm.

Opened in the early 1980s, this is an established institution on the *Madrileño* gay scene, with regulars of all ages, a pool table upstairs and great parties during *Carnaval*.

Gula Gula

Map 6, H8. Gran Vía 1 ☎915 228 764. Metro Gran Vía; c/Infante 5 ☎914 202 919. Metro Antón Martín. Mon–Thurs 1–4.30pm & 9pm–2am, Fri & Sat 1–4.30pm & 9pm–3am.

Spacious salad-bar-type restaurant that does an eat-as-much-as-you-can self-service buffet for €10, and has live shows featuring drag queens and dancers every night. Popular for "hen nights" as well as with the gay crowd.

La Sastrería

Map 6, H6. C/Hortaleza 74. Metro Chueca. Mon–Thurs 8.30am–1.30am, Fri 8.30am–3am, Sat 10am–3am, Sun 10am–1.30am.

On the site of a former military tailor's shop, this popular two-floored café/bar is a great place for an afternoon coffee, tea or fruit juice, as well as an evening drink.

Stars Dance Café

Map 6, I8. C/Marqués de Valdeiglesias 5. Metro Gran Vía. Mon–Wed 1pm–2am, Thurs 1pm–3am, Fri 1pm–3.30am, Sat 5.30pm–3.30am. ⊛www.stars cafedance.com.

Quiet and low key during the day, this place gradually livens up in the evening with dancing, music and cabaret on most nights. Popular meeting spot for gays, but the clientele is mixed.

XXX Café

Map 6, H7. Corner of c/Clavel and c/Reina. Metro Gran Vía. Daily 1pm–1.30am.

This pleasant café has a mainly gay clientele, but is

open to everyone. A good place to read the paper while sampling some of the very good carrot cake and coffee.

GAY BARS AND DISCOTECAS

Bar LL
Map 6, H6. C/Pelayo 11. Metro Chueca. Daily 6pm–3am.
Upstairs, there's a bar with live acts at the weekend (striptease and drag queens). Downstairs, there's a more intimate room, where people sit and talk or watch hardcore gay porn on the video screen. Attracts a slightly older, mainly singles crowd.

Black and White
Map 6, I6. C/Libertad 34. Metro Chueca. Daily 9pm–4am, Fri & Sat till 5am.
Very popular strip shows upstairs and a disco downstairs at this well-established gay nightspot.

Cruising
Map 6, H6. C/Pérez Galdós 5. Metro Chueca. Daily 8pm–3.30am, Fri & Sat till 4.30am.
This *discobar* is strictly for leather boys, with a dark room showing porn films and a bar upstairs. Downstairs is a disco playing a good variety of music.

Heaven
Map 3, G5. C/Veneras 2. Metro Santo Domingo/Callao. Daily midnight–late. €6.
Just behind Plaza Callao, this mixed disco becomes very popular with the gay crowd as an "after hours" venue. Good DJs playing a selection of house music. During the week it organizes parties, live acts and strip shows.

La Lupe
Map 4, F3. C/Torrecilla del Leal 12. Metro Antón Martín. Daily 9pm–2.30am.
Mixed gay and lesbian bar. Good music, cheap drinks and occasional cabaret.

Liquid
Map 6, J7. C/Barquillo 8. Metro Chueca. Tues–Sun 9pm–3am.

Smart and stylish relative newcomer on the gay scene. The two bars are lined with video screens playing a selection of modish music and there's a clientele to match.

New Leather Bar
Map 6, I5. C/Pelayo 42. Metro Chueca. Daily 8pm–3am, Fri & Sat till 4am.
Refurbished bar on two floors with a mixed gay crowd. Dance floor, dimly lit rooms, erotic parties and strip shows.

OHM/Weekend
Map 6, E7. Plaza del Callao 4. Metro Callao. OHM: Fri & Sat midnight–6.30am; Weekend: Sun midnight–5am. €6–10.
One of the most popular venues on the gay club scene. Weekend is the "after hours"

club *par excellence* for those who still find their appetite for dancing isn't satisfied.

Ricks
Map 6, I7. C/Clavel 8. Metro Gran Vía. Daily 11pm–5am.
Mixed straight/gay *discobar* which gets wild at weekends, when every available space is used for dancing. Open and light, with a friendly atmosphere and fine music ranging from house classics through disco to hi-NRG – plus table football at the back. Pricey drinks.

Shangay Tea Dance
Map 3, I5. C/Mesonero 13. Metro Callao. Sun 9pm–2am. €6 including first drink.
A compulsory Sunday night stop, featuring live shows and 70s disco hits.

LESBIAN BARS AND DISCOTECAS

Ambient
Map 6, H4. C/San Mateo 21. Metro Alonso Martínez. Tues–Thurs & Sun 8pm–4am, Fri & Sat 9pm–5am.

Thriving lesbian bar, serving decent pizzas. Also pool, table football, exhibitions, occasional live acts and a market on Sunday.

Medea

Map 4, E2. C/Cabeza 33.
Metro Lavapiés/Antón Martín.
Daily Tues–Sun 11pm–5am. €6.
The city's premier lesbian
disco – though accompanied
men are admitted. Cabaret on
Thursday & Sunday, smart
decor, great music and a pool
table. Gets going from about
1am.

La Rosa

Map 5, B2. C/Tetuán 27. Metro
Sol. Daily 11pm–6am. €5.

Lesbian disco run by a
women's collective, although
men are admitted if
accompanied. Good selection
of music and friendly
atmosphere.

Truco

Map 6, I6. C/Gravina. Metro
Chueca. Mon–Thurs & Sun
8.30pm–2.30am. Fri & Sat
9pm–5am.
Very popular women's bar
that spills out on to the street
near the lively Plaza Chueca.

LESBIAN BARS AND DISCOTECAS

Live music

Madrid's **music** scene is as varied as anything else in the city and ranges from classical and opera to salsa and flamenco. Often, it's the smaller, offbeat clubs that are the more enjoyable, though there are plenty of large auditoriums – including the sports stadiums and bullring – for big-name concerts. In summer, events are supplemented by the council's *Veranos de la Villa* cultural programme, and in autumn by the *Festival de Otoño*.

Forthcoming events are well covered in
Madrid's listings magazines; see p.7.

CLASSICAL AND OPERA

Madrid's classical music scene may not be able to compete with its offerings on the fine art front, but it still has a number of interesting venues, which attract leading Spanish and international performers. The **Teatro Real** is the city's prestigious opera house and, along with the **Auditorio Nacional de Musica**, is home to the Orquesta Nacional de España. There are also a host of other lesser concert venues for which it's much easier to get tickets, as well as a number of highly enjoyable salons and small auditoriums for chamber orchestras and groups. Madrid's own form of operetta, the *zarzuela* (see box p.54), can be seen at several venues across the city, but is probably at its most authentic when seen at the open-air tenement block *La Corrala* in the summer.

Auditorio Nacional de Música

C/Príncipe de Vergara 146
☎913 370 100, ⓦwww.auditorio
nacional.mcu.es.
Metro Cruz del Rayo.
This is the home of the Orquesta Nacional de España and host to most international visiting orchestras.

Centro de Arte Reina Sofía

Map 4, I5. C/Santa Isabel
☎914 675 062,
ⓦmuseoreinasofia.mcu.es.
Metro Atocha.
The modern art museum also has a concert hall which often hosts programmes of contemporary music.

Centro Cultural de la Villa

Map 8, C9. Plaza de Colón.
☎915 756 080. Metro Colón.
The arts centre underneath the fountains in Plaza de Colón is a popular venue for *zarzuelas*.

La Corrala

Map 4, E5. C/Mesón de Paredes ☎915 309 600.
Metro Lavapiés.
A surviving tenement block, once typical of working-class Madrid, which stages open-air *zarzuelas* during the *Veranos de la Villa* summer season.

La Fídula

Map 5, E6. C/Huertas 57.
Metro Antón Martín.
A chamber orchestra plays most nights at 11.30pm in this café from June to September and then weekends in the summer. Make sure you arrive on time, as the doors are closed during performances.

Fundación Juan March

C/Castelló 77 ☎914 354 240.
Metro Núñez de Balboa.
Small auditorium in this interesting exhibition space in the Salamanca *barrio* used for recitals two or three times a week.

CLASSICAL AND OPERA

Teatro Calderón

Map 5, B5. C/Atocha 18 ☎916 320 114. Metro Sol.

Venue for a very popular annual opera season between September and July – a lot easier to get tickets here than at the Teatro Real.

Teatro Monumental

Map 4, G2. C/Atocha 65 ☎914 298 119. Metro Antón Martín.

A large theatre, offering orchestral concerts, opera, *zarzuela* and flamenco recitals. Tickets are sold for stalls (*butaca de patio*) or a series of dizzying circles (*entresuelo*).

Teatro Real

Map 3, E6. Plaza Isabel II. Info ☎915 160 660, tickets ☎902 244 824 or 915 588 787 from abroad, ⊛www.teatro-real.com. Metro Ópera.

Madrid's opulent opera house hosts suitably lavish opera productions and classical concerts. Ticket prices range from €12 to €150, but are very hard to get your hands on and you need to book well in advance for the best seats.

La Zarzuela

Map 5, E3. C/Jovellanos 4 ☎915 245 400, ⊛teatro zarzuela.mcu.es. Metro Sevilla.

As the name suggests, this is the leading venue for Spanish operetta.

FLAMENCO

Flamenco has undergone something of a revival since the 1990s, in large part due to the "new flamenco" artists, like Ketama, Pata Negra and the dancer Joaquín Cortés, who are unafraid to mix it with a bit of blues, jazz, and even rock. More traditional artists such as José Mercé and Agujetas remain extremely popular and Madrid is one of the best places in Spain to see leading performers.

The following club and café listings span the range from purist flamenco to crossover experiments, and some host performances by the major stars. Opening hours are variable

---

For the latest information on flamenco artists try the excellent website Ⓦ www.flamenco-world.com.

---

and those given below are only a rough guideline. Look out, too, for the annual week-long **Flamenco Festival** in May, usually in the Teatro Albéniz (Map 3, I9. C/Paz 11 ☎ 915 318 311; Metro Sol).

In addition, try the **Salas Rocieras**, places where the public get up and perform *sevillanas*, the complex and sensual courtship dance of southern Spain. Even if you don't want to have a go yourself, it's worth paying a visit just to watch the spectacle. Drinks and food are, however, very pricey. Good options are *Al Andalús*, c/Capitán Haya 19 (Metro Cuzco; Mon–Sat 11pm–6am; minimum bar/tapas charge of €15–20) and *Almonte*, c/Juan Bravo 35 (Metro Núñez de Balboa; daily 9pm–6am; minimum bar/tapas charge of €12).

Café de Chinitas
Map 3, E4. C/Torija 7 ☎ 915 471 502. Metro Santo Domingo. Mon–Thurs 9pm–2am, Fri & Sat 9pm–3am. Drinks and show €27.

One of the oldest flamenco clubs in Madrid, hosting a dinner-dance spectacular. Keep an eye on the prices, as it's very expensive and rather touristy, but the music is authentic. Reservations are essential, though you may get in late when people start to leave an hour before closing (at this time you don't have to eat and the entrance fee includes your first drink).

Candela
Map 4, F3. C/Olmo 2 ☎ 914 673 382. Metro Antón Molina. Daily 10.30pm–late.

A legendary bar frequented by musicians, with occasional shows too. The late, great Camarón de la Isla is reputed to have sung here until 11am on one occasion. The cellar area is only accessible by invitation.

FLAMENCO

Caracol

Map 4, F7. C/Bernardino Obregón 18 ☎915 308 055. Metro Embajadores. Daily 9.30pm–2am. €10.
The top names tend to appear at this sometime club, sometime disco. Flamenco is often mixed with jazz and blues; pure flamenco is usually on Thursday night, but call beforehand to check.

Las Carboneras

Map 4, E10. Plaza Conde de Miranda ☎915 428 677. Metro Sol. Shows Mon–Thurs 9pm & 10.30pm, Fri & Sat 9pm & 11pm.
A relative newcomer to the restaurant/tablao scene, geared to the tourist market and slightly cheaper than its rivals, but a good alternative if you just want to get a taste of flamenco.

Cardamomo

Map 5, D4. C/Echegaray 15. Metro Sevilla/Sol. Daily 9pm–4am.
Noisy and fun flamenco bar close to Santa Ana with live acts every Wednesday and Sunday. Draws its fair share of big names in an unpretentious atmosphere that couldn't be more different from the more formal tablaos that are geared up to the tourist market. No entry charge and drinks are standard prices.

Casa Patas

Map 4, E2. C/Cañizares 10 ☎913 690 496. Metro Antón Martín. Daily midnight–3am. €12.
Authentic club with a bar and restaurant that gets its share of big names. The best nights are Thursday and Friday.

Corral de la Morería

Map 3, C11. C/de la Morería 17 ☎913 658 446. Metro La Latina. Daily 9pm–3am. Around €27.
A good, if expensive, venue for serious flamenco acts. Worth staying until late in case there are any spontaneous contributions from the audience. Frank Sinatra, Ava Gardner and Che Guevera are among the celebrities who've seen the show.

FLAMENCO

La Soleá

Map 3, F11. C/Cava Baja 27 ☎913 653 308. Metro La Latina. Mon–Sat 8.30pm–3am. Closed Aug.

This long-established flamenco bar is the genuine article. People sit around in the tiny salon, pick up a guitar or start to sing and gradually the atmosphere builds up until everyone is clapping or dancing. Has to be seen to be believed.

ROCK AND BLUES

Madrid is very much on the international **rock** tour circuit, and you can catch big (and small) American and British acts playing to enthusiastic audiences. In early summer, the Parque el Soto in Mostoles, to the south of the city, plays host to the Festimad rock festival (Ⓦ www.festimad.es), which features international groups ranging from heavy metal to indie and dance. Regular concerts are also held as part of the *Veranos de la Villa* season (see "Festivals" chapter, p.232) in the Centro Cultural Conde Duque. **Tickets** for most big rock concerts, as well as for the Festimad and *Veranos de la Villa*, are sold by Madrid Rock, Gran Vía 25; Fnac, c/Preciados 28 (both Metro Callao; daily 10am–10pm; all cards); and branches of El Corte Inglés.

You'll find a thriving Celtic music scene in many of Madrid's Irish pubs; see box on p.192.

Madrid has also long been the heart of the **Spanish rock** scene, and in the smaller clubs you'll see a very wide range of local bands. In most cases you can just turn up and pay on the door – keep an eye out for posters scattered around the city and check the *Guía del Ocio*.

ROCK AND BLUES

CLUBS

Café Libertad 8

Map 6, I7. C/Libertad 8. Metro Chueca. Mon–Thurs 5pm–2am, Fri 5pm–3am, Sat 7pm–3am, Sun 6pm–1am.

The place to hear budding *cantautores* (singer-songwriters). Some big names such as Rosana and Pedro Guerra started off in this café, which has now been going for nearly 30 years.

Chesterfield Café

Map 6, A2. C/Serrano Jover 5. Metro Argüelles. Daily 1.30pm–3.30am.

As well as the Tex-Mex food,

La Coquette

Map 3, G7. C/Hileras 14. Metro Ópera. Daily 8pm–2.30am. Closed Aug.

Small, smoky basement bar, where people sit around in the near dark, watching bands perform on a tiny stage. Wednesday and Thursday are the blues nights.

Maravillas

Map 6, F4. C/San Vicente Ferrer 33. Metro Tribunal. Thurs–Sat 9pm–late.

Small, but usually uncrowded, indie venue, a favourite with the young crowd, where bands play anything from jazz to funk to reggae, often till around 4am.

The club Arena also hosts concerts; see "Nightlife", p.202.

---

this club is a live rock venue from Wednesdays to Sundays. Sets begin at midnight (1am on Fridays and Saturdays) and there's a happy hour from 8 to 10pm.

Siroco

Map 6, D3. C/San Dimas 3. Metro San Bernardo/Noviciado. Tues–Thurs 9.30pm–3am, Fri–Sun 10pm–6am.

Live local bands most nights at this popular little club/disco, just north of Gran Vía. Music ranges from soul and funk to rock and indie.

ROCK AND BLUES

MAJOR CONCERT VENUES

The city's main indoor arena, the **Palacio de Deportes**, recently burned down, so the following venues are likely to feature more frequently when big groups play the Spanish leg of their European tours.

Caracol
Map 4, F7. C/Bernardino Obregón 18 ☏915 308 055. Metro Embajadores.
Originally a leading flamenco night spot, but now also one of the most popular venues for touring groups including, of late, Eagle Eye Cherry and the Manic Street Preachers. Good acoustics and visibility.

La Cubierta
Plaza de Toros de Leganés, c/Maestro 4 ☏917 651 890. Local train from Atocha to Leganés and then bus 484.
Bullring in the southern industrial suburb of Leganés, increasingly used as a venue for heavy rock artists of the Iron Maiden, Megadeth variety, although, as a complete contrast, Soft Cell also appeared recently.

La Katedral
C/Fundadores 7. Metro Manuel Becerra/O'Donnell.
A relatively new venue, which started off with a host of concerts by indie bands, including Echobelly and Supergrass. However, most of the big names now seem to be heading for *La Riviera*.

Palacio de Congresos
Paseo de la Castellana 99. Metro Santiago Bernabéu.
Large, comfortable, though somewhat sterile, venue used by a number of middle-of-the-road artists such as the king of Spanish crooners Julio Iglesias.

Palacio de Vistalegre
Avenida Plaza de Toros. Metro Oporto/Vista Alegre.
Since the demise of the Palacio de Deportes, this covered bullring in the south-west of the city has become the temporary home to the Estudiantes basketball team, as

ROCK AND BLUES

well as a major venue for leading artists such as Lenny Kravitz and Santana.

Plaza de Toros de las Ventas

Las Ventas. ⓦwww. las-ventas.com. Metro Ventas. The bullring is a pretty good concert venue, put to use during the summer festival. Tickets are usually all one price, though the best reserved seats (*asiento*

reservado) often carry an extra charge.

La Riviera

Map 2, A7. Paseo Bajo Virgen del Puerto s/n, Puente de Segovia. Metro Puerta del Angel. Fri–Sun 11pm–5am. Right next to the river, fun disco and concert venue that has hosted some of the big names in recent years, ranging from Suede and Garbage to Salif Keita and David Byrne.

LATIN MUSIC

Madrid attracts big-name **Latin** artists, and if you happen to coincide with the summer festival you'll stand a good chance of catching someone of the stature of Juan Luis Guerra from the Dominican Republic. Gigs by top artists tend to take place at the rock venues listed on pp.221–222. The local scene is a good deal more low-key, but there's enjoyable salsa, nonetheless, in a handful of clubs.

Café del Mercado

Map 4, A6. Ronda de Toledo 1, in the Mercado Puerta de Toledo ☎913 653 786. Metro Puerta de Toledo. Live music daily in a spacious, comfortable club and a *Gran Baile de Salsa* every Friday and Saturday at 2am.

Oba-Oba

Map 3, G4. C/Jacometrezo 4. Metro Callao. Daily 11pm–5.30am. Live Brazilian music as you refine your samba and lambada technique with the help of lethal Brazilian caipirinhas from the bar.

Salsipuedes

Map 6, F6. C/Puebla 6. Metro Callao/Gran Vía. Daily 11pm–6am. €6 including first drink.

Serious salsa to a live orchestra most weekdays in a "tropical" setting. You need to be smartly dressed to get in.

Suristan

Map 5, B5. C/Cruz 7 ☎915 323 909. Metro Sol.

A wide range of ethnic music at this venue, including Cuban rock and other Latin sounds. Wednesday night is usually Flamenco night. Closed Sunday.

JAZZ

Madrid doesn't rank with London, Paris or New York on the **jazz** front, but the clubs are friendly, unpretentious places. Look out for the annual jazz festival staged at a variety of venues in November.

Café Central

Map 5, B5. Plaza del Angel 10. Metro Sol. Mon–Sat noon–1.30am, Fri & Sat till 2.30am. €9–11 for gigs, otherwise free.

Sixth in the "Best Jazz Clubs of the World" poll in *Wire* magazine some time back, this is certainly an attractive venue – small, relaxed and covered in mirrors – and it gets the occasional big name, plus strong local talent. The Art Deco café is worth a visit in its own right.

Café Jazz Populart

Map 5, C6. C/Huertas 22. Metro Antón Martín. Daily 6pm–2.30am. Live music supplement €6.

Twice nightly sets (11pm and 12.30am) from jazz and blues bands. Another friendly and relaxed venue. Tends to start a little earlier than the *Café Central*, which is a few minutes' walk away, so you can combine the two if you fancy an overdose of laid-back rhythms.

JAZZ

Bar Clamores

Map 6, G1. C/Albuquerque 14 ☎914 457 938, ⒲www.salaclamores.com. Metro Bilbao. €3–6 for gigs, otherwise free.

Large, low-key and enjoyable jazz bar with accomplished (if not very famous) artists, not too exorbitant drinks and a nice range of snacks. Last set finishes around 1.30am, though the bar stays open to 4am.

Downtown

Map 6, I1. C/Covarrubias 29. Metro Alonso Martínez. Mon–Thurs & Sun 10pm–3am, Fri & Sat 10pm–3.30am.

Just north of Alonso Martínez, *Downtown* hosts good jazz nights on Mondays and Tuesdays, while blues bands often play here at weekends.

Segundo Jazz

C/Comandante Zorita 8. Metro Nuevos Ministerios. Daily 7pm–3.30am.

Jazz on most nights of the week at this atmospheric basement club, but also some Latin sounds (usually Wed & Thurs). Shows normally get going at around midnight, with last set at 2.15am. No entry charge, but you have to buy a drink.

JAZZ

Theatre
and cinema

I n a city that has been home to so many of Spain's great
writers and dramatists, it's not surprising that Madrid's
theatrical tradition is strong. In the golden age, writers
such as **Cervantes**, **Lope de Vega** and **Tirso de Molina**
all lived in the streets in and around Plaza de Santa Ana,
and, later, a number of great poets and writers such as
García Lorca and **Antonio Machado** converged on the
city, further contributing to Madrid's literary heritage.
Madrileños have always been enthusiastic theatregoers, and
today you can catch anything from the classics to contemporary experimental productions, cabaret and comedy
acts.

Details of **performances**, which usually begin after
9pm, are to be found in *La Guía del Ocio* and the Friday
supplement of *El Mundo*. Look out also for what's on offer
in the annual *Festival de Otoño* (late Sept to Nov), sponsored
by the Comunidad de Madrid. This is often the time when
international shows and performers visit the city. Madrid
also hosts a dance season between mid-May and mid-June
and an alternative festival of theatre, dance and music,

which is now in its tenth year and usually takes place around February.

As with the theatre, *Madrileños* are enthusiastic and knowledgeable **cinema** devotees, flocking to the openings of Spanish and international films, lapping up the extensive press and TV coverage, and keeping up with all the latest gossip about the stars. Major releases are dubbed into Spanish, though a number of cinemas have regular **original-language** screenings, with subtitles; these are listed in a separate *versión original subtitulada* (*v.o.*) section in the newspapers and *La Guía del Ocio*.

The city itself has been a star in its own right: the elegant apartment blocks on the edge of the Retiro, sleazy nightclubs and bars in the centre, and the decaying slum areas on the outskirts have all featured as backdrops in the post-*Movida* films of Almodóvar and others.

For more on the Spanish film industry, see the box on p.230.

THEATRES

Credit-card **bookings** can be made over the phone through La Caixa Catalunya and Caja de Madrid (see "Directory", p.273, for telephone numbers), or you can buy directly from the theatre. Prices range from €6 to €25, but many venues operate a **día del espectador** ("audience day", usually Mon or Wed), when prices are halved – demand for these is high, so book as early as possible.

Berlin Cabaret
Map 3, D11. Costanilla de San Pedro 11 ☎913 662 034. Metro La Latina. Mon–Thurs 11pm–5am, Fri & Sat 11pm–6am.
Varied cabaret and comedy in a traditional, slightly seedy club setting. Admission is free, but drinks are expensive.

Centro Cultural de la Villa

Map 8, C9. Plaza de Colón ☎915 756 080. Metro Colón. This is where you're likely to see more experimental companies on tour, as well as popular works and *zarzuela* performances. It also hosts a puppet season for children.

La Muralla Arabe

Map 3, B9–10. C/Cuesta de la Vega (no street number). Metro Ópera. Atmospheric outdoor setting for plays from the Spanish golden age, staged in the summer months as part of the *Veranos de la Villa* season. There are side shows and street entertainers, too, and you'll need to arrive early if you want a table where you can eat and drink during the performance. Tickets are available from the booth outside the entrance.

Teatro de la Abadía

C/Fernández de los Ríos 42 ☎914 481 627. Metro Quevedo/Argüelles. Beautifully decorated theatre, set in pleasant grounds just off the main street. The two stages, both with an intimate atmosphere, have put on some very successful productions and are especially popular venues during the *Festival de Otoño*.

Teatro Albéniz

Map 5, A4. C/Paz 11 ☎915 318 311. Metro Sol. Another popular venue for *Festival de Otoño* productions. Also hosts small-scale dance performances and the annual flamenco festival in May.

Teatro Bellas Artes and Círculo de Bellas Artes

Map 5, E2. C/Marqués de Casa Riera 2 ☎915 324 437. Círculo ☎913 605 400, ⒲www.circulobellasartes.com. Metro Banco de España. A beautiful old theatre with a reputation for quality, while the Círculo also has a theatre staging more adventurous productions.

Teatro Español

Map 5, C4. C/Príncipe 25 ☎914 296 297. Metro Sol/Sevilla. Classic Spanish theatre in a

THEATRES

majestic venue, built on the site of one of the original *corrales* (courtyards) where drama was first performed for ordinary *Madrileños* in the golden age. Works by Lope de Vega, Calderón de la Barca and Tirso de Molina often feature.

Teatro Lope de Vega

Map 6, D7. C/Gran Vía 57 ☎915 238 098.

Metro Callao/Santo Domingo. Large, old-style theatre on the Gran Vía that puts on its fair share of big-budget musical productions such as *Beauty and the Beast*.

Teatro de Madrid

Avda de la Ilustración (no street number) ☎917 405 374.

Metro Barrio del Pilar. Large, modern theatre next to the large La Vaguada shopping centre in the north of the city, presenting some excellent ballet, drama and touring cultural shows.

Teatro María Guerrero

Map 6, K6. C/Tamayo y Baus 4 ☎913 194 769. Metro Colón. This is the headquarters of the Centro Dramático Nacional which stages high-quality Spanish and international productions in a beautiful neo-*Mudéjar* interior.

Teatro Nuevo Apolo

Map 4, D2. Plaza Tirso de Molina 1 ☎914 295 238.

Metro Tirso de Molina. An old music-hall-style venue with traditional decor and a good atmosphere, if a little cramped. Madrid's principal venue for major musicals and popular with flamenco stars such as Joaquín Cortés and Eva Yerbabuena.

CINEMA

Cinemas (*cines*) can be found all over the city centre. Tickets cost around €5.50, but, as with theatres, most cinemas have a *día del espectador* ("audience day", usually Mon or Wed), when admission is €3.50–4. Be warned that on

Sunday night half of Madrid goes to the movies and queues can be long – it's usually best to buy tickets early and then spend time in a bar before the show starts.

Alphaville, Renoir & Princesa

Map 6, A4. C/Martín de los Heros 14 ☎915 593 836. Metro Plaza de España/ Ventura Rodríguez.
A trio of multiscreen cinemas, within 200m of each other just beside Plaza de España. Original-language-version new releases and old classics make up the majority of films.

Bellas Artes

Map 5, E2. C/Marqués de Casa Riera 2 ☎915 225 092. Metro Banco de España.
A varied diet of mainstream releases and art-house productions. Comfortable environment and pleasant café.

Cines Ideal

Map 5, B6. C/Doctor Cortezo 6 ☎913 692 518. Advanced ticket sales ☎902 124 134. Metro Sol/Tirso de Molina.
A massive nine-screen complex south of Sol with something for everyone – a mixture of mainstream, art-house, independent and Spanish films.

Filmoteca/Cine Doré

Map 4, F2. C/Santa Isabel 3 ☎915 490 011. Metro Antón Martín. **Closed Monday.**
Beautiful old cinema, now home to a two-screen art-film centre, with imaginative programmes of classic and contemporary films, and popular open-air summer screenings – buy tickets in advance. Entrance costs just €1.35 and a ten-session ticket is an even better value €10.22.

Imax Madrid

Parque Tierno Galván, C/Meneses ☎914 674 800, ⊚www.imaxmadrid.com. Metro Méndez Alvaro.
Three different types of screen at this futuristic cinema – a giant flat one, a dome-shaped one for

CINEMA

MADE IN SPAIN – MODERN SPANISH CINEMA

Ever since the surrealist classics of Luis Buñuel, and even during four decades of Francoist censorship, the Spanish film industry has had a reputation for producing innovative and thought-provoking cinema. However, in recent years the industry has scaled new heights with many seeing it as a golden era in the history of Spanish cinema.

It was Pedro Almodóvar who broke new ground with his post-*Movida* films *Women on the Edge of a Nervous Breakdown*, *Kika* and *Tie Me Up, Tie Me Down*. With a powerful cocktail of strong leading women, black comedy, dysfunctional relationships and a generous helping of sex, the man from La Mancha soon made a name for himself. Later efforts such as the Oscar-winning *All About My Mother* provided a showcase for his more mature skills.

In 1995, the year after Fernando Trueba won the Best Foreign Film Oscar for *Belle Epoque,* the most successful of Spain's younger directors, former Madrid university film student Alejandro Amenábar, debuted his brilliant *Tesis*. Three years later he produced the critically-acclaimed thriller *Abre los Ojos* (remade by Hollywood as *Vanilla Sky*), and soon had Nicole Kidman agreeing to star in *The Others*, his first English-language film and a big hit worldwide.

Though the success of other young directors, including Fernando Barrio, Ramón Salazar and Julio Menem, has been largely restricted to domestic audiences, Spanish actors are making it big on both sides of the Atlantic. For a long time Málaga-born Antonio Banderas was Hollywood's token Spaniard, but now Penelope Cruz and Javier Bardem, both stars of Bigas Lunas's 1992 study of food, sex and machismo *Jamón Jamón*, have joined the Hollywood ranks and are proof that the Spanish film industry is making its mark internationally.

all-round viewing and one for 3D projections. Continuous shows: Mon–Fri 11.20am–1pm & 3.45pm–1am, Sat & Sun 11.20am–2.15pm & 3.45pm–1am; €5.40–6.60.

Luna

Map 6, E6. C/Luna 2 ☎915 224 752. Metro Callao. Four-screen cinema showing some of the latest releases (mostly in *v.o.*) located in a grim-looking square just north of the Gran Vía.

CINEMA

Festivals

I t's worth checking out which **festivals** (fiestas) your visit to Madrid coincides with. There are dozens throughout the year, some involving the whole city, others just an individual barrio. The important dates are listed below.

Religious fiestas aside, the city council organizes cultural festivals, in particular the *Veranos de la Villa* (July–Sept) and *Festival de Otoño* (Sept–Nov) with concerts, theatre and cinema events. Many are free and they're often open-air, taking place in the city's parks and squares. **Annual festivals** for alternative theatre (Feb), flamenco (Feb), dance (mid-May to mid-June), photography (mid-June to mid-July) and jazz (Nov) are also firmly established on the cultural agenda. Full programmes are published in the monthly *En Madrid* tourist hand-out, free from any of the tourist offices (see p.8 for addresses).

JANUARY

Cabalgata de los Reyes (Cavalcade of the Three Kings)
January 5. A very popular evening procession through the city centre to celebrate the arrival of the Three Kings, in which children are showered with sweets. Most Spanish children receive their Christmas presents the next day.

FEBRUARY

Carnaval

Taking place the week before Lent, the *Carnaval* is an excuse for a lot of partying and fancy-dress parades, especially in the gay zone around Chueca. The end of *Carnaval* is marked by the bizarre and entertaining parade, *El Entierro de la Sardina* (The Burial of the Sardine), on Paseo de la Florida. The parade reputedly originates from the time of Carlos III, when a delivery of rotting sardines arrived in the city, prompting the king to order their immediate burial. The burial thus signifies the end of *Carnaval* and the arrival of the abstinence of Lent.

MARCH/APRIL

Semana Santa

Easter Week is celebrated with processions of penitents in Madrid although they're not quite as impressive and moving as those in Toledo.

Look out for the Jesús Nazareno "El Pobre" procession that winds its way through La Latina on Easter Thursday and the Cristo de Medinaceli that begins at the church behind the Palace Hotel on Good Friday. Route and times of procession available from any of the tourist offices.

MAY

Fiesta del Dos de Mayo

May 2. Celebrated especially in Malasaña, where there are bands and partying around the Plaza Dos de Mayo. It was the funkiest festival in the city during the 1980s, but has been a bit low-key in recent years.

Fiestas de San Isidro

May 15. The festival of Madrid's patron saint extends a week either side of May 15, with a non-stop round of carnival events, parades and free entertainment. Bands play every night in the Jardines de las Vistillas (see p.205), and there's traditional

FEBRUARY–MAY

chotis music and dancing. The festival also heralds the start of the bullfighting season.

La Feria del Libro

At the end of May, Madrid's great book fair takes place, with hundreds of stands set up in El Retiro.

JUNE

Fiesta de la Ermita de San Antonio de la Florida

June 13. Events based around the church (see p.136) and in the adjacent Parque de la Bombilla.

Fiestas de San Juan

June 17–24. Bonfires and fireworks in El Retiro, marking the traditional start of summer.

JULY

La Virgen del Carmen

July 9–16. Local fiesta in the barrio of Chamberí, to the north of the city centre.

AUGUST

Castizo fiestas

August 6–15. Traditional fiestas of *San Cayetano*, *San Lorenzo* and *La Virgen de la Paloma* in La Latina and Lavapiés barrios. Much of the activity takes place around the Plaza de la Paja, Las Vistillas and around c/Toledo.

DECEMBER

Navidad

During Christmas, Plaza Mayor is filled with stalls selling all manner of decorations and displaying a large model of a crib. El Corte Inglés, at the bottom of c/Preciados, has an all-singing-all-dancing clockwork Christmas scene over the entrance facing c/Maestro Vitoria, which plays at certain times of the day to enthusiastic children.

Nochevieja

December 31. New Year's Eve is celebrated in bars, restaurants and parties all over the city, with bands in some of the squares. Puerta del Sol is the traditional place to gather, waiting for the twelve chimes of midnight to sound on the clock above the plaza – it's traditional to swallow a grape on each strike for luck.

Sport and bullfighting

Spaniards, and *Madrileños* in particular, are **sport** crazy. Basketball, cycling, handball, tennis and motorcycling all generate plenty of interest, but without a doubt, the great national obsession is **fútbol** (*el deporte rey*, the king of sports). Fierce rivalry between Madrid and Barcelona dominates both football and the other major national sport, basketball, but there is also stiff competition within the city between football clubs **Real Madrid** and **Atlético Madrid** and basketball's Real Madrid and Estudiantes.

The biggest-selling daily paper in Spain is the sports tabloid *Marca*, and ninety percent of its pages are taken up with football (mainly coverage of Real Madrid).

Sports facilities in the capital are good, though heavily used. You shouldn't have much difficulty finding somewhere to swim (in summer), play tennis or go running – there are plenty of *polideportivos* (sports centres) run by the council and scattered across the city – and even obscure sports can be tracked down through the Consejo Superior de Deportes (☎915 896 700).

While many Spaniards regard **bullfighting** as a refined art form, it does have much in common with professional sport with its multimillion euro turnover, highly paid preening stars and massive exposure on television. It's a phenomenon linked very closely to the history, culture and character of Spain and if you're keen for an insight into a world that dominates visitors' images of the country, then Madrid is one of the best places to see a bullfight, though it certainly isn't to everyone's taste.

FOOTBALL

Madrid has three football clubs in the *Primera División* (First Division): **Atlético Madrid**, their star-studded neighbours **Real Madrid** and the more modest **Rayo Vallecano**. In addition, the Second Division (*Segunda A*) has Leganés and Getafe, local stalwarts from the tough industrial suburbs whose names they bear. The **season** runs from September to June, and league matches are usually played on Sunday afternoon at 5 or 6pm. Many of the bigger matches are shown live on pay-per-view TV, while one match a week, played on a Saturday evening, is shown on regular TV.

A massive influx of expensive **foreign players** has seen Real Madrid break the world transfer record on three occasions in recent years, bringing Nicolas Anelka – who only stayed for one season – Luis Figo and Zinedine Zidane to the club. Brazilian World Cup star Ronaldo is the latest addition to Real's glittering squad. Atlético were also big spenders in the past, with Juninho, Christian Vieri and Jimmy Hasselbaink all involved in big-money signings, but a spell in the second division saw them off-load many of their big stars.

As well as major foreign imports, there are plenty of classy **Spanish players** on the scene, notably Real's Raul, their

FOOTBALL

237

young keeper Iker Casillas and veteran skipper Fernando Hierro. Atlético can also claim to have one of the country's most promising rising stars in the shape of Under-21 international striker Fernando Torres. Entertainment on the pitch is matched by the antics off it, with the flamboyant owner of Atlético, Jesús Gil, presently embroiled in a long-running series of legal battles over alleged misuse of funds, which have resulted in him spending short spells in prison.

Atlético owner Gil is no stranger to controversy and was jailed in the late 1960s after a building he owned collapsed, killing 58 people. He was subsequently pardoned by Franco after serving 18 months.

Tickets usually only go on sale a couple of days before matches, with massive queues building up outside the stadium box offices. Real Madrid has a telephone booking system through the bank Caja Madrid (☎902 324 324), but you still have to queue to collect the tickets before the match. For big matches you may have to resort to the touts, who can be bargained down quite substantially. For smaller games, however (those that are not Madrid derbies or don't involve Barcelona), tickets can be obtained relatively easily.

Fans tend to congregate in the bars that ring the stadiums well before kick-off, as alcohol is banned inside the ground, although it's a common sight to see a *bota* (hide pouch full of cheap red wine) being passed around the crowd. At half-time there's a general rustle of tin foil as almost everyone settles down to enjoy a homemade *jamón* or *tortilla bocadillo* – the food inside the grounds is pretty poor.

FOOTBALL

Atlético Madrid
Estadio Vicente Calderón,
Paseo de la Virgen del Puerto

67 ☎913 664 707,
🌐www.clubatleticodemadrid.
com. Metro Pirámides.

Ticket office Mon–Fri 5–8pm; two days before each match also 11am–2pm. Tickets from €12.

Atlético Madrid, given the not-so-glamorous nickname of *Los Colchoneros* (The Mattress Makers) because of the colours of their shirts which resemble the formerly ubiquitous red and white Spanish mattresses, have always been the rather poor relations of Real Madrid. Originally set up by young Basques and *Madrileños* as a branch of Athletic de Bilbao, the club soon became independent (although its strip is still the same colour as the Basque club) and has enjoyed considerable success since its foundation in 1903. They have won nine league titles and nine cups, as well as the Cup Winners' Cup in 1962, the high point being the *doblete* (league and cup double) in the 1995–96 season, when their loyal and long-suffering fans at last had an excuse to celebrate in the Neptuno fountain on the Paseo del Prado. Although not as impressive as Real Madrid's Bernabéu stadium, the newly equipped all-seater **Vicente Calderón Stadium** has a not insubstantial 55,000 capacity and usually enjoys a far better atmosphere than its more glamorous counterpart.

Real Madrid

Estadio Santiago Bernabéu, c/Concha Espina
℡913 984 300; information line ℡902 271 708,
tickets ℡902 324 324;
ⓦwww.realmadrid.com.
Metro Santiago Bernabéu.
Ticket office Mon–Fri 5–8pm; match days 11am–1.30pm. Tickets from €15 go on sale three days before each match.
Of the three main Madrid football clubs, the one with the best record and richest heritage is **Real Madrid**, nine times winners of the European Cup and 28 times winners of the Spanish League. *El Equipo Merengue* (The Meringues), named after their traditional all-white strip, maintained their reputation by winning the European Cup three times between 1998 and 2002. To

FOOTBALL

the delight of their fans they have also eclipsed arch-rivals Barcelona on the domestic scene in recent seasons. Much of Real's reputation is based on the **golden era** of the 1950s when they dominated not just Spanish,

permanent trophy exhibition at the Bernabéu where you can see the cabinets groaning under the weight of their accumulated silverware (Tues–Sun 10.30am–7.30pm; €3.61; entrance by gate 5 of the stadium).

Real Madrid played in arguably the greatest football match on British soil. Their 7–3 humbling of Eintracht Frankfurt in the final of the European Cup at Hampden Park in 1960 gave them their fifth title in a row.

---

but European and world football.

Their magnificent **Santiago Bernabéu Stadium**, venue of the 1982 World Cup Final, is one of the greatest grounds in the world, even with its reduced capacity of 75,000. A small but highly repellent neo-fascist group of hooligan followers known as the *Ultra Sur*, are heavily outnumbered by decent fans at the frequently packed ground. Whenever they have something to celebrate, Real fans throng the fountain of Cibeles at the top of Paseo del Prado. Real have a

Rayo Vallecano

Estadio de María Teresa Rivero, Avda Payaso Fofó ☎914 782 253, ⓦwww.rayovallecano.es. Metro Portazgo. Ticket office Mon–Sat 5.30–8.30pm & two hours before each match. Tickets from €12.

Rayo Vallecano bounced back to top-league status in the 1998–99 season and despite regular scares have stayed there ever since. Their modest stadium in the working-class suburb of Vallecas holds a mere 15,500, but there's still plenty of atmosphere. They openly admit they cannot

THE REAL DEAL

Under Franco's regime Real Madrid became the showcase of
Spanish sport, enjoying privileges not afforded to other clubs.
This preferential treatment is said to continue to this day, with
the most recent episode concerning a miraculous turn-around
in the club's financial position.

By the year 2000 Real had run up a debt of over $250 million
– but were still able to break the then world transfer record
with Luis Figo for $56 million – yet within months new club
president Florentino Perez, a former politician and head of
one of Spain's biggest construction empires, had done a deal
with Madrid city council that allowed the club to clear its debts
with the stroke of a pen. The agreement, which according to
the opposition parties on the local council breached building
regulations, allowed the club to sell off its city-centre training
grounds for office development, while building new facilities on
a cheaper out-of-town green-field site. Depending on your
footballing allegiances, the deal, which was worth close to
$400 million, was either the product of astute financial man-
agement on Perez's behalf or evidence that Real were still very
much the regime team. Whatever the truth of the matter Real
went from the red into the black in a matter of days and celebrated by breaking the world transfer record once again, buying Zidane from Juventus for a cool $66 million. The whole
series of events formed yet another intriguing chapter in the
history of a sport that has become more intertwined with politics and regionalism than in practically any other European
country.

compete financially with big
brothers Real and Atlético
and frequently reschedule
games so as not to clash with
their neighbours' fixtures.
The best position they have
managed in the league was
ninth in 1999–2000. The

FOOTBALL

fact that the club has the only female football president in Spain, María Teresa Rivero, wife of the controversial entrepreneur, José María Ruiz Mateos, adds a little extra colour to this friendly local club.

BASKETBALL

Basketball is the second most popular spectator sport in Spain, and Madrid has two top-class teams, **Estudiantes** and **Real Madrid** (part of the football club). Following a fire that burnt down their previous stadium in the centre of the city, Estudiantes have moved out to the Palacio de Vistalegre in the southwest of the city (Metro Vista Alegre/Oporto; stadium ☏ 914 220 780, club ☏ 915 624 022, tickets through El Corte Inglés ☏ 902 400 222; Ⓦ www.clubestudiantes.com; tickets €10–12). Real Madrid play at the Pabellón Raimundo Saporta at the northern tip of the Paseo de la Castellana (Metro Begoña; tickets in advance through Caja Madrid ticket line ☏ 902 488 488; Ⓦ www.realmadrid.com; from €5). The **season** runs from September to May, the high points being the playoffs from April onwards and the Torneo de Navidad in the last week in December.

Several polideportivos (sports centres) around the city cater for most sports: Polideportivo de la Chopera, Parque del Retiro (Metro Atocha; daily 8.30am–9.30pm; ☏ 914 201 154); Estadio de Vallehermoso, Avda Islas Filipinas (Metro Cuatro Caminos/Ríos Rosas; daily 8am–10pm; ☏ 915 347 723); Parque Deportivo La Ermita, c/Sepúlveda 3–5 (Metro Puerta del Angel; Mon–Fri 9am–11pm, Sat 10am–8pm, Sun 10am–3pm; ☏ 914 700 111).

BOWLING

You'll find plenty of ten-pin **bowling alleys** in Madrid. Two of the most central are Star Bowl Azca, Paseo de la Castellana 77 (Metro Nuevos Ministerios; daily 11am–midnight, Fri & Sat till 2am; ☏915 557 626; €3.40–5) and AMF Bowling Centre, La Vaguada (Metro Herrera Oria/Barrio del Pilar; daily 10pm–1am, Fri & Sat till 4am; ☏917 301 811; €3.50–5).

GOLF

Golf is prohibitively expensive at the private clubs in Madrid. The most accessible **public facilities** are the two courses (18 and 9 holes) at Olivar de la Hinojosa on the eastern outskirts of the city – Avda de Dublin, Campo de las Naciones (Metro Campo de las Naciones; daily 8.30am–8pm; ☏917 211 889). It costs between €15.50 and €37.50 depending on how many holes you play. You need to bring notification of your handicap and a membership card from your own club to get access. There is also a **driving range** in the Parque Empresarial de la Moraleja (daily 10am–10.30pm; opens 9am at weekends; €16.53 per person for nine holes; €2 for a bucket of 25 balls on the driving range; ☏916 614 444), just outside the city on the N-I road to Burgos.

GYMS AND FITNESS CENTRES

Some private **gyms** provide short-term membership: try Club Abascal, c/José Abascal 46 ☏914 420 749; Palestra, c/Bravo Murillo 5 ☏914 489 822; Holiday Gym Castellana, Plaza Carlos Trías Bertrán 4 ☏915 559 624; or Holiday Gym Princesa c/Serrano Jover 3 ☏915 474 033.

RUNNING

There are plenty of places to **run** in the major parks, Parque del Oeste, Casa de Campo and the Retiro; the last two have specially marked-out routes for *footing* (jogging) – the one in the Casa de Campo is by the lake; the one in the Retiro is on the north side of the park. There's a popular **marathon** held in the city in late April.

SKIING

There are several **ski stations** in the mountains to the north of Madrid which provide limited skiing in the winter months, and can make for a fun day-trip escape from the city (see p.314 for more on this area).

SWIMMING

Madrid is well supplied with **open-air pools** (*piscinas*), which is just as well given that summer temperatures can soar above 40°C. Most have shade and pleasant sunbathing areas, restaurants and/or bars, and some offer other activities such as volleyball. Open-air pools generally open daily from mid-May to mid-September, 10.30am–8pm and admission is usually around €3. The most central pools include: Barrio del Pilar, c/Monforte de Lemos (Metro Barrio del Pilar/Begoña; ☎913 147 943); Canal de Isabel II, Avda de las Islas Filipinas 54 (Metro Ríos Rosas; ☎915 339 642); Casa de Campo, Avda del Angel (Metro Lago; ☎914 630 050); Chamartín, Plaza del Perú (Metro Pío XII; ☎913 501 223); Concepción, c/José del Hierro (Metro Concepción/Quintana; ☎914 039 020); La Elipa, Parque de la Elipa, c/O'Donnell (Metro Estrella; ☎914 303 511); José María Cacigal, c/Santa Pola (Metro Príncipe Pío; ☎915 413 716); and Estadio de Vallehermoso, Avda Islas

Filipinas (Metro Cuatro Caminos/Ríos Rosas; ℡ 915 347 723).

The pleasant *parque deportivo* at Puerta de Hierro on the banks of the River Manzanares is an option for open-air swimming; take bus 83 or 133.

An expensive alternative is the rooftop pool at the *Hotel Emperador*, Gran Vía 53 (Metro Gran Vía). It costs an exorbitant €24, but you get spectacular views of the city as you swim. In addition, there are **indoor pools** at Moratalaz, c/Valdebernardo (Metro Pavones; closed Aug; ℡ 917 727 121) and **La Latina**, Plaza de la Cebada 1 (Metro La Latina; ℡ 913 658 031). For **aquaparks**, see "Kids' Madrid", p.267.

TENNIS

Most of the *polideportivos* and the Casa de Campo (Metro Lago, near the lake) have a variety of **courts** for rent at around €2.25 an hour, but you need your own equipment. The city's exclusive Club de Campo hosts the annual Spanish Open women's tennis tournament in May.

BULLFIGHTING

Bullfighting (*los toros*) is a multimillion-euro business and around half a million Spaniards are employed either directly or indirectly in the bullfighting world. Nevertheless, there are many Spaniards who have never been to a bullfight and may only have seen one on TV; there is even some opposition to the activity from animal welfare groups, but it's not widespread, and the last few years have seen bullfighting become even more fashionable. *Los toros* is culture and ritual rolled into one, where the emphasis is on the way man (and occasionally woman) and bull "perform" together – the art is at issue rather than the cruelty. *Aficionados* (fans) argue that the life of a bull destined for the ring is infinitely preferable and more honourable than that of the majority which end ignominiously in the slaughterhouse.

Regular **corridas** (bullfights) are held in the smaller bullrings of a number of towns surrounding Madrid during their fiestas. Many also feature **encierros**, where young bulls pursue often drunk runners along a set route into the *plaza de toros*. The more famous of these *ferias* (all late Aug) include: **Chinchón**, a picturesque setting in the ancient plaza; **Colmenar Viejo**, a prestigious *feria* in the heart of bull-breeding country; **Manzanares el Real**; and **San Sebastián de los Reyes**, which features highly rated *encierros*. Towns to the north and west of Madrid, such as Pozuelo and Las Rozas, hold their *ferias* in September.

All manner of taurine-related memorabilia, including the *traje de luces* worn by Manolete in his last and fatal corrida, is displayed in the Museo Taurino, Plaza de las Ventas (Tues–Fri 9.30am–2.30pm, Sun & hols 10am–1pm, closed Sun between Nov and Feb; free; Metro Ventas). It's a little unimaginative and old-fashioned, but there's just about enough to keep budding Hemingways satisfied.

Among the established and popular **matadores** – Enrique Ponce, César Rincón, Joselito, Litri, Jesulín de Ubrique, Ortega Cano, Finito de Córdoba and El Cordobés – are two new stars, **El Juli** and **José Tomás**, who both hail from the Madrid area and who have had rave reviews from the normally hard-to-please critics.

Plaza de Toros de Las Ventas

C/Alcalá 237 ☎917 264 800 or 913 562 200, ⊛www. las-ventas.com. Metro Ventas. Box office March–Oct Thurs–Sun 10am–2pm & 5–8pm; Cajamadrid ticket line ☎902 488 488 and from authorised agents in booths along c/Victoria near Sol; tickets €12–100.

Madrid's neo-*Mudéjar* bullring, **Las Ventas**, with its 23,000 capacity, is probably the most illustrious in the world. The season lasts from March to October and *corridas* are held every Sunday at 7pm and every day during the three main *ferias*: *La Comunidad* (early May), *San Isidro* (mid-May to June) and *Otoño* (late Sept to Oct). **Tickets** go on sale at the ring only a couple of days in advance, with many already allocated to season-ticket holders. The cheapest seats are *gradas*, the highest rows at the back, from where you can see everything that happens without too much of the detail; the front rows are known as the *barreras*. Seats are also divided into *sol* (sun), *sombra* (shade), and *sol y sombra* (shaded after a while). The *sombra* seats are more expensive, mainly for reasons of comfort. On the way in, you can rent cushions – two hours sitting on concrete is not much fun. Beer and soft drinks are sold inside.

BULLFIGHTING

Shopping

Shopping districts in Madrid are pretty clearly defined. The biggest range of **shops** is along Gran Vía and around Puerta del Sol, and this is where you'll find the main branches of **department stores** such as the ubiquitous El Corte Inglés and leading chain stores such as Zara, Cortefiel and Mango. If you want international or speciality shops, head for Madrid 2, a huge hypermarket next to Metro Barrio de Pilar or the upmarket ABC Serrano at c/Serrano 61 and Paseo de la Castellana 34 (Metro Rubén Darío/Nuñez de Balboa).

Although Madrid has its fair share of stylish designer shops it has also managed to retain many of its **traditional establishments**, and these eccentric little shops, still serving the local community, provide the greatest interest for casual browsers and shopaholics alike.

For **fashion** (*moda*) and designer labels, the smartest addresses are calles Serrano, Goya, Ortega y Gasset and Velázquez in Salamanca, north of the Retiro, while more alternative designers are to be found in Malasaña and Chueca (on c/Almirante especially). For **shoes** the road to head for is c/Augusto Figueroa in Chueca where there are a number of factory outlets selling a wide range at very good prices and for fans of **street fashion** there is plenty on offer in the shops in and around c/Fuencarral. Anything **electrical**, particularly sound systems, can be found in nearby c/Barquillo. The **antiques** trade is concentrated on and around c/Ribera de Curtidores, near the Rastro, and in the Puerta de Toledo shopping centre; while for truly idiosyncratic items, it's hard to beat the shops just off Plaza Mayor, where luminous saints rub shoulders with surgical supports and fascist memorabilia. The cheapest, trashiest **souvenirs** can be collected at the Todo a un Euro (Everything One Euro) shops scattered all over the city.

OPENING HOURS AND LATE-NIGHT SHOPS

Usual opening hours are Monday–Friday 9.30am–2pm & 5–8pm, Saturday 10am–2pm, but the big department and chain stores don't tend to close for lunch. Nearly all shops close on Sunday, but the larger stores do open on up to nineteen Sundays in the year, usually the first in each month, and all those in August and December. All the bigger places take credit cards, but many require photographic identification, for example a passport, as well.

There are also two chains of late-night shops, VIPS and 7 Eleven, which stay open into the early hours and on Sundays. Each branch sells newspapers, cigarettes, groceries, books and CDs – all the things you need at 3am. Larger branches also have café/restaurants, one-hour photo developing and other services. Central branches include:

VIPS (daily 9am–3am): Glorieta de Quevedo (Metro Quevedo); Gran Vía 43 (Metro Gran Vía); c/Fuencarral 101 (Metro Bilbao); c/Miguel Ángel 11 (Metro Rubén Darío); c/Serrano 41 (Metro Serrano); c/Velázquez 84 & 136 (Metro Velázquez).

7 Eleven (daily 24hr): c/Arenal 28 (Metro Sol/Ópera); c/Toledo 80 (La Latina); Agustín de Foxá 25 (Metro Plaza de Castilla); Avda. de América 18 (Metro Avda. de América); Capitán Haya 17–19 (Metro Lima); San Bernardo 33 (Metro Noviciados).

Most areas of the city have their own *mercados del barrio* (indoor **markets**), devoted mainly to food. Among the best are those in Plaza San Miguel (just west of Plaza Mayor); La Cebada in Plaza de la Cebada (Metro La Latina); Antón Martín in c/Santa Isabel (Metro Antón Martín); and Maravillas, c/Bravo Murillo 122 (Metro Cuatro Caminos). The city's biggest market is, of course, the **Rastro** – the flea market – which takes place on Sunday in the area south of Plaza Mayor. Other specialized markets include a second-hand **book market** on the Cuesta de Moyano, at the southwest corner of El Retiro (see p.109), and the stamp and coin market in Plaza Mayor every Sunday (Metro Sol; 9am–2pm), where collectors gather to buy, sell and inspect.

For more on the Rastro see box, p.53.

BOOKS, MAPS AND POSTERS

In addition to specialist **bookshops**, the museum and art galleries, especially in the Centro Arte de Reina Sofía, all have a good range of posters, prints and books.

Casa del Libro
Gran Vía 29 (Map 6, F7) and c/Maestro Victoria 3 (Map 6, E8). Both Metro Callao. Mon–Sat 9.30am–9.30pm. The Casa del Libro's Gran Vía branch is the city's biggest bookshop, with four floors covering just about everything, including a wide range of fiction in English and translations of classic Spanish works. The branch at Maestro Victoria has a good section on maps, guides and books about Madrid.

Crisol
Map 2, K3. C/Serrano 24 (Metro Serrano) and C/Juan Bravo 38 (Metro Diego de León). Mon–Sat 10am–10pm, Sun & public holidays 11am–3pm & 5–9pm.

Good selection of English-language books, plus records and foreign newspapers too.

Desnivel
Map 5, D6. Plaza Matute 6 (Metro Antón Martín). Mon–Sat 10am–2pm & 4.30–8.30pm. ⊛www.libreria desnivel.com.
More centrally located than La Tienda Verde (see below), this bookshop stocks a good range of guides and maps covering all parts of Spain.

The International Bookshop
Map 3, F5. C/Campomanes 13. Metro Ópera/Santo Domingo. Mon–Fri 10.30am–2.30pm & 4.30–8.30pm, Sat 10.30am–3pm. Aug Mon–Sat 11am–3pm.
Wide range of secondhand books in most European languages.

Librería Antonio Machado
Map 6, I4. C/Fernando VI 17. Metro Alonso Martínez. Mon–Sat 10am–2pm & 5–8pm.
The city's best literary

bookshop. All credit cards accepted.

La Librería
Map 3, D9. C/Mayor 78. Metro Sol. Mon–Fri 10am–2pm & 4.30–7.30pm, Sat 11am–2pm.
Tiny place full of books just about Madrid. Also a good place to pick up old postcards, historic maps and photos of the city.

Pasajes
Map 6, J3. C/Genova 3. Metro Alonso Martínez. Mon–Fri 10am–2pm & 5–8pm, Sat 10am–2pm.
Specializes in English and foreign-language books, also has a useful noticeboard where people advertise flats for rent, Spanish classes, and so on.

La Tienda Verde
C/Maudes 23 & 38. Metro Cuatro Caminos. Mon–Sat 9.30am–2pm & 4.30–8pm. ⊛www.tiendaverde.org.
A pair of small shops crammed with trekking and mountain books, guides and survey (*topográfico*) maps. The helpful staff will point you in the right direction.

BOOKS, MAPS AND POSTERS

CLOTHES AND SHOES

Chain stores selling good-value **clothes** can be found all over the city; look out for Massimo Dutti, Springfield, Milano Trajes for men, and Zara and Mango for women, while Cortefiel caters for both sexes.

Adolfo Domínguez
Map 8, D6 & E3. C/José Ortega y Gasset 4 and c/Serrano 96. Both Metro Serrano. Mon–Sat 10am–2pm & 5–8.30pm. The c/Serrano branch doesn't close for lunch. The classic modern Spanish look – sober colours, little extra decoration and free lines. Domínguez's designs are quite pricey, but he has a cheaper *Básico* range. Both branches have men's clothes; women's are only available at the Ortega y Gasset branch.

Agatha Ruiz de la Prada
Map 8, B5. C/Marqués de Riscal 8. Metro Rubén Darío. Mon–Fri 10am–2pm & 5–8pm, Sat 10am–2pm. *Movida* designer who shows and sells her brightly-coloured clothes and accessories at this outlet.

Ararat
Map 6, K6 & J6. C/Conde Xiquena 13; c/Almirante 10 & 11. Both Metro Chueca. Mon–Sat 11am–2pm & 5–8.30pm. A trio of shops with clubby Spanish and foreign designs at reasonably modest prices. Men's clothes are at c/Conde Xiquena 13, women's in c/Almirante. No.10 specializes in more formal wear, while no.11 goes for a younger, more modern look.

Berlín
Map 6, J6. C/Almirante 10. Metro Chueca. Mon–Sat 11am–2pm & 5–8.30pm. Next door to Ararat. Women's clothes from a selection of vanguard European and American designers, as well as Spaniard Roberto Torretta.

Camper

Map 6, D6. C/Gran Vía 54.
Metro Callao. Mon–Sat
10am–2pm & 5–8.30pm.
Spain's best shoe-shop chain,
selling practical and
comfortable designs at modest
prices, with the odd quirky
fabric and unusual heel
thrown in. There are lots of
other branches around the
city.

Ekseptión

Map 2, L3. C/Velázquez 28.
Metro Velázquez. Mon–Sat
10.30am–2.30pm & 5–8.30pm.
A dramatic walkway bathed
in spotlights leads to some of
the most *moderno* women's
clothes in Madrid, from
Sybilla and Antoni Miró,
among others.

Excrupulus Net

Map 6, J6. C/Almirante 7.
Metro Chueca. Mon–Sat
11am–2pm & 5–8.30pm.
Groovy shoes from Spanish
designers Muxart and Looky,
starting at around €100. Also
sells some original and stylish
accessories. Men and women.

Glam

Map 6, G6 & H6. C/Fuencarral
35 (Metro Gran Vía/Chueca);
c/Hortaleza 62 (Metro Chueca).
Mon–Sat 10am–2pm & 5–9pm.
Club/street-style clothes,
which wouldn't look out of
place in an Almodóvar film.
Good-value shirts and tops.

Hernanz

Map 3, G10. C/Toledo 30.
Metro Tirso de Molina. Mon–Fri
9.30am–1.30pm & 5–8.30pm,
Sat 9.30am–1.30pm. No cards.
Established more than a
hundred and fifty years ago,
and good enough for King
Juan Carlos, this shoe shop
stocks over one hundred
different types of *alpargata*
(espadrille) in just about every
imaginable colour and style.
Prices range from €6 to €20.

Sybilla

Map 2, K3. C/Jorge Juan 12.
Metro Retiro. Mon–Sat
10am–2pm & 4.30–8.30pm.
Sybilla was Spain's top
designer of the 1980s and
remains at the forefront of the
scene – with prices to show
it. The shop is a comfortable
place to while away the time,

CLOTHES AND SHOES

253

with its armchairs and sofas, clashing with Sybilla's

trademark vivid colours. Women's clothes only.

CHILDREN

Bazar Mila
Map 6, F7. Gran Vía 33. Metro Gran Vía/Callao. Mon–Sat 9.30am–8.30pm.
Standard toy shop that is just the place to get your Spanish set of Monopoly or your plastic models of Real and Atlético players.

Caramelos Paco
Map 3, F12. C/Toledo 55. Metro La Latina. Mon–Sat 9.30am–2pm & 5–8pm, Sun 11am–3pm.
A child's dream and a dentist's nightmare, with a window crammed full of every sugary confection. Giant lollipops, sugar-coated figures and almond-flavoured sticks of rock are among the delights.

Mothercare
Madrid 2, La Vaguada, Avda. Monforte de Lemos. Metro Barrio del Pilar; C/Claudio Cuello 44 (**Map 8, C9**), Metro Serrano. Mon–Sat 10am–9pm.

Wide range of clothes and every accessory you might need for a young child.

Prénatal
C/Fuencarral 17. Metro Quevedo (**Map 6, G7**); c/San Bernardo 97–99 (**Map 6, D6**), Metro Santo Domingo. Mon–Sat 10am–1.45pm & 4.30–8pm.
The Spanish version of Mothercare, and generally a little cheaper; if you need something in an emergency this is probably your best bet.

Puck
C/Duque de Sesto 30. Metro Goya. Mon 4.30–8pm, Tues–Sat 10am–1.30pm & 4.30–8pm.
An old-fashioned toy shop now celebrating 25 years in business. The fabulous dolls' houses are complete down to the very smallest detail, and customers can select their own decor. Not a Nintendo or Playstation in sight.

CHILDREN

CRAFTS AND SOUVENIRS

Alvarez Gómez

Map 2, J4. C/Serrano 14.
Metro Serrano; branch at
c/Sevilla 2 (**Map 5, C3**), Metro
Sevilla. Mon–Sat 9.30am–2pm
& 4.45–8.15pm.

Gómez has been making the
same perfumes in the same
bottles for the last century.
The fragrances – carnation,
rose and violet – are as simple
and straight as they come.
The elegant shop, complete
with chandeliers, also sells
stylish toilet bags, hats and
umbrellas.

Area Real Madrid

C/Carmen 3, Metrol Sol.
Mon–Sat 10am–9pm.

Newly opened club
superstore located just off Sol
where you can pick up
replica shirts and all manner
of – not cheap – souvenirs
related to the historic club.
There is a smaller branch in
the shopping centre on the
corner of Real's massive
Bernabéu stadium at
c/Concha Espina 1 (metro
Santiago Bernabéu).

El Arco de los Cuchilleros

Map 3, G9. Plaza Mayor 9.
Metro Sol. Mon–Sat
11am–8pm, Sun 11am–2.30pm.

El Arco houses thirty or so
workshops and artesans, who
reflect Spanish *artesanía* at its
most innovative and
contemporary. Crafts include
ceramics, leather, wood,
jewellery and textiles, and
there's a gallery space used for
five or six exhibitions each
year. Prices are very
reasonable and staff helpful.

Casa Jiménez

Map 3, H5. C/Preciados 42.
Metro Callao. Mon–Sat
10am–1.30pm & 5–8pm. Closed
Sat afternoon in July and all
day Sat in Aug.

One of the oldest shops in
Spain, where you can buy
embroidered *mantones*
(shawls) made in Seville, with
prices ranging from €100 to
€600, as well as gorgeous
fans from around €40.

CRAFTS AND SOUVENIRS

Casa Postal

Map 6, I6. C/Libertad 37. Metro Chueca. Mon–Fri 10am–2pm & 5–8pm, Sat 10am–2pm.

Marvellous old-fashioned shop packed to the rafters with old postcards, posters and other mementos of the city.

Casa Yustas

Map 3, G8. Plaza Mayor 30. Metro Sol. Mon–Sat 9.30am–9.30pm, Sun 11am–9.30pm.

Madrid's oldest hat shop, established in 1894. Every conceivable model and price, from pith helmets and commando berets to panamas and bowlers. Also sells a large range of souvenir-style goods including Lladró porcelain figurines.

El Flamenco Vive

Map 3, E7. C/Unión 4. Metro Ópera. Mon–Sat 10.30am–2pm & 5–9pm.

This place specializes in all things Andalusian: flamenco music, guitars, percussion, dance accessories, books and more.

Fútbol Total

C/Cardenal Cisneros 80. Metro Quevedo. Mon–Sat: July–Sept 10.30am–2pm & 5.30–8.30pm; Oct–June 10.30am–2pm & 5–9pm.

Just the place to get your Real, Atlético or even Rayo shirt. In fact the strip of practically every Spanish team is available, for around €50.

Intermon

Map 6, C1. C/Alberto Aguilera 15. Metro Argüelles. Mon–Sat 10am–2pm & 5–8pm.

Arts and crafts from Asia, Africa and South America, with some of the profits invested in development programmes.

José Ramírez

Map 3, H10. C/Concepción Jerónima. Metro Sol/Tirso de Molina. Mon–Fri 9.30am–2pm & 5–8pm, Sat 10am–2pm.

One of the most renowned guitar workshops in Spain; it even has a museum of antique instruments. Prices start at around €100 and head skywards for the quality models and fancy woods.

Mercado de Artesanos

Map 6, D3. Plaza de las Comendadoras. Metro San Bernardo. Every Sat afternoon. The weekly market in this pleasant plaza is a good place to pick up handicrafts and souvenirs. There are also performances and workshops to add to the interest.

Palomeque

Map 3, G7. C/Hileras 12. Metro Ópera. Mon–Fri 10am–2pm & 5–8pm, Sat 10am–2pm. A religious department store stocking everything from rosary beads and habits down to your very own plastic baby Jesus. If you want to complete your postcard collection of Spanish saints and virgins, this is the place.

Seseña

Map 5, B4. C/Cruz 23. Metro Sol. Mon–Sat 10am–1.30pm & 4.30–8pm. Tailor specializing in traditional *Madrileño* capes for royalty and celebrities. Clients include Luis Buñuel, Gary Cooper and Hilary Clinton.

El Templo del Fútbol

Map 6, F7. Gran Vía 38. Metro Callao. Mon–Sat 10am–8.30pm. Atlético Madrid shop where the ground floor has the standard replica kits, while downstairs anything from keyrings to a commemorative bottle of wine can be purchased.

DEPARTMENT STORES

El Corte Inglés

Map 3, I7. C/Preciados 1–4. Metro Sol. Branches at c/Princesa 42 (Metro Argüelles); c/Goya 76 & 87 (Metro Goya); Paseo de la Castellana 71 & 85 (Metro Nuevos Ministerios). Mon–Sat 10am–9.30pm.

The Spanish department store *par excellence*. It's not cheap, but the quality is very good and the advantage is that you can get practically anything you want under one roof. Highly professional staff (the majority of whom speak English) and a classy food department. Good for sports equipment and not bad for CDs.

Fnac

Map 3, H5. C/Preciados 28. Metro Callao. Mon–Sat 10am–9.30pm, Sun noon–9.30pm. Not a true department store, but it does have excellent sections for books, videos, CDs and electrical equipment. The book department is good for English-language fiction and has a decent section for English-language teachers/learners. The store has a price promise that it will return your money if you find any article cheaper anywhere else. Also sells concert tickets.

FOOD AND DRINK

Bruin

Map 2, A1. Paseo del Pintor Rosales 48. Metro Argüelles. Daily 10am–midnight. Great ice-cream parlour with a nice *terraza* next to Parque del Oeste. Over twenty different flavours, plus the full range of chilled drinks.

Casa Mira

Map 5, D4. Carrera de San Jerónimo 30. Metro Sevilla. Mon–Sat 10am–2pm & 5–9pm. The place to go for *turrón* (flavoured nougat) – eaten by nearly all Spaniards at Christmas – and marzipan. The family business has been open for nearly a hundred and fifty years since the founder, Luis Mira, arrived from Asturias and set up a stall in Puerta del Sol.

Mallorca

Map 2, J4. C/Serrano 6. Metro Serrano. Daily 9.30am–9pm. The main branch of Madrid's best deli chain – a pricey but fabulous treasure trove for picnics, cakes and chocolates. All branches have small bars serving drinks and canapés.

La Mallorquina

Map 3, I7. Puerta del Sol 2. Metro Sol. Mon–Sat

9am–9.45pm.
Wonderful-smelling pastry shop and café selling everything you've always been told not to eat. Try the small ball-shaped *buñuelos* filled with cream or the tray of assorted *pasteles*. Upstairs there's a salon which overlooks Puerta del Sol.

Mariano Aguado
Map 6, D5. C/Echegaray 19. Metro Sevilla. Mon–Fri 9.30am–2pm & 5.30–8.30pm, Sat 9.30am–2pm.
Atmospheric wine seller's with a reassuringly musty atmosphere, and fine selection of Spanish wines, especially sherries (*vinos de Jerez*), at prices to suit every pocket.

Mariano Madrueño
Map 3, H5. C/Postigo San Martín 3. Metro Callao. Mon–Fri 9.30am–2pm & 5–8pm, Sat 9.30am–2pm.
Great traditional wine seller's established back in 1895. There's an overpowering smell of grapes as you peruse its vintage-crammed shelves. Intriguing tipples include powerful Licor de Hierbas

from Galicia and homemade Pacharán sloe gin.

Museo del Jamón
Map 5, B3. Carrera de San Jerónimo 6. Metro Sol. Mon–Sat 9am–midnight, Sun & public holidays 10am–midnight.
A fantastic range of hams hanging from the ceiling, but it'll set you back a bit – a quality *Jamón de Jabugo* from pigs fed exclusively on acorns weighs in around €50 a kilo. Staff are always willing to provide advice. Branches all over town.

Patrimonio Comunal Olivarero
Map 6, I4. C/Mejía Lequérica 1. Metro Alonso Martínez. Mon–Sat 9.30am–2.30pm & 5.30–7.30pm.
Outlet for an olive-growers' co-operative, with information sheets to guide you towards purchasing the best olive oils. A vast range of grades and quantities are available from all over the peninsula.

Reserva y Cata
Map 6, K5. C/Conde de

FOOD AND DRINK

Xiquena 13. Metro Colón/Chueca. Mon–Fri 11am–2.30pm, Sat 11am–2.30pm. ⓦwww.reservaycata.com.
The well-informed staff at this friendly specialist shop will help you select from some of the highest quality new wines from the Iberian peninsula. There is a constantly-changing selection on display at prices ranging from a bargain €2 right through to an exorbitant €300.

MUSIC

Fnac
Map 3, H5. C/Preciados 28. Metro Callao. Mon–Sat 10am–9.30pm, Sun noon–9.30pm.
Large music department with Spanish, Latin American, international and classical sections. Also sells concert tickets.

Garrido Bailén
Map 3, C9. C/Mayor 88. Metro Ópera. Mon–Fri 10am–1.30pm & 4.30–8.15pm, Sat 10am–1.45pm.
Fascinating musical instrument shop on the corner of c/Bailén, stocking everything from Celtic bagpipes and sitars to Andean panpipes and drum machines. Worth a browse even if you aren't particularly musically-minded.

Madrid Rock
Map 6, G7. Gran Vía 25. Metro Callao. Daily 10am–10pm.
By Spanish standards this is a huge record store, selling a good range of rock, jazz, Pop Español and flamenco CDs. Tickets for most concerts are available too.

La Metralleta
Map 3, G6. Plaza de San Martín. Metro Ópera. Mon–Sat 10am–2.30pm & 4.30–8.30pm.
Down the steps on the edge of the plaza, La Metralleta buys and sells CDs, records, film posters, calendars and anything connected with the entertainment industry. Lots of bargains, with CDs at around €6 – a good place to find more obscure stuff.

Kids' Madrid

Although many of the main sights and museums in Madrid lack child-specific services or activities, there's plenty in the city to keep **children** occupied and interested for a short stay. Most of the parks have playgrounds and, in addition to the city's swimming pools (see p.244), there are a couple of aquaparks situated out of town. The colourful parades and events during fiestas are also worth investigating, particularly during *Carnaval* and Christmas.

For shops stocking toys and children's goods, see "Shopping", p.254.

Children are, in general, doted on in Spain and are welcome in nearly all cafés and restaurants. Most are more than willing to provide special child portions, while the VIPS chain of café/restaurants and all the burger bars provide children's menus. Spanish children stay up later than in many other countries and frequently accompany parents for a late evening stroll or drinks at a *terraza*.

MUSEUMS AND SIGHTS

Acuarium de Madrid

Map 3, H6. C/Maestro Vitoria 8 ☎915 318 172. Metro Callao/Sol. Daily 11am–2pm & 5–9pm. €4.75, under-8s €3.45, under-2s free.

A small-scale but interesting exhibition of fish, reptiles and spiders located in the heart of the shopping zone of Madrid.

Imax Madrid

Parque Tierno Galván Meneses ☎914 674 800, ⓦwww.imax madrid.com. Metro Méndez Álvaro. Continuous shows: Mon–Fri 11.20am–1pm & 3.45pm–1am, Sat & Sun 11.20am–2.15pm & 3.45pm–1am. €5.40–6.60.

Three different types of screen – a giant flat one, a dome-shaped one for all-round viewing and one for 3D projections – showing largely natural-history-style documentaries.

Mirador del Faro

Avda del Arco de la Victoria. Metro Moncloa. Tues–Sun: June–Aug 11am–1.45pm & 5.30–8.45pm; Sept–May 10am–2pm & 5–8pm. €1, €0.50 for 3–10-year-olds.

The futuristic *mirador* (viewing gallery) provides fantastic views over the city and is very popular with children.

Museo de Cera (Wax Museum)

Map 6, L5. Paseo de Recoletos 41 ☎913 080 825, ⓦwww.museoceramadrid.com. Metro Colón. Mon–Fri 10am–2.30pm & 4.30–8.30pm, Sat, Sun & holidays 10am–8.30pm. €7.20, under-10s & over-65s €4.20, under-4s free.

Over 450 different personalities including a host of VIPs, heads of state and, of course, Real Madrid's Zinedine Zidane in this expensive and tacky museum, which is nevertheless popular with children. There's also a chamber of horrors and a film history of Spain, for which you pay a supplement.

Museo de Ciencias Naturales

C/José Gutiérrez Abascal 2
⊕914 111 328. Metro Nuevos
Ministerios. Tues–Fri
10am–6pm, Sat 10am–8pm,
Sun 10am–2.30pm. €2.40,
under-14s €1.50.

The Natural History Museum is the most interactive of the traditional museums in the city centre, with audiovisual displays on the evolution of life on earth and plenty of dinosaur exhibits. Children's activities on Saturday and Sunday mornings.

Museo del Ferrocarril

Paseo de las Delicias 61 ⊕902
228 822, ⊛www.museode
lferrocarril.org. Metro Delicias.
Tues–Thurs 10am–5pm, Fri–Sun
10am–3pm. €3.50, under-12s
€2, under-4s free.

An impressive collection of engines, carriages and wagons that once graced the railway lines of Spain, as well as memorabilia from around the world. The museum is also home to a fascinating collection of model railways and there's an atmospheric little cafeteria housed in one of the elegant carriages.

Planetario

Avda del Planetario 16, Parque
Tierno Galván ⊕914 673 461,
⊛www.planetmad.es. Metro
Méndez Álvaro. Tues–Sun
11am–1.45pm & 5–7.45pm;
shows at 11.30am, 12.45pm,
5.30pm & 6.45pm. €3, under-
14s €1.20.

Exhibition halls, audiovisual displays and projections on a variety of astronomical themes (all in Spanish).

Teleférico

Map 2, A2. Paseo del Pintor
Rosales ⊕915 417 450,
⊛www.teleferico.com. Metro
Argüelles. April–Sept daily
11am–3pm & 5pm–dusk;
Oct–March Sat, Sun & public
holidays only. €2.80 single, €4
return, under-7s half price,
under-3s free.

**The Museo Thyssen-Bornemisza (see p.86) offers
children's workshops for accompanied five- to ten-year-olds
on Saturdays at 10am. Ring to confirm.**

MUSEUMS AND SIGHTS

A popular cable-car ride over to the restaurant/bar on the far side of Casa de Campo, with great views of the city. You can't use it to get to the zoo or Parque de Atracciones, however, as they're on the other side of the park.

Zoo–Aquarium

Casa de Campo ℡917 119 950, ⓦwww.zoomadrid.com. Metro Batán/bus #33. Daily 10am–dusk. €12.15, under-7s €9.80, under-3s free.

The zoo, on the southwestern edge of Casa de Campo, is laid out in sections corresponding to the five continents. Most animals are kept in by moats and have plenty of space to move around. There are over 2000 different species, including a new pair of koalas and venomous snakes, plus a children's zoo and parrot show. Boats can be rented and there are train tours too.

THEME PARKS

Faunia

Avda de las Comunidades 28 ℡913 016 210, ⓦwww.faunia-es.com. Metro Valdebernardo, bus #130, 8, 71; special buses from Metro Pavones on Sat, Sun & hols. Daily 10.30am–9pm. €16.20, under-10s €11.40, under-3s free.

An innovative nature park providing an entertaining and educational experience for children of all ages, recreating a series of ecosystems to provide a home to 720

different animal species. Highlights include the Arctic zone and its spectacular "penguinarium", the *polinario* with its host of giant butterflies and a tropical rainforest complete with toucans, lizards, exotic fish and periodic thunderstorms.

Parque de Atracciones

Casa de Campo ℡915 268 030 or 914 632 900, ⓦwww.parque deatracciones.es. Metro Batán/bus #33 & #65. June–Sept daily noon–1am, Fri

& Sat till 2am; Oct–June Fri–Sun and holidays only noon–11pm, Sat open till 1am. Entry without rides €4.50; entry with unlimited access to rides (*Calco Adulto*) €19.50, under-7s (*Calco Infantil*) €11.50.

A theme park full of rides, whose attractions include the 63-metre vertical drop (*la lanzadera*), the stomach-churning *la máquina*, the whitewater raft ride (*los rápidos*), and the haunted mansion, *el viejo caserón*. Spanish acts perform in the open-air auditorium in the summer and there are frequent parades. Plenty of places to eat and drink of the burger/pizza variety too.

Parque Secreto

Map 6, D1. Plaza del Conde Valle Suchil 3 ☏915 931 480. Metro San Bernardo. Mon–Fri 5–9pm, Sat, Sun & hols 11.30am–2pm & 4.30–9pm. First half-hour costs €3, and after that €2.50.

Indoor activity park for kids up to eleven years old with a massive maze, including a host of obstacles, slides, swings and bouncy mats. There's a special area reserved for younger kids and a small café where parents can relax.

Warner Brothers Movie World

San Martín de la Vega. Carretera Andalucia (N-IV) km 22. ☏918 211 234, ⓦwww. warnerbrospark.com. Trains from Atocha every half hour, change at Pinto. Open April–May Thurs–Sun, June–Sept daily, Oct–Nov Fri–Sun: weekdays 10am–8pm, weekends & hols 10am–midnight, but subject to variations. €32, under-12s €24, under-3s free.

All-American theme park divided into five different themed areas, each with its own set of rides and Warner Bros. characters. The rollercoasters, raft rides and the 40-metre-high free-fall tower are undeniably impressive, but queues are lengthy, the entrance fee exorbitant and it's a long way out of town.

THEME PARKS

PARKS AND GARDENS

Capricho de la Alameda de Osuna

Paseo de la Alameda de Osuna. Metro Canillejas; bus #101, #105. Open Oct–March Sat, Sun & hols 9am–6.30pm, April–Sept 9am–9pm.

A fascinating and little-known park located between the Parque Juan Carlos I and the airport. The shady gardens that were commissioned for the powerful Duquesa de Osuna in the late eighteenth century are scattered with a series of romantic follies, artificial canals, waterfalls and lakes. A wonderful escape from the heat and bustle of the city.

Casa de Campo

Metro Lago/Batán.
The zoo, Parque de Atracciones and boating lake are all here. However, be aware that many areas of the park have become increasingly populated by prostitutes and their kerb-crawling clients (see p.137).

Parque Juan Carlos I

Metro Campo de las Naciones.
There's plenty to do here, including boat and train rides, playgrounds and kite flying. The large greenhouse-style building – *la estufa fria* – contains a variety of exotic plants and exhibitions (Tues–Sun 10am–5pm; €1.20, €0.60 children) and from mid-June to mid-September a spectacular *son et lumière* show takes place at the fountains (10.30pm Thurs–Sun; €3, €1.20 children).

Parque del Oeste

Map 2, A2. Metro Moncloa/Príncipe Pío.
Very pleasant shady parkland with a small river, the Egyptian Templo de Debod and the starting point of the Teleférico cable car (see p.135).

Parque del Retiro

Map 7. Metro Retiro/Ibiza/Atocha.
Plenty of activities for

children, including a boating lake, puppet shows (all year round Sat & Sun 1pm; also July–Sept Mon, Wed, Fri, Sat & Sun 7.30pm & 10.30pm) and playgrounds. Room for roller skating and cycling too.

AQUAPARKS

Aquamadrid

Carretera de Barcelona (N-II) km 15.5 ☎916 731 013. Bus Continental Auto #281, #282, #284, or #385 from Avda de América. Train cercanías C-2 or C-7 to San Fernando. June & Sept daily noon–7pm, July & Aug Mon–Fri noon–8pm, Sat & Sun 11am–8pm. €12, under-10s €8.15.

Busy waterpark with the usual monster slides set around a large lake, plus toddlers' pool and nighttime disco.

Aquópolis

Villanueva de la Cañada, Carretera de la Coruña (N-VI) km 25 ☎918 156 911, ⒲www.aquopolis.es. Free bus from Plaza de España weekdays 11am & noon, Sat & holidays 11am, noon, 1pm. Open mid-June & Sept daily noon–7pm; July & Aug noon–8pm. €12.85, under-10s €8.45, under-3s free.

The largest of the waterparks, with a variety of giant slides, including the 65-metre-long "black hole", a wave machine, a water-based assault course and plenty of grass for a picnic. Smaller rides for younger kids too.

AQUAPARKS

FOOD

Hard Rock Café
Map 8, C9. Paseo de la Castellana 2 ☏914 364 340. Metro Colón. Daily 12.30pm–2am. **Moderate.** A children's favourite, with its tried-and-tested formula of burgers, merchandising and rock memorabilia.

Planet Hollywood
Map 5, F5. Plaza de las Cortes 7 ☏913 601 400. Metro Banco de España. Daily 12.30pm–12.30am. **Moderate.** Similar to the *Hard Rock Café* – just substitute film for the rock memorabilia.

Directory

Airlines Aer Lingus ☎915 414 216; American Airlines ☎901 100 000 or 914 531 400; Air France ☎901 112 266 or 913 300 440; British Airways ☎913 769 666 or 902 111 333; Iberia ☎902 400 500 or 915 878 156; KLM ☎912 478 100 or 902 222 747; TWA ☎913 103 094; Virgin Express ☎915 411 494 or 916 625 261

Airport information Flights ☎902 353 570; general enquiries ☎913 958 343

American Express Plaza de las Cortes 2, entrance on Marqués de Cubas (Metro Sevilla; ☎915 720 303). Open Monday–Friday 9am–5.30pm, Saturday 9am–noon for mail, transactions and exchange.

Banks and exchange The main Spanish banks are concentrated on c/Alcalá and Gran Vía. Opening hours are normally Mon–Fri 9am–2pm, but they're also often open Sat 9am–1pm from Oct to May. In addition to the banks, branches of El Corte Inglés have exchange offices with long hours and competitive rates; the most central is on Puerta del Sol. Barajas airport has a 24-hour currency exchange office. Although they don't usually charge commission, the rates at the exchange bureaux scattered around the city are often very poor. Western Union, Gran Vía 16 (☎914 428 180 or 900 633 633; Metro Gran Vía) provide money transfer services.

Bicycles Madrid is a highly bike-unfriendly city, but determined cyclists should try Bicicletas Chapinal, c/Alcalá 242 (Metro El Carmen; Mon–Fri

10am–1.30pm & 4.30–8pm, Sat 10am–2pm; ☏914 041 853); Calmera, c/Atocha 98 (Metro Antón Martín; Mon–Sat 9.30am–1.30pm & 4.30–8pm; ☏915 277 574); Karacol, c/Montera 32 (Metro Gran Vía/Sol; Mon–Fri 10am–2pm & 5.30–8.30pm, Sat 10.30am–2pm; ☏915 329 073, Ⓦwww.karakol.com) and branch at c/Tortosa 8 (Metro Atocha; ☏915 399 633).

Car rental Atesa ☏915 711 931 or 902 100 101; Avis ☏915 472 048, reservations ☏902 135 531, Ⓦwww.avisworld.com; Easy-Rent-a-Car ☏0906 586 0586 (telephone bookings available from Britain only); Europcar ☏917 211 222 or 901 102 020; Hertz ☏914 681 318 or 917 330 400, Ⓦwww.hertz. es; Rent Me ☏915 590 822

Disability Madrid is not particularly well geared up for the disabled (minusválidos), although the situation is gradually improving. The Organizacíon Nacional de Ciegos de España (ONCE) at c/Prado 24 (Metro Sevilla; ☏915 894 600 or 915 773 756) provides good specialist advice as does the Coordinadora de Minusválidos Físicos de Madrid at c/Ríos Rosas 54 (Metro Ríos Rosas; ☏915 350 619). Major museums and some of the larger, more expensive hotels have adapted facilities. Some buses have been altered for wheelchairs, all metro trains and buses have designated seats, and the new metro and train stations have lifts. Wheelchair-adapted taxis can be ordered from Radio Taxi (☏915 478 200).

Doctors English-speaking doctors are available at the Anglo-American Medical Unit, c/Conde de Aranda 1 (Metro Retiro; Mon–Fri 9am–8pm, Sat 10am–1pm; ☏914 351 823).

Driving The head office of the Real Automobile Club de España can be found at c/José Abascal 10 (☏900 200 093; Metro Alonso Cano) and will be able to help out with all queries related to driving in Spain.

Electricity 220 volts AC. Most European appliances should work as long as you have an adaptor for European-style two-pin plugs. North Americans will need this plus a transformer.

Embassies Australia, Plaza Descubridor Diego Ordás 3

(Metro Ríos Rosas; ☎914 419 300, ⊛www.emaustralia.es); Canada, c/Núñez de Balboa 35 (Metro Núñez de Balboa; ☎914 314 300, ⊛www.canada-e.org); France, c/Salustiano Olozaga 9 (Metro Banco de España; ☎914 355 560); Germany, c/Fortuny 8 (Metro Rubén Darío; ☎913 199 100); Ireland, Paseo de la Castellana 46 (Metro Rubén Darío; ☎913 190 200); Italy, c/Lagasca 98 (Metro Núñez de Balboa; ☎915 776 529); Netherlands, Paseo de la Castellana 178 (Metro Cuzco; ☎913 590 914); New Zealand, Plaza Lealtad 2 (Metro Banco de España; ☎915 230 226); Norway, Paseo de la Castellana 31 (Metro Rubén Darío; ☎913 103 116); South Africa, c/Claudio Coello 91 (Metro Núñez Balboa; ☎914 356 688); Sweden, c/Caracas 25 (Metro Sevilla; ☎913 081 535); UK, c/Fernando el Santo 16 (Metro Alonso Martínez; ☎913 190 200); USA, c/Serrano 75 (Metro Serrano; ☎915 774 000)

Emergencies For police, medical services and the fire brigade call ☎112.

Health Residents of European Union countries get free medical treatment under the Reciprocal Medical Treatment arrangement, provided they have a completed E111 form (available from post offices in Britain and Social Security offices elsewhere). Citizens of non-EU countries are charged at private hospital rates, so take out medical insurance before travelling.

Hospitals The most central are: El Clínico, Plaza de Cristo Rey (Metro Moncloa; ☎913 303 747); Hospital Gregorio Marañón, c/Dr Esquerdo 46 (Metro O'Donnell; ☎915 868 000); Ciudad Sanitaria La Paz, Paseo de la Castellana 261 (Metro Begoña; ☎913 582 831) and Hospital Ramón y Cajal, Carretera de Colmenar Viejo km 9.1 (Metro Begoña; ☎913 368 000). First aid clinics, scattered throughout the city, are open 24-hours: one of the most central is at c/Navas de Tolosa 10 (Metro Callao; ☎915 210 025).

Internet access The best equipped and most central internet cafés are: BBigg, c/Alcalá 21 (⊛www.BBIGG. com, ☎916 647 700; Metro Sevilla); Easy Everything, c/Montera 10–12

EMERGENCIES–INTERNET ACCESS

(ⓦwww.easyeverything.com/spain; Metro Sol); and Ono.com, Gran Vía 59 (open 24hr; ☎915 474 930; Metro Plaza de España). Prices range from €1.20–€3.50 per hour, often with a drink included.

Language courses Madrid has numerous language schools, offering intensive courses in Spanish. One of the best-established is International House, c/Zurbano 8 (Metro Alonso Martínez; ☎913 101 314, ⓦwww.ihmadrid.es).

Laundry Central *lavanderías* include: c/Barco 26 (Metro Gran Vía); c/Cervantes 1–3 (Metro Sol); c/Donoso Cortés 17 (Metro Quevedo); c/Hermosilla 121 (Metro Goya); c/Palma 2 (Metro Tribunal).

Left luggage There are *consignas* at the airport (between terminals 1 and 2; open 24hr), Estación Sur (daily 6.35am–11.45pm), the Conde de Casal bus station (Mon–Thurs 7am–10pm, Fri 7am–1am, Sat 7am–2pm), as well as lockers at Atocha (6.30am–10.30pm) and Chamartín (8am–9pm) train stations.

Pharmacies *Farmacias* are distinguished by a green cross;

each district has a rota with one staying open through the night. For details call ☎098 (Spanish only) or check the notice on the door of your nearest pharmacy or the listings magazines. Madrid also has quite a number of traditional herbalists, best known of which is Maurice Méssegue, c/Goya 64 (Metro Goya; Mon–Fri 10am–2pm & 5–8pm, Sat 10am–2pm).

Police The headquarters of the Policía Nacional are near to Plaza de España at c/Fomento 24 (☎915 417 160). Other centrally located police stations (*comisarías*) are at c/Luna 29 (Metro Callao; ☎915 211 236) and c/Huertas 76 (Metro Antón Martín; ☎912 490 994). To report a crime you have to make an official statement or *denuncia* – often a time-consuming and laborious business, especially as few policemen speak English, but a necessary procedure for any insurance claim. If you have had something stolen call ☎900 100 333 (English spoken). In an emergency call ☎112.

Post office The main one is the Palacio de Comunicaciones in Plaza de la Cibeles (Metro

Banco de España; Mon–Sat 8.30am–9.30pm, Sun 8.30am–2.30pm for stamps and telegrams; Mon–Fri 9am–8pm, Sat 9am–2pm for poste restante or *lista de correos*. Branch offices open Mon–Sat 9am to 2pm, but the easiest places to buy stamps are the *estancos*, small shops selling stamps and tobacco, recognizable by their brown and yellow signs bearing the word *Tabacos*.

Public holidays The main national holidays when shops and banks close are: Jan 1 (*Año Nuevo*); Jan 6 (*Reyes*); Easter Thursday (*Jueves Santo*); Good Friday (*Viernes Santo*); May 1 (*Fiesta del Trabajo*); May 2 (*Día de la Comunidad*); May 15 (*San Isidro*); Aug 15 (*Virgen de la Paloma*); Oct 12 (*Día de la Hispanidad*); Nov 1 (*Todos los Santos*); Nov 9 (*Virgen de la Almudena*); Dec 6 (*Día de la Constitución*); Dec 8 (*La Inmaculada*); Dec 25 (*Navidad*).

Public toilets There are very few public toilets in Madrid, so your best bet is to pop into a local bar, café or department store.

Telephones International calls can be made from any phone box or from any *telefónica*. The main *telefónica* at Gran Vía 30 (Metro Gran Vía) is open until midnight. Minimum charge is 20 cents, but you won't usually get any change from a 50 cent coin. Phones that accept coins, phonecards and credit cards are increasingly common and many have instructions in English and other languages. Phonecards cost €6 or €12 and can be bought at post offices or *estancos*. For international directory enquiries ring ☏025; for national directory enquiries ring ☏1003; for the international operator ☏1008 (Europe), ☏1005 (rest of the world). To make a reverse charge call ask the operator (☏1009) for *cobro revertido*. For mobile phones, check with your provider whether it works abroad and what the call charges are.

Tickets For theatre and concert tickets, plus some sports events, credit-card booking services are run by BBVA ticket (☏902 150 025), Caixa Catalunya (☏902 101 212), Caja Madrid (☏902 488 488), Servicaixa (☏902 332 211) or Caja de Catalunya

PUBLIC HOLIDAYS–TICKETS

273

(Ⓣ902 101 212). Tickets are also available from El Corte Inglés (Ⓣ902 400 222, Ⓦwww.elcorteingles.es). Localidades Galicia, Plaza del Carmen 1 (Metro Sol; Ⓣ915 312 732 or 915 319 131, Ⓦwww.eol.es/lgalicia) sells tickets for football games, bullfights, theatres and concerts. Fnac, c/Preciados 28 (Metro Callao; Ⓣ915 956 200) and Madrid Rock, Gran Vía 25 (Metro Gran Vía; Ⓣ915 232 652) sell tickets for major rock concerts.

Trains Information Ⓣ902 240 202; reservations Ⓣ915 623 333. Tickets can be bought at the individual stations, or at Barajas airport arrivals and the city-centre RENFE office, c/Alcalá 44 (Metro Banco de España; Mon–Fri 9am–7pm, Sat 9am–1.30pm; Ⓣ915 623 333, Ⓦwww.renfe.es).

Travel agencies Viajes Zeppelin, Plaza Santo Domingo 2 (Metro Santo Domingo; Ⓣ915 425 154), is an English-speaking and very efficient company, offering excellent deals on flights and holidays. Nuevas Fronteras, c/Velázquez 75 (Metro Velázquez; Ⓣ914 316 464 or 902 212 120) and in the Torre de Madrid, Plaza de España (Metro Plaza de España; Ⓣ912 474 200) can be good for flights, or try Top Tours, c/Capitán Haya 20 (Metro Cuzco; Ⓣ915 550 604). Many other travel agents are concentrated on and around the Gran Vía. For student travel go to TIVE, c/Fernando el Católico 88 (Metro Moncloa; Ⓣ915 430 208).

OUT OF THE CITY

BEYOND THE CITY

El Escorial and El Valle de los Caídos

Fifty kilometres northwest of Madrid, in the foothills of the Sierra de Guadarrama, lies one of Spain's best-known and most visited sights – Felipe II's vast monastery-palace complex of **El Escorial**. An exceptional building in itself, it also provides an unprecedented insight into the mindset of Spain's greatest king. The town around the monastery, **San Lorenzo del Escorial**, is an easy day-trip from Madrid and you can also take in **El Valle de los Caídos** (The Valley of the Fallen), 9km further north. This is an equally megalomaniacal, yet far more chilling monument: an underground basilica hewn under Franco's orders, allegedly as a monument to the Civil War dead of both sides, though in reality a memorial to the Generalíssimo and his regime.

Regular **trains** run from Estación de Atocha on the Cercanías line C-8a (daily 5.45am–11.30pm; 50min; €4.80–5.20 return), calling at Chamartín on the way. From the station at El Escorial take the local bus or make the twenty-minute walk up the hill to the monastery. **Buses** run by Autocares Herranz leave from Moncloa bus station every thirty minutes on weekdays and hourly at weekends (Mon–Fri 7.15am–10pm, Sat 9am–9.30pm, Sun & public holidays 9am–11pm; 55min; €5.50. Metro Moncloa). The **Turismo** in San Lorenzo del Escorial is at c/Grimaldi 2 (Mon–Thurs 11am–6pm, Fri–Sun 10am–7pm; ☎918 901 554, ⓔoflocaalt@worldonline.es), the small street to the north of the visitor's entrance to the monastery.

To visit El Valle de los Caídos from El Escorial, a local bus run by *Herranz* goes from the office in Plaza de la Virgen de Gracia, just north of the visitors' entrance to the monastery, departing at 3.15pm and returning at 5.30pm (Tues–Sun).

El Escorial

Map 1, C4. Tues–Sun: April–Sept 10am–6pm, Oct–March 10am–5pm. €6 non-guided, €6.91 guided, concessions €3, free Wed for EU citizens; combined ticket for monastery and El Valle de los Caídos €8.40.

El Escorial was the largest Spanish building of the Renaissance. Rectangular, overbearing and severe, from the outside it resembles more a prison than a palace. Built between 1563 and 1584 by Juan Bautista de Toledo and Juan de Herrera, **Felipe II** planned the enormous complex as part monastery, part mausoleum and part palace, where he would live the life of a monk and "rule the world with two inches of paper". Seven kilometres out of town, on the Ávila road, there are great views of the monastery from the Silla de Felipe (Philip's Seat), a chair carved into a rocky outcrop from where Felipe II is supposed to have watched the construction.

The **monastery** itself commemorates the victory over the French at St Quentin on San Lorenzo's feast day

MONASTERIO DE
SAN LORENZO
DEL ESCORIAL

La Casa del Rey

Panteón
Real

Felipe II's
apartments

Panteón de
Infantes

Museos Nuevos

Sacristía

Palacio de
los Borbones

Sala de las Batallas

Claustro Grande

Basílica

Salas capitulares

Visitor's entrance

Vestíbulo

Colegio

Monasterio

Colegio

Patio de
los Reyes

Monasterio

Biblioteca

Colegio entrance

Main entrance

(August 10, 1557), and above the **west gateway** is a gargantuan statue of the patron saint holding the gridiron on
which he was burned to death. The gridiron emblem is also
present on the builders' trowels displayed in the basement
exhibition, and the whole complex is said to have been
designed around this pattern. Within is the **Patio de los
Reyes**, named after the six statues of the kings of Israel
which adorn the facade of the Basílica, on one side of the
Patio. Linking the secular and religious zones of the
monastery complex is the **Biblioteca**, a splendid hall with
multicoloured vivid frescoes by Tibaldi, showing the seven

EL ESCORIAL

Liberal Arts. The Biblioteca's collections include Santa Teresa's personal diary, some gorgeously executed Arabic manuscripts and a Florentine planetarium of 1572 demonstrating the movement of the planets.

The enormous, cold, dark interior of the **Basílica** contains over forty altars, designed to allow simultaneous Masses to be held. Behind the main altar lies some of Felipe's mammoth collection of saintly relics, including six whole bodies, over sixty heads and hundreds of bone fragments set in fabulously expensive caskets. The two bronze sculptural groups at the east end, depicting Carlos V with his family and Felipe II with three of his wives, were carved by the father-and-son team of Leone and Pompeo Leoni.

Many of the monastery's religious treasures are contained in the **Sacristía** and **Salas Capitulares** (Chapter Houses) around the Basílica and include paintings by Titian, Velázquez and José Ribera. Below these rooms is the **Panteón Real**, where past Spanish monarchs lie in their gilded marble tombs, while just above the entrance you pass the doorway to the **Pudrería**, a separate room in which the bodies rotted for twenty years or so before the skeletons were moved downstairs. The royal children are laid in the **Panteón de los Infantes** and there's also a wedding-cake babies' tomb with room for sixty infants.

What remains of the Escorial's **art collection** – works by Bosch, Gerard David, Dürer, Titian, Zurbarán and many others, which escaped transfer to the Prado – is kept in the elegant suite of rooms known as the **Museos Nuevos**. Don't miss the newly-restored **Sala de Batallas**, a long gallery lined with an epic series of paintings depicting important imperial battles. Finally, there are the treasure-crammed **Salones Reales** (Royal Apartments), containing the austere quarters of Felipe II, with the chair that supported his gouty leg and the deathbed from which he was able to contemplate the high altar of the Basílica.

EL ESCORIAL

The outlying lodges, the **Casita del Príncipe** (aka Casita de Abajo; June–Sept Sat & Sun 10am–1pm & 3.30–6.30pm; €3.46; compulsory tours every 30min for a maximum of 10 people; currently under restoration) and the **Casita del Infante** (aka Casita de Arriba; Easter & mid-July to mid-Sept Tues–Sun 10am–6pm; €3, Wed free for EU citizens) are two eighteenth-century royal lodges, both full of decorative riches, and built by Juan de Villanueva, Spain's most accomplished Neoclassical architect.

To escape the worst of the crowds, especially
in the Royal Apartments, avoid Wednesdays
and try visiting just before lunch.

EATING AND DRINKING

For **refreshments** head away from the monastery, up c/Reina Victoria into town. *La Genara*, at Plaza San Lorenzo 2, is a good-value restaurant filled with theatrical mementos, while the more expensive *Charolés*, c/Floridablanca 24, is renowned for its fish and stews. The best bar is the friendly *Cervecería Los Pescaítos*, c/Joaquín Costa 8, which also serves fish dishes.

El Valle de los Caídos

Map 1, C4. Tues–Sun: April–Sept 9.30am–7pm, Oct–March 10am–6pm. €4.80, free Wed for EU citizens; combined ticket with El Escorial €8.40.

The **basilica complex** belies its claims of being a

memorial "to the Civil War dead of both sides" almost at a glance. The dour, grandiose architectural forms employed, the constant inscriptions "Fallen for God and for Spain", and the proximity to El Escorial clue you in to its true function – the glorification of **General Franco** and his regime. The dictator himself lies buried behind the high altar, while the only other named tomb is that of his guru, the Falangist leader José Antonio Primo de Rivera, who was shot dead by Republicans at the beginning of the war. The "other side" is present only in the fact that the complex was built by the Republican army's survivors – political prisoners on quarrying duty.

From the entrance to the basilica a shaky **funicular** (Tues–Sun: April–Sept 11am–1.30pm & 4–6.30pm, Oct–March 11am–1.30pm & 3–5.30pm; €3) ascends to the base of a vast cross, reputedly the largest in the world, offering superlative views over the Sierra de Guadarrama and of the giant, grotesque figures propping up the cross.

EL VALLE DE LOS CAÍDOS

Aranjuez
and Chinchón

little oasis on the way to Toledo, the town of
Aranjuez was used by the eighteenth-century
Bourbon rulers as a spring and autumn retreat, and
you can still see their legacy of palaces with luxuriant gardens, most notably the Palacio Real. If you're travelling by
train you can break your journey here and then continue
on to Toledo. The nearby picturesque town of **Chinchón**
is also worth a visit, and is home to Spain's best-known *anís*
(aniseed liqueur) – a mainstay of breakfast drinkers across
the country.

A visit in summer is enhanced by stalls dotted along the
roads selling strawberries and cream – *fresas con nata*.

Aranjuez is served by **trains** from Estación de Atocha
(Cercanías line C-3; daily every 15–30min, 6am–11.55pm;
45min; €4.68–5.16 return) and by regular **buses** from
Estación Sur (40min; €5.80 return). An old wooden **steam
train**, *El Tren de la Fresa*, also makes weekend runs between
Madrid and Aranjuez (mid-April to July & mid-Sept to

Oct; 1hr; info ☏902 228 822). It leaves Atocha at 10.05am and returns from Aranjuez at 6.12pm (Sat & Sun). The €21 (€13.50 for children between 2-12) fare includes a guided bus tour in Aranjuez, entry to the monuments, plus strawberries on the train. The **Turismo** in Aranjuez is in the Casa de Infantes, facing the Plaza de San Antonio (daily: summer 10am–7.30pm, winter 10am-6.30pm; ☏918 910 427, ⓦwww.aranjuez.net).

Chinchón is connected to Aranjuez by sporadic buses from c/Almíbar 138, Aranjuez (Mon–Fri 4 daily; Sat 2 daily), and to Madrid by regular services on the La Veloz bus from Avenida del Mediterraneo 49 (Metro Conde de Casal; 1hr; €5.60 return).

Aranjuez

The beauty of **Aranjuez**, 50km from the capital (map 1, F8), is in its greenery, studded with opulent palaces and luxuriant gardens. In summer, Aranjuez functions principally as a weekend escape from Madrid, and most people come out for the day, as there's no accommodation.

The centre-piece of the town is the eighteenth-century **Palacio Real** (Tues–Sun: April–Sept 10am–6.15pm, Oct–March 10am–5.15pm; €4.81, concessions €2.40, free Wed for EU citizens) and its **gardens** (daily: April–Sept 8am–8.30pm, Oct–March 8am–6.30pm; free). Although there has been a summer residence for the royals on this site since the late sixteenth century, the present building dates from the eighteenth century and was an attempt by the Spanish Bourbon monarchs to create a Versailles in Spain. Aranjuez clearly isn't in the same league, but it's a pleasant place to while away a few hours. The palace is more remarkable for its interior ornamental fantasies than for any architectural virtues. The **Porcelain Room**, for example, is entirely covered in decorative ware from the factory which used to stand in Madrid's Retiro park, while the **Smoking Room** is a copy of one of the finest halls of the Alhambra in Granada, though executed with less subtlety. Most of the palace dates from the reign of the "nymphomaniac" Queen Isabel II, and many of the scandals which led to her eventual abdication were played out here.

Outside, on a small island, are the fountains of the **Jardín de la Isla**, though the **Jardín del Príncipe**, on the other side of the main road, is more attractive, with shaded walks along the river and plenty of spots for a siesta. At its far end stands the **Casa del Labrador** (Peasant's House; same hours as Palacio Real; visits by appointment only – ☎918 910 305, phone at least a week in advance; €3, concessions €1.50, Wed free for EU citizens), which is anything but what the name implies, crammed as it is with silk, marble, crystal and gold, as well as a huge collection of fancy clocks. Also in the gardens, by the river, is the small Casa de los Marinos (Sailors' House), containing the **Museo de Faluas** (same hours as Palacio Real; €3, concessions €1.50, Wed free for EU citizens), a museum displaying the brightly coloured launches in which royalty would take to the river.

A bus service occasionally connects the various sites, but all are within easy walking distance of each other, and it's a lovely place to stroll around.

Look out for the suitably regal eighteenth-century **Plaza de Toros** and the newly inaugurated exhibition space entitled *Aranjuez – una gran fiesta* (summer Tues–Sun 10am–6.30pm, winter Tues–Sun 10am–5.30pm; €3, concessions €1.20, Wed free for EU citizens), part local history exhibition, part bullfighting museum. Nearby in c/Naranja and c/Rosa are a number of **corrales**, traditional-style wooden-balconied tenement blocks.

EATING AND DRINKING

Casa José
C/Asbastos 32.
Tasty and expensive *nouvelle cuisine*. Closed Sun eve and Mon.

Casa Pablete
C/Stuart 108.
An offshoot of *Casa Pablo* and one of the best places in town for tapas. Closed Tues and Aug.

Casa Pablo
C/Almíbar 42.
A traditional place, the walls of which are covered with pictures of local dignitaries and bullfighters. Closed Aug.

Mercado de San Antonio
C/Stuart near the Jardines Isabel II.
Just the place to buy your own food for a picnic.

El Rana Verde
C/Reina 1.
Probably the best-known restaurant in Aranjuez, this pleasant riverside establishment dates back to the late nineteenth century and serves a wide-ranging *menú* at around €11.

ARANJUEZ

Chinchón

Chinchón, 45km southeast of Madrid (map 1, G7), is a highly picturesque little town, with a fifteenth-century castle and a medieval Plaza Mayor, encircled by wooden-balconied houses. Next to the plaza stands the **Iglesia de la Asunción**, containing a panel by Goya of *The Assumption of the Virgin*. Most visitors, however, come to visit the three **anís distilleries**, a couple of which are housed in the castle. If you want to buy a bottle try the *Alcoholera de Chinchón* on the Plaza Mayor. After the tastings, the modestly priced *Mesón del Duende* and *Mesón del Comendador*, both on the Plaza Mayor are good places for a **meal**; alternatively, there's the more expensive, former olive-oil mill *Mesón Cuevas del Vino*.

The best bet for **accommodation**, though it's not cheap, is the *parador* at c/Generalíssimo 1 (☎918 940 836, ✉chinchon@parador.es; ❺), housed in a sixteenth-century convent, with wonderful Moorish-style gardens and a magnificent seventeenth-century dining room. A more modest option is the pleasant *Hostal Chinchón* (☎918 935 398, ℻918 940 108; ❷), also close to the Plaza Mayor in c/José Antonio.

If you're visiting over **Easter**, you'll be treated to the townsfolk's own enactment of the *Passion of Christ*, when participants and audience process through the town. In 1995, Chinchón launched its **Fiesta del Anís y del Vino**, an orgy of anis- and wine-tasting; understandably, it was an immediate success and is now held every year in mid-April. An older annual tradition takes place on July 25, when the feast of St James (Santiago) is celebrated with a bullfight in the Plaza Mayor.

CHINCHÓN

Toledo

Toledo (map 1, D9) epitomizes the soul of Spain and shares many of its contradictions. From imperial greatness it declined into isolation, and from religious toleration it came to be dominated by a stark vision of Catholicism. Home to many artists, most notably **El Greco**, and a setting for Cervantes' writing, the city is also famous for its majestic **cathedral**, its Toledan swords and the towering **Alcázar**.

Surrounded on three sides by the Río Tajo, slowly meandering its way towards Lisbon, every available inch of this rugged outcrop has been built on. Churches, synagogues, mosques and houses are heaped upon one another in a haphazard spiral which the cobbled lanes infiltrate as best they can. Certainly, it's a city redolent of past glories, and is packed with sights, although the extraordinary number of day-trippers has taken the edge off what was once the most extravagant of Spanish experiences. Still, the setting is breathtaking, and if you're an El Greco fan, you'd be mad to miss this city. Toledo also hosts one of the best celebrations of **Corpus Christi** (late May/early June) in the country. Other local festivals take place on May 25 and August 15 and 20, and the **Easter processions** here are much more impressive than those in Madrid.

To see Toledo at its best, you'll need to stay at least a

night. A day-trip will leave you hard-pressed to see everything and, more importantly, in the evening, when the crowds have gone, the city is a completely different place, lit up by floodlights, and resembling one of El Greco's moonlit paintings. However, as it's such a tourist honeypot, booking a **hotel** in advance is important, especially at weekends and during the summer.

Getting to Toledo, some 70km south of Madrid, is straightforward. There are nine **trains** a day (fewer on Sat & Sun) from Estación de Atocha (7am–8.30pm; 1hr 15min; €8.72 return). Toledo's train station is some way out, so either make the beautiful twenty-minute walk into town or take bus #5 or #6. **Buses** from Madrid operate every thirty minutes from Estación Sur de Autobuses (6.30am–10pm; 1hr; €8.52 return), dropping you just outside the old city, from where regular buses head into the heart of town. If you're **driving**, park in the streets around the Circo Romano – the remains of an old Roman chariot-racing circuit – and make your way up to the old city via the new **escalator** (*escaleras mecánicas*; Mon–Fri 7am–10pm, Sat, Sun & hols 8am–10pm).

Toledo's main **Turismo** is also outside the city walls at Puerta de Bisagra (July & Aug Mon–Sat 9am–7pm, Sun 9am–3pm; Sept–June Mon–Fri 9am–6pm; ☏925 220 843). There's also a smaller, but more central turismo opposite the cathedral (Mon–Fri 9am–2pm & 4–6pm; ☏925 254 030) and a small booth at the bottom of the escalator service (Mon–Fri 9.30am–2pm & 3.30–6pm; Sat & Sun 10am–2pm & 3.30–6.30pm).

SANTO DOMINGO EL ANTIGUO

The late-sixteenth-century **Convento de Santo Domingo Antiguo**, is a natural first stop if you enter the town via the escalator. The convent's chief claim to fame is

Circo
Romano

CAMPO
ESCOLAR

AVENIDA DE CARLOS III

Puerta de
Alfonso V
(Antigua de
Bisagra)

PASEO DEL CIRCO ROMANO

GLORIETA DE LA
RECONQUISTA

PASEO DE LOS CANONIGOS

SANTIAGO

Escaleras
Mecánicas

CUESTA DE
LA GRANJA

PASEO DE RECAREDO

Convento de Santo
Domingo el Real

AVENIDA DE LA CAVA

CALLEJON DE LA MERCED

BUZONES

PLAZA DE
SANTA EOCADIA

Convento de las
Capuchinas

Convento de
Carmelitas
Descalzas

Convento de Santo
Domingo Antiguo

San Ildefonso

Convento
de Santa
Clara

Torreón de
los Abades

PLAZA DE LAS
CARMELITAS

SANTA
EOCADIA

Santa
Eulalia

Casa de
Mesa Academia
de Bellas Artes

Palacio
Lorenzana

Puerta del
Cambrón

Museo de Arte Visigodo

SAN MARTÍN

Convento de
San Clemente

CUESTA DE SAN MARTIN

LA CAVA

LAS BULAS

Monumento
de San Pedro
Mártir

PLAZA DEL
P. MARIANA

San Juan de
los Reyes

Casa de la Cadena
(Museo de Arte
Contemporáneo)

ALFONSO XII

Puente de
San Martín

SANTA ANA

REYES

ANGEL

Sinagoga de
Santa María
la Blanca

Santo
Tomé

SANTO TOME

San Marcos

La Trinidad

El Salvador

N

JUDERÍA

Sinagoga del
Tránsito

PLAZA
DEL
CONDE

Taller
del Moro

Santa
Ursula

Museo
Victorio
Macho

Casa
del Greco

Palacio de
Fuensalida

PASEO DEL TRANSITO

Río Tajo

EL CALVARIO

Convento de
Santa Isabel

RESTAURANTS AND BARS

Restaurante Adolfo	D
Alex	A
Restaurante Los Cuatro Tiempos	E
Bar Ludeña	B
Restaurante Palacios	C
La Perdiz	F
Bar El Tropezón	G

Convento
de San Gil
o Gilitos

SAN CIPRIANO

San
Sebastián

TOLEDO

0   100m

TOLEDO

ACCOMMODATION

El Cardenal	1
Parador Conde de Orgaz	6
Pensión Descalzos	5
Hostal Maravilla	3
Hotel Santa Isabel	4
Hotel Sol	2

that El Greco's remains lie in the crypt, which can be glimpsed through a peephole in the floor of the church. The nuns display their art treasures in the old choir (Mon–Sat 11am–1.30pm & 4–7pm, Sun 4–7pm; €1.20), but more interesting is the high altarpiece of the church, El Greco's first major commission in Toledo. Unfortunately, most of the canvases have gone to museums and are here replaced by copies, leaving only two *St Johns* and a *Resurrection* in situ.

ALCÁZAR AND HOSPITAL Y MUSEO DE SANTA CRUZ

Dominating the main **Plaza de Zocódover**, indeed all of Toledo, is the bluff, imposing **Alcázar** (Tues–Sun 9.30am–2pm; €2), entered off Cuesta del Alcázar. It was founded by Carlos V in the sixteenth century, but has been burned and bombarded so often that almost nothing of the original building remains. The most recent destruction occurred in 1936 during one of the most symbolic and extraordinary episodes of the Civil War, involving a two-month siege of the Nationalist-occupied Alcázar by the Republican town. The besieged Nationalists under Colonel José Moscardo were eventually relieved by a Nationalist army heading for Madrid, which then took severe retribution on the town – not one prisoner was taken. After the war, Franco's regime completely rebuilt the fortress as a monument to the glorification of its defenders, and their propaganda models and photos are still displayed.

Just north of Plaza de Zocódover is the **Hospital y Museo de Santa Cruz** (Mon 10am–2pm & 4–6.30pm, Tues–Sat 10am–6.30pm, Sun 10am–2pm; €1.20, but free while being renovated), a superlative Renaissance building with a magnificent Plateresque main doorway, housing some of the greatest El Grecos in Toledo, including *The Coronation of the Virgin* and *The Assumption of the Virgin*. As well as outstanding works by Goya and Ribera, the museum also contains a huge collection of ancient carpets and faded tapestries, a military display, sculpture, ceramics and a small archeological collection.

THE CATHEDRAL

Mon–Sat 10.30am–6.30pm, Sun 2pm–6pm; Treasury, Sacristy, Chapter House and the New Museums (Mon–Sat 10.30am–6.30pm, Sun 2–6.30pm); €4.80, free Wed for EU citizens. The *Coro* is closed on Sun morning, and the New Museums on Mon.

Toledo's **cathedral**, situated to the south of Plaza de Zocódover down c/Comercio, is something special, reflecting the importance of the city that for so long outshone its near neighbour, Madrid. A robust Gothic construction, which took over two hundred and fifty years (1227–1493) to complete, it's richly decorated in almost every conceivable style, with masterpieces of the Gothic, Renaissance and Baroque periods. The exterior is best appreciated from outside the city, where the hundred-metre spire and the weighty buttressing can be seen to advantage. The cavernous interior is home to some magnificent stained glass, an outstanding **Coro** (Choir) and a wonderfully Gothic **Capilla Mayor**, depicting a synopsis of the entire New Testament. Directly behind the main altar is an extraordinary piece of fantasy – the **Transparente**, a Baroque chapel, wonderfully and wildly extravagant, with its marble cherubs sitting on fluffy marble clouds. It's especially magnificent when the sun reaches through the hole punched in the roof for that purpose.

There are well over twenty **chapels** embedded in the walls, all of which are of some interest, and many housing fine tombs. The **Tesoro** (Treasury), the **Sacristía**

THE CATHEDRAL

(Sacristy), the **Sala Capitular** (Chapter House) and the **Nuevos Museos** (New Museums) house hugely impressive accumulations of wealth and artistic riches, including paintings by El Greco, Goya and Velázquez, as well as one of El Greco's few surviving pieces of sculpture.

SANTO TOMÉ AND THE CASA DEL GRECO

Domenikcos Theotokopoulos, or **El Greco** (the Greek), was born in Crete in 1541, but settled in Toledo in about 1577, and it's mainly through the portrayal of the city in his extraordinary mystical paintings that the skyline of Toledo has become so famous. El Greco's masterpiece, *The Burial of the Count of Orgaz*, is housed, alone, in a small annexe of the church of **Santo Tomé** (daily 10am–6pm, summer till 7pm; €1.20, free Wed after 2.30pm for EU citizens) to the west of the cathedral, and depicts the count's funeral, at which St Stephen and St Augustine appeared and lowered him into the tomb. It combines El Greco's genius for the mystic, exemplified in the upper half of the picture, where the count's soul is being received into heaven, with his great powers as a portrait painter and master of colour. El Greco himself (seventh on the left) and his son (in the foreground) are said to be amongst the onlookers portrayed in the lower half. A search for the count's bones came to an end in 2001, when they were unearthed from a tomb located, appropriately enough, directly below the painting.

The rather misleadingly named **Casa y Museo del Greco**, just to the south of Santo Tomé in Plaza del Conde (Tues–Sat 10am–2pm & 4–6pm, Sun 10am–2pm; €1.20 while Casa is closed, free Sat pm and Sun), was never actually the artist's home, but is a reconstruction of a typical Toledan residence of the period. The living quarters are closed for restoration, but the museum displays many of El Greco's classic works, including his famous *View and Map of Toledo* and a complete series of the Twelve Apostles.

For thrilling, uncluttered views of Toledo head for the ring road Carretera de Circunvalación which runs along the south bank of the Tajo, the opposite bank from the city. It takes about an hour to walk from one of the medieval fortified bridges to the other.

THE JEWISH QUARTER

The area to the west of the Casa del Greco was once the *Judería*, the Jewish quarter of medieval Toledo. The synagogues, **El Tránsito** (closed for restoration) and **Santa María de la Blanca** (daily 10am–1.45pm & 3.30–6pm, summer until 7pm; €1.20), both built by *Mudéjar* craftsmen, are stunning reminders of Toledo's cosmopolitan past; while the superb church of **San Juan de los Reyes** (daily May–Sept 10am–1.45pm & 3.30–6.45pm; Oct–April 10am–1.30pm & 3.30–5.45pm; €1.20), whose exterior is bizarrely festooned with the chains worn by Christian prisoners from Granada released on the reconquest of their city, is a legacy of more intolerant times under the *Reyes Católicos*.

As you wind your way back towards Plaza de Zocódover, the **Museo de Arte Visigodo** (Tues–Sat 10am–2pm & 4–6.30pm, Sun 10am–2pm; €0.60, free Sat pm and Sun) stands on c/San Clemente in the impressive church of San Román. Moorish and Christian elements (horseshoe arches, early murals and a splendid Renaissance dome) combine to make this the most interesting church in Toledo. Visigothic jewellery, documents and archeological fragments make up the bulk of the collection.

MUSEO VICTORIO MACHO

Just east of the *Judería* along c/de los Reyes Católicos is the Victorio Macho Museum (Mon–Sat 10am–7pm, Sun 10am–3pm; €3.01), dedicated to the sculptor who spent the last fourteen years of his life in Toledo. Apart from compelling sculptures of leading Spanish personalities and assorted heroic figures, the main attractions are the gardens which have outstanding views across the Tajo and down towards the Puente de San Martín. The auditorium on the ground floor shows a short documentary film about the city and its history (a commentary is available in English).

HOSPITAL DE TAVERA

Situated outside the city walls to the north of the Puerta de Bisagra, the private collection of the Duke of Lerma is housed in the **Hospital de Tavera** (daily 10.30am–1.30pm & 3.30–6pm; €3.01), a Renaissance palace with beautiful twin patios. Ring the bell on the stairs to the left of the entrance and wait for the guide to arrive. The quick tour of the musty interior passes some fine paintings by Bassano, El Greco, Giordano and Canaletto. Look out for Ribera's bizarre painting *La Mujer Barbuda*, a portrait of Magdalena Ventura, a 37-year-old woman who grew a beard after giving birth to the third of her seven children. The church contains Alonso de Berruguete's ornate marble tomb of Cardinal Tavera, the hospital's founder.

ACCOMMODATION

El Cardenal
Paseo de Recaredo 24 ☏925 224 900,

©cardenal@macom.es.
Splendid old palace with famous restaurant and a

beautiful garden, located near Puerta Nueva de Bisagra. Very good value given its facilities and location. ❺

Parador Conde de Orgaz
Cerro del Emperador
☎925 221 50,
📧toledo@parador.es.
Across the river and a couple of kilometres uphill is Toledo's top hotel offering superb views from its terrace. ❻

Pensión Descalzos
C/Descalzos 30
☎ & 📠925 222 888,
📧h-descalzos@jet.es.
Centrally located *pensión*, handy for the main sights. Some of the en-suite rooms have great views across the Tajo. ❸

Hostal Maravilla
Plaza Barrio Rey 5 & 7

☎925 228 317,
📠925 228 155.
A prime location just off Plaza de Zocódover. All rooms are en suite and air conditioned. ❷

Hotel Santa Isabel
C/Santa Isabel 24
☎925 253 120,
📠925 253 136.
One of the best of the mid-range hotels, right in the centre and with safe parking. ❷

Hotel Sol
C/Azacanes 15
☎925 213 650,
📠925 216 159.
A good-value place on a quiet side street just off the main road up to the Plaza de Zocódover. The owners also run the cheaper hostal across the street – ask at reception. ❷

EATING AND DRINKING

Restaurante Adolfo
C/Granada 6.
One of the best restaurants in town, tucked behind a marzipan café, in an old

Jewish town house (ask to see the painted ceiling downstairs). Expect to pay €30 a head. Closed Sun eve.

ACCOMMODATION

Alex
Plaza de Amador de los Ríos 10, top of c/Nuncio Viejo.
Reasonable-value restaurant in a lovely location, with a much cheaper café at the side.

Bar El Tropezón
Travesía de Santa Isabel 2.
A stone's throw from the cathedral, this outdoor bar offers generous meals for around €6. The fish is particularly good.

La Perdiz
C/Reyes Católicos 7.
Quality restaurant which does a very good *menú de degustación*, which includes half a roast partridge, for €19, and has a good selection of local wines.

Restaurante Los Cuatro Tiempos
C/Puerta Llana, at the southeast corner of the cathedral.
Excellent mid-price restaurant with local specialities and good tapas.

Bar Ludeña
Plaza Magdalena 13.
One of many places around this square just off Plaza de Zocódover, offering a cheap *menú* and the best *carcamusa* (meat stew in a spicy tomato sauce) in town.

Restaurante Palacios
C/Alfonso X El Sabio 3.
Friendly and popular local restaurant, with two *menús* from €6.

EATING AND DRINKING

Segovia

After Toledo, **Segovia** (map 1, D2) is the best day-trip from Madrid. A relatively small city, strategically sited on a rocky ridge, it's deeply and haughtily Castilian, with a panoply of squares and mansions from its days of golden-age grandeur. For a city of its size, Segovia has an amazing number of architectural monuments. Most celebrated are the **Roman aqueduct**, the **cathedral** and the fairy-tale **Alcázar**, but the less obvious attractions – the cluster of ancient churches and the many mansions in the lanes of the old town, all in a warm, honey-coloured stone – are what really make Segovia worth visiting. Also, just a few kilometres outside the city, is the Bourbon palace of **La Granja**.

Well connected by road and rail, Segovia is an easy trip from Madrid. Eight **trains** leave daily from Atocha (6am–8pm; 2hr; €8.92 return) and up to fifteen **buses** operated by La Sepulvedana make the run from their terminal at Paseo de la Florida 11 (Metro Príncipe Pío; Mon–Sat 6.30am–10.30pm, Sun 8am–10.15pm; 1hr 45min; €8.20 return). It's worth noting that buses also operate between Ávila and Segovia (2–4 daily; 1hr), so you could consider combining the two in a day-trip. Segovia's own **train station** is some distance out of town and you'll need to take bus #3 to the Plaza Mayor. If you're **driving**, park outside

Convento de
las Carmelitas

Monasterio
del Parral

Iglesia de
la Vera Cruz

CARRETERA DE ZAMARRAMALA

Río Eresma

San
Marcos

CALLE SAN MARCOS

SAN MARCOS

Casa de
la Moneda

PASEO DE SANTO

Muralla

Puerta de
Santiago

PLAZA DE LA REINA
VICTORIA EUGENIA

CALLE DE VELARDE

San
Esteban

Alcázar

CALLE DE

LAS
CANONIGAS

SAN
ESTEBAN

PLAZA
DE SAN
ESTEBAN

Río Clamores

PASEO DE DON JUAN II

DADIZ

San Andrés

PLAZA DE
LA MERCED

A

DESAMPARADOS

C. MARQUES DEL ARCO

Muralla

Casa del Sol
(Museo de Segovia)

Catedral

ESCUDEROS

Puerta de
San Andrés

LA JUDERÍA

N

PASEO DE LOS HOYOS

ACCOMMODATION

Hostal Don Jaime	4
Hotel Infanta Isabel	2
Hostal Juan Bravo	3
Hotel Los Linajes	1

RESTAURANTS AND BARS

Mesón El Campesino	C
Mesón de Cándido	F
La Cocina de San Millán	E
Bar-Mesón Cuevas de San Esteban	A
Mesón José María	B
La Vinatería de José Luis	D

SEGOVIA

0   100m

SEGOVIA

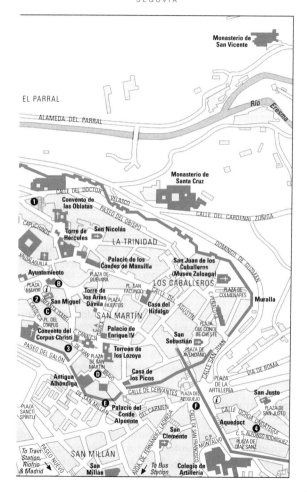

Monasterio de
San Vicente

EL PARRAL

Río Eresma

ALAMEDA DEL PARRAL

Monasterio de
Santa Cruz

CALLE DEL DOCTOR VELASCO

CALLE DEL CARDENAL ZÚÑIGA

❶ Convento de
las Oblatas

PASEO DEL OBISPO

CAPUCHINOS

Torre de
Hércules   San Nicolás

LA TRINIDAD

DOMINGO DE GUZMÁN

VALDELAGUILA

Palacio de los
Condes de Mansilla

San Juan de los
Caballeros
(Museo Zuloaga)

Ayuntamiento

PLAZA DE
GUEVARA

LOS CABALLEROS

PLAZA DE
COLMENARES

PLAZA
MAYOR   ⓘ   Ⓑ

PL. SAN
FACUNDO

CALLE DEL

C. PERAROS.

Muralla

❷   San Miguel   Ⓒ

Torre de
los Arias
Dávila

PLAZA
HUERTOS

Casa del
Hidalgo

AGUSTÍN

PLAZA
DEL CONDE
DE CHESTE

PL. DE ISABEL

C. ESCUDEROS

SAN MARTÍN

C. CANALEJA

Palacio de
Enrique IV

San
Sebastián

PLAZA DE
AVENDAÑO

Convento del
Corpus Christi   ❸

PL. DEL
CORPUS

CALLE SAN JUAN

VIA DE ROMA

PASEO DEL SALÓN

C. DE JUAN BRAVO

Torreón de
los Lozoya

PLAZA
DE SAN
MARTÍN

Ⓓ

Casa de
los Picos

PLAZA
DE LA
ARTILLERÍA

Antigua
Alhóndiga

CALLE DE CERVANTES

PLAZA DEL
AZOGUEJO

San Justo

PLAZA
SANCTI
SPIRITU

DE SAN MILLÁN

Ⓔ   Palacio del
Conde
Alpuente

Ⓕ

CALLE OCHOA ONDATEGUI

ⓘ

PLAZA DE
SAN JUSTO

PLAZA DE
DÍAZ SANZ

CALLE DEL CARMEN

Aqueduct

C. S. ALFONSO RODRÍGUEZ

❹

C.P.
MONTALVO

San
Clemente

SAN MILLÁN

AVDA. DE FERNÁNDEZ LADREDA

CALLE DE SAN FRANCISCO

To Train
Station,
Ríofrío
& Madrid

PASEO NUEVO

San
Millán

To Bus
Station

Colegio de
Artillería

the old city below the aqueduct. The **Turismo** (Mon–Fri 9am–3pm & 5–7pm, Sat & Sun 10am–2pm & 5–8pm; ☎921 460 334) is centrally located in the Plaza Mayor. There's also a small kiosk in Plaza de Azoguejo below the aqueduct (daily 10am–8pm; ☎921 462 914).

THE CATHEDRAL AND THE ALCÁZAR

Segovia's **cathedral** (daily summer 10am–6.30pm, winter 9am–5.30pm; museums €2), just behind the Plaza Mayor in the heart of the old town, was the last major Gothic building constructed in Spain, and arguably the last in Europe. Pinnacles and flying buttresses are tacked on at every conceivable point, although the interior is surprisingly bare and its space is cramped by a great green marble choir in the very centre. The treasures are almost all confined to the museum which opens off the cloisters.

From the cathedral, c/de Daoiz leads to the **Alcázar** (daily: May–Sept 10am–7pm, Oct–Apr 10am–6pm; €3.10), an extraordinary fantasy of a castle, with its narrow towers and flurry of turrets. It seems eerily familiar to just about every visitor, having served as the model for the original Disneyland castle in California. Although it dates from the fourteenth and fifteenth centuries, it was almost completely destroyed by a fire in 1862 and rebuilt as a deliberately exaggerated version of the original. It's worth visiting if only for the magnificent panoramas from the tower.

THE AQUEDUCT

The most photographed site in Segovia is its stunning **aqueduct**. Over 800m long and at its highest point towering some 30m above the Plaza de Azoguejo, it stands up without a drop of mortar or cement. No one knows exactly when it was built, but it was probably around the end of the first century AD under the Emperor Trajan. It no longer carries water from the Río Frío to the city and in recent years traffic vibration and pollution have been threatening to undermine the entire structure, but the recent completion of a meticulous restoration programme should ensure it remains standing for some time to come. Stairs beside the aqueduct lead up to a surviving fragment of the city walls, giving an excellent view.

For the best view of Segovia take the main road north for 2km or so towards Cuéllar, and a panorama of the whole city, including the aqueduct, gradually unfolds.

VERA CRUZ

The best of Segovia's ancient churches is undoubtedly **Vera Cruz** (Tues–Sun 10.30am–1.30pm & 3.30–6pm, open till 7pm in summer; closed Nov; €1.50), a remarkable twelve-sided building in the valley facing the Alcázar, reached by taking one of the paths that descend from the north side of the city walls. The church was built by the Knights Templar in the early thirteenth century on the pattern of the Church of the Holy Sepulchre in Jerusalem, and once housed part of the supposed True Cross (hence its name). You can climb the tower for a highly photogenic view of the city.

Nearby is the prodigiously walled **Convento de las Carmelitas** (daily summer 10am–1pm & 4–8pm, winter 10am–1.30pm & 4–7pm; closed Tues 10am–1.30pm; free), also referred to as the monastery of San Juan de la Cruz, which contains the gaudy mausoleum of its founder-saint.

LA GRANJA

Just 10km southeast of Segovia on the N601 Madrid road, and connected by regular bus services, lies the Bourbon summer palace of **La Granja** (map 1, D3), built by the first Bourbon king of Spain, Felipe V, no doubt homesick for the luxuries of Versailles. Its glories are the mountain setting, and the extravagant wooded grounds and gardens, but it's worth casting an eye over the **palace** (June–Sept Tues–Sun 10am–6pm, Oct–May Tues–Sat 10am–1.30pm & 3–5pm, Sun 10am–2pm; compulsory guided tour €4.81, concessions €2.40, Wed free for EU citizens). Though destroyed in parts and damaged throughout by a fire in 1918, much has been well restored. Everything is furnished in plush French imperial style but it's almost all of Spanish origin, and the palace is also home to one of the most valuable collections of sixteenth-century tapestries in the world.

The highlight of the **gardens** (daily 10am–7pm; €3.01, concessions €1.50) is the series of fountains, which culminate in the fifteen-metre-high jet of La Fama. They're a fantastic spectacle, but usually only operate at 5.30pm at weekends and on Wednesdays, with special displays on May 30, July 25 and August 25 (check at the turismo first).

ACCOMMODATION

Hostal Don Jaime
C/Ochoa Ondátegui 8
℡921 44 47 87.
Excellent *hostal* near Plaza de Azoguejo. All doubles have their own bathroom. ➋

Hotel Infanta Isabel
C/Isabel la Católica 1
℡921 461 300,
℻921 462 217.
Comfortable hotel – and better value than the *parador* outside town – ideally positioned on Plaza Mayor.

**Rooms can be hard to come by, even out
of season, so it's worth booking ahead.**

Hostal Juan Bravo
C/Juan Bravo 12
☎921 463 413.
Lots of big, comfortable
rooms and plant-festooned
bathrooms. ②

Hotel Los Linajes
C/Dr Velasco 9
☎921 460 475,
⊕921 460 479.
Good-value, atmospheric
hotel located in a quiet corner
of the walled city, with a fine
garden overlooking the river
valley. ④

EATING AND DRINKING

Segovia takes its cooking seriously, and culinary specialities
include **roast suckling pig** (*cochinillo asado*) and **lamb**
(*cordero*). There's a concentration of cheaper **bar/
restaurants** on c/Infanta Isabel, off the Plaza Mayor, and
late-night bars on c/Escuderos and c/Judería Vieja, and
along Avenida Fernández Ladreda.

Mesón El Campesino
C/Infanta Isabel 14.
One of the best budget
restaurants in town, serving
decent-value *menús* and
combinados to a young crowd.
Closed Aug.

Mesón de Cándido
Plaza Azoguejo 5
☎921 428 103.
The city's most famous
restaurant, run by the

founder's son and still the
place for *cochinillo* and the
like. The *menú* is around
€20, although with the
cochinillo you're more likely to
top €25.

La Cocina de San Millán
C/San Millán 3
☎921 436 226.
Nestling below the steps
which lead up to the old
town, this cosy restaurant

305

serves up imaginative cooking at reasonable prices. Closed Sun eve & Jan 7–31.

Bar-Mesón Cuevas de San Esteban

C/Valdeláguila 15, off the top end of Plaza San Esteban.
A cavern-restaurant and bar (serving draught beer), popular with locals. Excellent value.

Mesón José María

C/Cronista Lecea 11, just off Plaza Mayor
℡ 921 461 111.

Currently reckoned to be the city's best and most interesting restaurant, with modern variations on Castilian classics. The *menú* is a hefty €25, but there are dishes costing around €12.

La Vinateria de José Luis

C/Herreria 3.
Imaginative tapas and good selection of wines in this friendly bar off c/Juan Bravo.

Ávila

To things distinguish **Ávila** (map 1, A4) – its eleventh-century **walls**, two perfectly preserved kilometres of which surround the old town, and the mystic writer **Santa Teresa**, who was born here and whose shrines are a major focus of religious pilgrimage. Set on a high plain, with the peaks of the Sierra de Gredos behind, the town is an impressive sight, especially if you time it right and approach with the evening sun highlighting the golden tone of the walls and its 88 towers. There are also a number of fine **Romanesque churches** dotted in and about the old town.

From **Madrid** (Chamartín and Atocha) there are up to 24 **trains** a day to Ávila (daily 6.40am–8.30pm; 1hr 30min; €10.70–27). **Buses** (operated by Larrea from Estación Sur de Autobuses; Metro Méndez Alvaro) are less frequent (eight on weekdays, three at weekends; 1hr 20min–2hr; €9.67 return). Buses also operate between Ávila and Segovia (2–4 daily; 1hr; ask at the turismo for details), so you could consider combining the two in one day. The main **turismo** (Mon–Fri 9am–2pm & 5–7pm, Sat & Sun 10am–2pm & 5–8pm; ☎920 211 387) is in the Plaza de la Catedral, and there's another, smaller office next to the Basílica de San Vicente (open July–Sept only; same hours).

SANTA TERESA IN ÁVILA

The obvious place to start a tour of Santa Teresa's Ávila is the **Convento de Santa Teresa** (daily 8.30am–1.30pm & 3.30–8.30pm; free), built over the saint's birthplace, just inside the south gate of the old town. Most of the convent remains *in clausura*, but you can see the very spot where she was born. In a small reliquary (daily 9am–1.30pm & 3.30–7.30pm, summer 10am–1pm & 4–7.30pm; free), beside the gift shop, is a **museum** (daily 10am–1pm & 4–7pm; €2) containing memorials of Teresa's life, including not only her rosary beads, but also one of the fingers she used to count them with.

In the **Convento de la Encarnación** (May–Sept Mon–Fri 9.30am–1.30pm & 3.30–6pm, Sat & Sun 10am–1pm & 3.30–6pm; Oct–April Mon–Fri 9.30–1pm &

SANTA TERESA DE ÁVILA

Santa Teresa (1515–82) was born to a noble family in Ávila and from childhood began to experience visions and religious raptures. Teresa's religious career began at the Carmelite convent of La Encarnación, where she was a nun for 27 years, and from this base, she went on to reform the movement and found convents throughout Spain. She was an ascetic, but her appeal – and her importance to the Counter-Reformation – lay in the mystic sensuality of her experience of Christ, as revealed in her autobiography – for centuries a bestseller in Spain. As joint patron saint of Spain (together with Santiago – or St James), she remains a pillar of Spanish Catholicism and schoolgirls are brought into Ávila by the busload to experience first-hand the life of the woman they're supposed to emulate. On a more bizarre note, one of the saint's mummified hands has now been returned to Ávila after spending the Franco years by the dictator's bedside.

ÁVILA

RESTAURANTS AND BARS	
El Molino de la Losa	B
Mesón del Rastro	C
Bar El Rincón	A

ACCOMMODATION

Hostería de Bracamonte	3
Hostal Don Diego	2
Parador Raimundo de Borgoña	1
Hostal El Rastro	4
Hospedería La Sinagoga	6
Palacio de Valderrábanos	5

4–6pm, Sat & Sun 10am–1pm & 3.30–6pm; €1.20), reached by leaving the old town through Puerta del Carmen and following c/de la Encarnación, each room is labelled with the act Teresa performed there, while everything she might have touched or looked at is on display. A small museum section also provides a reasonable introduction to the saint's life.

Also outside the walls, a third sight connected with the saint lies a couple of blocks northeast of Plaza de Santa Teresa. The **Convento de San José** (daily 10am–1.30pm & 3–6pm; €1) was the first monastery founded by Teresa, in 1562. Its museum contains relics and memorabilia, including the coffin in which Teresa once slept, and assorted personal possessions. Lastly, you might want to make your way up to **Los Cuatro Postes**, a little four-posted shrine, 1.5km along the Salamanca road west of town. It was here, aged seven, that the infant Teresa was recaptured by her uncle after she had run away with her brother to seek Christian martyrdom fighting the Moors in North Africa.

THE CATHEDRAL AND OTHER SIGHTS

Ávila's **cathedral** (Mon–Sat 10am–7pm, Sun midday–7pm; closed 1–6 Jan, 15 Oct & 25 Dec; €1.20) was started in the twelfth century, but has never been finished, as evidenced by the missing tower above the main entrance. The earliest Romanesque parts were as much fortress as church, and the apse actually forms an integral part of the city walls. Inside, the succeeding changes of style are immediately apparent; the Romanesque parts are made of a strange red-and-white mottled stone, then there's an abrupt break and the rest of the main structure is pure white stone and Gothic forms.

Although the proportions are exactly the same, this newer half of the cathedral seems infinitely more spacious. Here you can admire the carved stalls in the *Coro* and the treasury-museum with its silver *custodia* (monstrance) and ancient religious images, and the tomb of a fifteenth-century bishop known as *El Tostado* (the "toasted" or "swarthy").

Just outside the city walls, on the northeast corner, is the basilica of **San Vicente** (daily 10am–1.30pm & 4–6.30pm; €1.20), which, like the cathedral, is a mixture of architectural styles. Its twelfth-century doorways and the portico which protects them are magnificent examples of Romanesque art, while the church itself shows the influence of later trends. San Vicente and his sisters were martyred on this site, and their tomb narrates the gruesome story of their torture and execution by the Romans. Legend has it that following their martyrdom a rich Jew who had been poking fun at them was enveloped and suffocated by a great serpent that miraculously emerged from the rocks. On the verge of asphyxiation, he repented and converted to Christianity, later building the church on the very same site; he, too, is said to be buried here. In the crypt you can see part of the rocky crag where San Vicente and his sisters were executed and from which the serpent later supposedly appeared. The warm pink glow of the sandstone of the church is a characteristic feature of Ávila, also notable in the church of **San Pedro**, on Plaza de Santa Teresa.

Just over half a kilometre to the southeast stands the **Monasterio de Santo Tomás** (daily 10am–1pm & 4–8pm; *Coro* and cloisters €1), a Dominican monastery founded in 1482, but greatly expanded over the following decade by Fernando and Isabel, whose summer palace it became. Inside are three exceptional cloisters, the largest of which contains an **oriental collection**, a strangely incongruous display built up by the monks over centuries of missionary work in the Orient. Notice also the elaborate tombs and the thrones occupied by the king and queen

THE CATHEDRAL AND OTHER SIGHTS

during services. The notorious inquisitor **Torquemada** is buried in the sacristy here.

Just outside the city walls, through the Puerta del Peso de la Harina, is Ávila's small **Museo Provincial**, housed in the sixteenth-century Palacio de los Deanes (Tues–Sat 10.30am–2pm & 4.30–7.30pm, Sun 10am–2pm; €1.20, free Sat & Sun), where the cathedral's deans used to live. Today, its exhibits include collections of archeological remains, ceramics, carpets and furnishings from around the Ávila province.

One of the best things to do in Ávila is to walk the small section of the **city walls** from Puerta del Alcázar to Puerta del Rastro (the only part still open to the public); the view of the city is stunning. Tickets (Tues–Sun 11am–8pm; €3.50) are available from the kiosk by the Puerta del Alcázar.

ACCOMMODATION

Hostería de Bracamonte
C/Bracamonte 6
☎920 251 280.
Atmospheric and elegant hotel, between the city walls and the Plaza de la Victoria, created from a number of converted Renaissance mansions. ❸–❹

Hostal Don Diego
C/Marqués de Canales y Chozas 5
☎920 255 475,
☎920 254 549.
Friendly, very good-value

hostal just opposite the *Parador*. All thirteen rooms have bath or shower. ❷

Parador Raimundo de Borgoña
C/Marqués de Canales y Chozas 2
☎920 211 340,
☎920 226 166.
A converted fifteenth-century mansion, set right next to the city walls. The rooms in the tower are a little cramped, but it's the cheapest of Ávila's top hotels. ❺

Hostal El Rastro
Plazuela del Rastro 1
☏920 211 218,
🖷920 251 626.
A good mid-range option, this characterful old inn, set against the walls, has a pleasant garden and popular restaurant. ❷

Hospedería La Sinagoga
C/Reyes Católicos 22
☏920 352 3321,
✉lasinagoga@airtel.net.
As the name suggests this marvellous little hotel was a synagogue in the fifteenth century. Modern, comfortable and good-value rooms in a tastefully restored and atmospheric building. ❸

Palacio de Valderrábanos
Plaza de la Catedral 9
☏920 211 023,
🖷920 251 691.
This former bishop's palace beats the *Parador* for ambience and the rooms are equally luxurious. ❺

EATING AND DRINKING

El Molino de la Losa
Bajada de la Losa 12
☏920 211 101.
Converted fifteenth-century mill, with a good reputation, and a play area for kids. The *menú* is around €20. Closed Mon & mid-Oct to mid-March.

Mesón del Rastro
Plazuela del Rastro 1.
Excellent bar, attached to the *hostal* of the same name, with a range of tapas. Behind it is a modest-priced restaurant, an old-fashioned place with solid, traditional food.

Bar El Rincón
Plaza Zurraquín 4.
To the north of Plaza de la Victoria, this bar serves a generous three-course *menú* for €10.

EATING AND DRINKING

The Sierra de Guadarrama

The closest the majority of visitors to Madrid get to the **Sierra de Guadarrama** is when they glimpse the mountain chain out of the aircraft window, unaware that less than an hour from the city centre lies a series of spectacular peaks that tower over the Castilian plains. A **day-trip** to the Sierra is a favourite *Madrileño* pastime with opportunities for a riverside picnic, a stroll through the cool mountain scenery, a more challenging hike up some of the higher peaks or just a hearty Castilian lunch in one of the mountain villages.

In the winter months there's even reasonable **skiing** at the two major stations of Cotos and Navacerrada, both accessible by train and providing a good starting point for some of the routes through the higher peaks, while the town of **Manzanares El Real**, with its medieval castle, makes an ideal base to experience the spectacular granite formations in the **Pedriza** regional park. A further attraction of the Sierra are the pretty little villages such as **Cercedilla**, which are perched on the lower slopes and make for a relaxing base for the less energetic.

If you do venture into the mountains remember that in summer the sun is strong so bring protection and plenty of water, while in winter stick to the lower slopes unless you're experienced in high-mountain conditions. Late spring and early autumn are probably the best times for walking. Maps and a compass are a must for all but the most straightforward routes.

The best walks in the Sierra de Guadarrama are outlined in the Sendirista guide by Juan Pablo Avisón. For maps of the Sierra try La Tienda Verde or Desnivel, see "Shopping", p.251.

The most impressive **wildlife** in the Sierra are the birds, with vultures, eagles and peregrine falcons all common in the mountains, while in the nearby villages storks nest on the rooftops and in the towers of local churches. More difficult to catch a glimpse of are the wild boar that inhabit the forests, but there are plenty of hares, rabbits, goats and squirrels. Lizards and amphibians are common too, but the only poisonous snakes are vipers which tend to keep to themselves unless molested.

Manzanares El Real and La Pedriza

Lying in the shadow of the Sierra Guadarrama and on the shores of the Santillana *embalse* (reservoir), lies **Manzanares el Real**, a town geared to Madrid weekenders, whose villas dot the landscape for miles around. Apart from the streetside cafés, the only attraction is the **castle** (daily 10am–1pm

& 3–5.30pm; free) which, despite its eccentric appearance is a genuine fifteenth-century construction, built around an earlier chapel. The interior has been heavily restored, but makes for an interesting visit and houses a fine collection of seventeenth-century Baroque tapestries from Brussels.

Buses from Madrid to Manzanares el Real run hourly (7.30am–9.30pm; €4.20 return) from Plaza de Castilla.

Near the town, the ruggedly beautiful **La Pedriza**, a spur of the Sierra de Guadarrama, has been declared a regional park (access limited to 350 cars a day at weekends; free; information centre open daily 10am–6pm; ☎ 918 539 978). There are some enjoyable walks around this granite kingdom with the huge egg-shaped rock El Yelmo dominating the surrounding landscape. The park also contains some much-revered technical **climbs**, notably the ascent to the jagged Peña del Diezmo and is home to a very large colony of griffon vultures.

Accommodation in town is expensive and limited to *Hostal Tranco* (☎ 918 530 423; ❷) and *Hotel Parque Real* (☎ 918 539 912; ❸). However, there's usually space at one of the two **campsites**, *El Ortigal* (☎ 918 530 120) at the foot of La Pedriza or the well-equipped *La Fresneda* (☎ & ℻ 918 476 523) on the Carretera M608 towards Soto del Real. **Food** is not cheap, but good meals can be had at *Los Arcos* in c/Real and the *Restaurante Parra* in c/Panaderos.

MANZANARES EL REAL AND LA PEDRIZA

Cercedilla and La Valle de Fuenfría

Cercedilla is an Alpine-looking village perched at the foot of the valley leading up to the **Puerto de la Fuenfría** (1796m) and makes an excellent base for summer walking. Like Manzanares el Real it's very popular with *Madrileños* at weekends, but has the advantage of being accessible by **train** from Madrid (over twenty a day, 6am–11pm from Atocha, calling at Chamartín; 1hr 20min; €5.32 return). **Buses** leave every half-hour from the Intercambiador de Autobuses de Moncloa (6.30am–10pm; 1hr 10min, €5.50 return).

The village is the starting point for a very pleasant five-hour round-trip **walk** along the pine-fringed Calzada Romana (old Roman road built in the first century AD) up to the Puerto. If you have your own transport you can reduce this by at least an hour by starting at the car park in **Las Dehesas**, a popular weekend picnic spot on the banks of the Río Guadarrama. Pop into the information centre (daily 9am–6pm; ☎918 522 213) on the way up for maps and advice. Once at the car park, carry on past the meadows alongside the river and then follow the indicated path up to the top for striking views of Segovia province. The *Casa Cirilo* restaurant near the car park is perfect for post- or pre-walk refreshments.

From Cercedilla, you can embark on a wonderful little **train ride** (6 daily; first train around 9.30am, last return to Cercedilla around 8.30pm; €1.82–1.92) up to the Puerto de Navacerrada, the most important pass in the mountains and the heart of the ski area, or a little further on to Puerto de Cotos where a number of well-maintained walks around the **Parque Natural de Peñalara** begin. Look out for roe deer and wild boar.

Accommodation can be found at the *Hostal El Aribel* on c/Emilio Serrano 71 (☎918 521 511, ☏918 521 561; ❷), or its sister hotel at no.3 on the same street, the *Hostal Frontón* (same phone number and price), and two **youth hostels** up on the Dehesas road: *Villa Castora* (☎918 520 334, ☏918 522 411) and, 2km up the road, *Las Dehesas* (☎918 520 135, ☏918 521 836). Further up still is a helpful **information booth** (daily 10am–6pm; ☎918 522 213). There are several **eating** places in town: *Los Frutales* on the Carretera de las Dehesas does good *croquetas*, *judías con perdiz* (partridge and beans) and *trucha* (trout), the train station has a restaurant on the first floor or you could try the restaurant at *Hostal Longinos El Aribel*.

Puerto de Navacerrada and Cotos

From Cercedilla the train winds its way up to **Puerto de Navacerrada** (1860 metres) and then on to the end of the line at **Puerto de Cotos** (Cotos), the two main **ski stations** in the Sierra. Navacerrada (Ⓦ www.puertonava cerrada.com) has eleven kilometres of runs for a range of abilities, with a day pass costing €24 at the weekends and on holidays and €16 at other times. All equipment can be hired locally, but long queues and traffic jams are common on winter weekends. The **Valdesquí** resort next to Cotos station has over twenty kilometres of runs, but is marginally more expensive.

Navacerrada is also the starting point for a number of impressive **walks** along the high peaks. To the west is the *Camino de Schmidt* which leads you past the Siete Picos

(Seven Peaks) and on to the Puerto de Fuenfría; while to the east is the *Cuerda Larga* which can be reached by heading up to the peak Bola del Mundo and following the route along the ridge to Puerto de la Morcuera. From there you can then drop down to the picturesque mountain village of Miraflores de la Sierra, which is linked to Madrid by bus.

Cotos is the gateway to the highest peak in the Sierra, **Peñalara** (2,430 metres). It can be reached in about four hours, but is a tough ascent and shouldn't be attempted in winter (ask at the information centre just above the small café close to the train station for advice and directions on all routes; ☏918 691 757; Mon–Fri 10am–6pm, Sat, Sun & hols 10am–8pm; winter daily 10am–6pm). For an interesting return route you can follow the ridge from the summit northwards along the narrow Risco de los Claveles ridge before dropping down the tricky slopes towards the glacial lakes Laguna de los Pájaros and Laguna Grande and an easy stroll back to the café. A less challenging, but highly enjoyable alternative is to take the gently sloping path up to the **Laguna Grande** – just follow the signs from the information booth.

El Paular and Rascafría

Cotos lies at the head of the beautiful **Valle de Lozoya**, the floor of which can be reached on foot by following the signposted path, half a kilometre beyond the ski station. The path takes you to within a short distance of the **Monasterio de Santa María de El Paular**, originally a Carthusian monastery founded at the end of the fourteenth century, and now home to a handful of Benedictine monks who provide guided tours (daily noon, 1pm and 5pm;

closed Thurs pm; free) of the silent cloisters and the main church. Part of the monastery has been turned into a parador-style hotel (☎918 691 011, ℱ918 691 006; ⑥) with a delightful courtyard bar, ideal for cool summer refreshments. A little further up the main road towards Cotos are the natural swimming pools at **Las Presillas**, a popular weekend picnic spot. Two kilometres in the opposite direction lies the pleasant little mountain village of **Rascafría**, where there's plenty of accommodation and a bus link back to Madrid (twice a day; 2hr 15min; €5.05).

CONTEXTS

History

A lthough there is some evidence of small-scale prehistoric settlements on the banks of the Manzanares, of
Roman villas around Carabanchel and a minor
Visigoth settlement on the banks of a stream running down
what is now c/Segovia, the city of Madrid was effectively
founded by the **Muslims** in the ninth century. Even then it
was more of a defensive outpost than a settlement in its
own right. Arabic engineers soon saw the military potential
of the escarpment, with its commanding views of the main
routes stretching south from the Sierra de Guadarrama, and
used it as a way of shoring up the communications to the
more prestigious city of **Toledo**. The area's other key
attribute was its ready supply of water, hence its early name
"mayrit" – place of many springs – successively modified to
Magerit and then Madrid. Fragments of the old **Arabic
wall** still remain on the Cuesta de la Vega beside the
Catedral de la Almudena.

In the late eleventh century, the town was taken by the
Christians under **Alfonso VI**, although the Muslims did
try to recapture it in an unsuccessful siege, launched from
below the Alcázar in the Campo del Moro in 1109.
Nevertheless, many Muslims remained in the tangled web
of streets and alleyways of **La Morería**, making the most of
their skills as builders and masons to help construct

churches and residences; the distinctive *Mudéjar* towers of San Nicolás and San Pedro el Viejo still remain from this era. Despite being used as a royal stopover for the itinerant Castilian monarchy and the establishment in the city of several powerful religious centres, such as the friary of San Francisco and the church of San Andrés, Madrid still remained a relatively insignificant backwater. The city was even given to Leo V of Armenia as a consolation for losing his kingdom to the Turks, although it later reverted to Castilian control.

Capital of the Empire

What changed Madrid's destiny from obscure provincial town into **capital** of the glittering Spanish empire was the caprice of one man, **Felipe II** (1556–98), who decided in 1561 to permanently locate the court here. His decision was prompted by the city's position in the centre of the recently unified Spain and his fear of giving undue influence to one of its overmighty regions. The population of Madrid immediately surged with the arrival of the royal entourage and there was a boom in the building industry. Much of this building was highly provisional, as few thought Madrid would last very long as the capital. However, they had underestimated the determination of Felipe II, who had also begun to construct the huge monastery complex-cum-mausoleum of **El Escorial** in the nearby mountains. Greater solidity and a touch of grandeur was added to the city with the appointment of **Juan Gómez de Mora** as city architect during the reign of Felipe III (1598–1621). He left his mark on the old city centre and his characteristic buildings of red brick, slate roofs and needle spires can still be seen in the Plaza Mayor and the Plaza de la Villa.

Between the mid-sixteenth and mid-seventeenth

centuries, Madrid's population grew from 20,000 to over 150,000. Building continued, with the foundation of a large number of **convents and monasteries** inside the city, including the Encarnación, Carboneras and Comendadoras, which survive today. It was during this period also that the palace **El Buen Retiro** was built on the east side of the city to house and provide entertainment for the court. The only parts of this royal village that remain today are the Casón del Buen Retiro (see p.85) and the Museo del Ejército (see p.106).

However, the city was still very much one of outsiders and immigrants, a city of consumption rather than production. All was not well with the overstretched and beleaguered Spanish empire, and the increasingly inbred Habsburg dynastic line dried up with the chronically ill and malformed Carlos II. He died in 1700, his demise hastened no doubt by the succession of cures doled out to him by his doctors.

With the emergence of the **Bourbon dynasty**, a touch of French style was introduced into the capital. Used to the luxuries of Versailles, **Felipe V** was somewhat disappointed with the capital that he'd inherited, and proceeded to construct a grand country villa at **La Granja**. In the wake of the 1734 fire at the Alcázar, he took the opportunity to build an altogether more sumptuous affair in the shape of the **Palacio Real**. Baroque flourishes were added to the city with the buildings of **Pedro de Ribera**, including the Hospice (now the Museo Municipal) and the Cuartel del Conde Duque; while under **Carlos III** (1759–88), the "Rey-Alcalde" (King-Mayor), more plans were made to make the city into a home worthy of the monarchy. The notoriously filthy streets were cleaned up, sewers and street lighting installed, and work began on the creation of an intellectual showcase of museums and research centres along the **Paseo del Prado**. Madrid undoubtedly became a more

CAPITAL OF THE EMPIRE

pleasant place to live in, but Carlos's foreign tastes didn't always meet with the approval of the *Madrileño* population. **Riots** broke out in 1766 over increased food prices and the introduction of a ban on long capes and wide-brimmed hats, which it was claimed were used by thieves to conceal their weapons.

Invasion and occupation

The improvements in Madrid lost momentum under the slothful **Carlos IV**, and the rise of the corrupt **Manuel Godoy** in the early years of the nineteenth century increasingly placed Spain under the influence of Napoleonic France. In March 1808, **French troops** entered the capital, and many suspected that the royal family was preparing to flee. Tension mounted until it culminated in a rising against the French troops on **May 2**, **1808**, with the heavily outgunned *Madrileños* eventually having to admit defeat. The rising and the subsequent reprisals by the French entered Spanish folklore and were immortalized by Goya in his two magnificent canvases now hanging in the Prado. **Napoleon** installed his brother Joseph (nicknamed "*Pepe Botella*" because of his alleged susceptibility to drink) on the throne, and, although highly unpopular, he did begin a whole series of projects designed to create more open spaces in the cramped city; his legacy can be seen in the plazas Santa Ana and Oriente. Nevertheless, there was also much **destruction**, with the plundering of the Prado and the virtual destruction of El Buen Retiro.

Division and instability

Once the French were removed by a combined Spanish and British army, the monarchy made a return under the myopic reactionary figure of **Fernando VII** in 1814, who soon annulled Spain's first – and decidedly liberal – constitution, drawn up by the Cortes (parliament) in Cádiz in 1812. The lines were now drawn that were to scar Spanish society and politics for the next hundred and fifty years, with progressive, anti-clerical and constitutional supporters lined up against conservative, Catholic and authoritarian forces. At first, these divisions confined themselves to the emerging café society and *tertulias*, but with the disputed succession after Fernando's death, they soon exploded into a series of conflicts known as the **Carlist wars** and led to constant political instability, including a brief period as a republic until the monarchy under **Alfonso XII** was restored in 1875.

At the same time, Madrid was experiencing significant **social changes**, with a rapid growth in population from 200,000 at the end of the eighteenth century to 300,000 by the 1860s. With the emergence of a **working class**, the socialist party, the **PSOE**, was founded in 1879 in *Casa Labra* in the city. Madrid began to expand north, with the construction of the working-class district of **Chamberí** and the development of **Salamanca** by the flamboyant speculator, the Marqués de Salamanca. The railway, improved water supply via the Canal Isabel II, the metro, electricity, trams and the construction of the Gran Vía all came to Madrid within the next 35 years. Despite these improvements, many of the underlying divisions remained. Confidence was further undermined and the monarchy further discredited by the loss of Cuba and the Philippines in 1898. This prompted a period of serious reflection by intellectuals and politicians, sparking off the great work of writers such as Baroja and Antonio Machado known as the "**Generation of '98**".

DIVISION AND INSTABILITY

The Second Republic and the rise of Franco

Despite Spanish neutrality in **World War I** and an accompanying economic boom, problems arose in the 1920s, and a hard-line military regime under the Captain-General of Barcelona, **Miguel Primo de Rivera**, took control from 1923 to 1930, with King Alfonso XIII relegated to the background. When Republican candidates unexpectedly swept the board in the 1931 municipal elections, the king decided to quit. The **Second Republic** was ushered in amid a host of unrealistic expectations, and had to cope not only with a divided Spanish society, but also with the impact of the Great Depression. Political polarization continued, and when the Popular Front won the 1936 elections the Right grew increasingly restless and called for the army to save the country. The ensuing **rising by the generals** in July 1936 was only partially successful and in Madrid the troops that barricaded themselves inside the Montaña barracks in Parque del Oeste were massacred by defenders of the Republic, making the capital a **Republican stronghold**. A revolutionary atmosphere prevailed and many of the city's churches and religious institutions were torched by Anarchists. By late October, the city was under attack by **Franco's Nationalists**, with some of the fiercest fighting of the war occurring along the Carretera de la Coruña and in the Ciudad Universitaria. However, the arrival of the International Brigades, the firm resistance of the *Madrileño* population and the discovery of the Nationalist plans to attack the city, thwarted Franco's efforts and a long drawn-out **siege** began. The city was regularly shelled by the Nationalists camped out in Casa de Campo, where traces of trenches and bunkers can still be found. There were severe food shortages, and meat and vegetables were hardly ever available. By 1939, divisions began to emerge between

Republican groups prepared to negotiate with Franco and those who, together with the Communists, saw this as tantamount to political suicide. **Franco** and his victorious Nationalists eventually entered the city in March 1939. There was little sign of graciousness in victory from the general – mass reprisals took place and Republicans were executed, imprisoned, forced into hiding or had to flee the country. While *El Caudillo* installed himself in the country residence of **El Pardo**, just to the north of the city, Republican prisoners were put to work on the monstrous war memorial – later to house *El Caudillo*'s tomb – **El Valle de los Caídos**.

Spain had to endure yet more suffering during the post-war years – *los años de hambre* (the years of hunger) until the turnaround in **American policy**, which rehabilitated Franco in a desperate search for anti-Communist Cold War allies. Madrid again experienced massive growth, with the population trebling between 1930 and 1970 to reach three million. The **monumentalist architecture** of this period can be seen in the buildings of the Ministerio del Aire, Nuevos Ministerios and the Edificio de España, while waves of **immigrants** set up home in the outskirts, many in shanty-town developments (*chabolas*). As the Spanish economy took off with mass tourism and the assistance of the IMF and World Bank, Madrid became more industrial with significant enterprises developing in the south and east of the city.

The return to democracy

By the early 1970s, Franco was clearly ailing, and the car bomb assassination by the Basque terrorist organization, ETA, of the man he was grooming to be his successor, **Admiral Carrero Blanco** in 1973, shook the regime to its foundations. Franco himself died in November 1975 and was succeeded by his appointee **King Juan Carlos**. The king eventually appointed **Adolfo Suárez** to take over the government and preside over the transition to democracy, with the holding of the first democratic elections since 1936 and the drawing up of a new constitution. Much greater power was given to Spain's regions and Madrid became a *Comunidad Autónoma*, with its own elected regional government. The military, however, hadn't quite given up and in its last-gasp attempt to re-establish itself, the Civil Guard commander, **Colonel Tejero**, stormed the Cortes in Madrid, firing his revolver and demanding everyone hit the floor. For a moment it looked as if the days of dictatorship were about to return, but lack of support from Juan Carlos in a TV broadcast and lack of commitment from a number of the army brigades saw it collapse. It was the Socialists under **Felipe González** who profited from the bungled coup attempt and proceeded to win the 1982 elections.

The new spirit: la Movida and beyond

In Madrid, the freedom from the shackles of military dictatorship and the release of long-pent-up creative forces helped to create **la Movida**, an outpouring of hedonistic, highly innovative and creative forces that was embodied by the rise of **Pedro Almodóvar** and his internationally acclaimed films. The work of the city's Socialist mayor, **Enrique Tierno Galván**, also helped make Madrid the place to be in the late 1970s and early 1980s. He rejuvenated the old fiestas of San Isidro, poured money into cultural events and helped oversee the **modernization** of the city. Many of the office blocks lining the Castellana were finished shortly after the demise of the dictator and, while ugly urban developments became a feature of the sprawling suburbs, much of the city centre was sensitively renovated, reinvigorating the old *barrios*. The nomination of Madrid as European Cultural Capital in 1992, along with the Barcelona Olympics and Seville Expo in the same year, placed Spain firmly on the international map once again.

However, the transition to democracy hasn't been quite as smooth as it may appear. The Socialists became increasingly discredited as they moved to the right and were engulfed in a web of ever-more incredible **scandals and corruption** until they lost control of Madrid in 1991 and the country in 1996 to the conservative Partido Popular (PP) under **José María Aznar**. Cuts in spending replaced generous funding and the days of *la Movida* were certainly over. The 1999 local elections saw the PP retain power in both the city and *comunidad* (region) of Madrid. The present authorities are committed to rehabilitating some of the more run-down areas in the centre and to improving the transport network throughout the city – although it's unlikely this will solve the city's acute traffic problem. The PP has more restrictive attitudes towards bar and club licensing, but this has done little to dent the city's appetite for enjoying itself. Madrid has made the transition from provincial backwater to major European capital, while preserving its stylish and quirky identity.

Books

The **book** reviews below represent a highly selective reading list on Spain in general and on Madrid in particular. Publishers are given UK first, then US. Only one publisher is listed if the UK and US publishers are the same. Out-of-print books are indicated by o/p. If you have difficulty finding any titles, an excellent source for books about Spain – new, used and out-of-print – is Books on Spain, PO Box 207, Twickenham TW2 5BQ, UK; ☎020/8898 7789, 🌐www.books-on-spain.com.

The best introductions

Ian Gibson *Fire in the Blood: The New Spain* (Faber/BBC, UK). A splendid, if dated, commentary on the Spanish which accompanied a 1992 television series. Gibson is a passionate writer who wears his heart on his sleeve, but he makes a valiant attempt to describe and explain the complexity and contradictions of modern Spain and Spanish society.

John Hooper *The New Spaniards* (Penguin). Revised, expanded and updated edition of Hooper's guide to contemporary Spain which first appeared as *The Spaniards*. It provides excellent and comprehensive coverage of all aspects of life in modern Spain. A perfect book for anyone wanting to scratch deeper.

History

J.H. Elliott *Imperial Spain 1469–1716* (Penguin). The standard work on the Spanish golden age. Elegantly written, highly readable and characterized by thorough research throughout.

Ronald Fraser *Blood of Spain* (Pantheon, US). Subtitled *The Experience of Civil War, 1936–39*, this is an impressive piece of research, constructed entirely of vivid oral accounts of these turbulent years.

Henry Kamen *The Spanish Inquisition* (Mentor, US). Highly respected examination of the causes and effects of the Inquisition and the long shadow it cast over Spanish history. Kamen's *Philip of Spain* (Yale UP) is the most thoroughly researched biography of the king most associated with the Inquisition.

Geoffrey Parker *Philip II* (Hutchinson, UK o/p). Entertaining, accurate and revealing portrait of the most powerful man of his age, based upon Philip's personal papers and memoranda.

Paul Preston *Franco* (HarperCollins). On a par with Thomas's epic account of the Civil War, this monumental biography of *El Caudillo* is a truly enthralling read, tracing the genesis of Franco's dictatorship right through to his final few hours. There are perceptive insights into Franco's background and upbringing and the evolution of his icy character.

Francisco Romero Salvadó *Twentieth-Century Spain* (Macmillan/St. Martin's Press). A good introduction to modern Spain, tracing its political, social and economic development throughout the twentieth century.

Hugh Thomas *Madrid, A Traveller's Companion* (Constable, UK); *The Spanish Civil War* (Penguin). The first is a varied anthology of travel writings on Madrid with a fine introduction to the city's history, while the latter gives a masterful account of the causes and course of the tragic history of the Spanish Civil War. An immense work of scholarship, this is the definitive account of the war. It's initially difficult to wade through the complexities of the prewar era, but this is ultimately an extremely rewarding book.

Recent Travels

David Gilmour *Cities of Spain* (Pimlico/Ivan R. Dee). Contains a well-written and evocative chapter on Madrid.

Michael Jacobs *Madrid Observed* (Pallas Athene, UK). Opinionated, witty and well observed, containing thoroughly researched thematic walks around Madrid.

Art and Architecture

Hugh Broughton *Madrid: A Guide to Recent Architecture* (Elipsis, UK). Pocket guide to a hundred of the best examples of architecture in Madrid, each with its own photo and directions on how to get there.

Jonathan Brown *Velázquez: Painter and Courtier* (Yale, US). A detailed study of the great painter.

J.H. Elliott and Jonathan Brown *A Palace for a King: The Buen Retiro and the Court of Philip IV* (Yale, US). Closely researched account of the grandeur of the Habsburg Court.

Pierre Gassier *Goya, A Witness of His Times* (Alpine, UK). A comprehensive biography of the painter and the period in which he lived.

Fiction

Miguel de Cervantes *Don Quixote* (Penguin/Signet). No apologies for including this classic sixteenth-century novel. The highly amusing account of the adventures of the eccentric knight is a key to understanding the Spanish character and outlook on life.

Benito Pérez Galdós *Fortunata y Jacinta* (Penguin). Late nineteenth-century classic piece of detailed social observation set against the backdrop of the political turmoil of 1860s Madrid.

Camilo José Cela *The Family of Pascual Duarte* (LittleBrown).

RECENT TRAVEL

The Nobel Prize-winner's portrayal of a family in the aftermath of the Spanish Civil War. Another masterpiece, *The Hive*, focuses on the comings and goings of a group of characters in a Madrid café in the postwar years.

Arturo Pérez Reverte *The Fencing Master* (Panther, UK). The story of an ageing fencing master is told against the backdrop of the political intrigues of nineteenth-century Madrid. The best-selling Spanish novelist has also met with critical acclaim for two of his other historical thrillers that have been translated into English: *The Dumas Club* (Harvill P, UK) and *The Seville Communion* (Harvill P, UK).

Ramón María Valle-Inclán *Luces de Bohemia/Lights of Bohemia* (David Brown, US). Renowned modernist work that satirizes Spanish society, written by a leading member of the famous Generation of '98.

Sport

Phil Ball *Morbo – The Story of Spanish Football* (When Saturday Comes Books, UK). Excellent account of the history of Spanish football from its nineteenth-century beginnings with British workers at the mines of Río Tinto in Huelva to the golden years of Real Madrid and the dark days of Franco.

SPORT

Language

Once you get into it, **Spanish** is the easiest language there is, and you'll be helped everywhere by people who are eager to try and understand even the most faltering attempt. English is spoken in the main tourist areas, but you'll get a far better reception if you try communicating with Spaniards in their own tongue.

PHRASEBOOKS, DICTIONARIES AND TEACHING YOURSELF SPANISH

Numerous Spanish phrasebooks are available, not least the *Spanish Rough Guide Phrasebook*, laid out dictionary-style for instant access. For teaching yourself the language, the BBC tape series *España Viva* and *Dígame* are excellent, as is their two-week crash-course *Get By in Spanish*. *Breakthrough Spanish* (Macmillan) is probably the best of the tape-and-book home study courses.

Many of the books available in North America are geared to Latin American usage – more old-fashioned publications may be better for Spain itself. Langenscheidt, Cassells, Collins and others all produce useful dictionaries; Berlitz and others publish separate Spanish and Latin American phrasebooks.

The rules of **pronunciation** are pretty straightforward and strictly observed. Unless there's an accent, words ending in d, l, r, and z are **stressed** on the last syllable, all others on the second last. All **vowels** are pure and short; combinations have predictable results.

A somewhere between the "A" sound of back and that of father.

E as in get.

I as in police.

O as in hot.

U as in rule.

C is lisped before E and I, hard otherwise: *cerca* is pronounced "thairka".

G is a guttural "H" sound (like the ch in loch) before E or I, a hard G elsewhere – *gigante* becomes "higante".

H is always silent.

J is the same as a guttural G: *jamón* is "hamon".

LL sounds like an English Y or LY: *tortilla* is pronounced "torteeya/torteelya".

N is as in English unless it has a tilde (accent) over it, when it becomes NY: *mañana* sounds like "manyana".

QU is pronounced like an English K.

R is rolled, RR doubly so.

V sounds more like B, *vino* becoming "beano".

X has an S sound before consonants, normal X before vowels.

Z is the same as a soft C, so *cerveza* becomes "thairbaitha".

SPANISH WORDS AND PHRASES

Basics

Yes, No, OK Sí, No, Vale

Please, Thank you Por favor, Gracias

Where?, When? ¿Dónde?, ¿Cuando?

What?, How much? ¿Qué?, ¿Cuánto?

Here, There Aquí, Allí

This, That Esto, Eso

Now, Later Ahora, Más tarde

Open, Closed Abierto/a, Cerrado/a

With, Without Con, Sin

Good, Bad Buen(o)/a, Mal(o)/a

Big, Small Gran(de), Pequeño/a

Cheap, Expensive Barato, Caro

Hot, Cold Caliente, Frío

More, Less Más, Menos

Today, Tomorrow Hoy, Mañana

Yesterday Ayer

Greetings and responses

Hello, Goodbye Hola, Adiós

Good morning Buenos días

Good afternoon/night Buenas tardes/noches

See you later Hasta luego

Sorry Lo siento/disculpe

Excuse me Con permiso/perdón

How are you? ¿Como está (usted)?

I (don't) understand (No) Entiendo

Not at all/You're welcome De nada

Do you speak English? ¿Habla (usted) inglés?

I (don't) speak Spanish (No) Hablo español

My name is... Me llamo...

What's your name? ¿Como se llama usted?

I am English/Soy inglés(a)/ Australian/australiano(a)/ Canadian/canadiense(a)/ American/americano(a)/ Irish/irlandés(a)

Needs – hotels and transport

I want Quiero

I'd like Quisiera

Do you know...? ¿Sabe...?

I don't know No sé

There is (is there)? (¿)Hay(?)

Give me...(one like that) Deme...(uno así)

Do you have...? ¿Tiene...?

the time la hora
a room una habitación
...with two beds/double bed
...con dos camas/cama
matrimonial
...with shower/bath ...con
ducha/baño
It's for one person Es para
una persona
(two people) (dos personas)
for one night para una noche
(one week) (una semana)
It's fine, how much is it? Está
bien, ¿cuánto es?
It's too expensive Es demasi-
ado caro
Don't you have anything
cheaper? ¿No tiene algo más
barato?
Can one...? ¿Se puede...?
camp (near) here? ¿. . .acam-
par aquí (cerca)?
Is there a hostel nearby?
¿Hay un hostal aquí cerca?
How do I get to...? ¿Por
donde se va a...?
Left, right, straight on
Izquierda, derecha, todo
recto
Where is...? ¿Dónde está...?
the bus station la estación de
autobuses

the railway la estación de
station ferro-carril
the nearest bank el banco
mas cercano
the post office el correos/la
oficina de correos
the toilet el baño/aseo/servi-
cio
Where does the bus to
...leave from? ¿De dónde
sale el autobús para...?
Is this the train for Toledo?
¿Es este el tren para Toledo?
I'd like a (return) ticket to...
Quisiera un billete (de ida y
vuelta) para...
What time does it ¿A qué
hora sale
leave (arrive in...)? (llega
a...)?
What is there to eat? ¿Qué
hay para comer?
What's that? ¿Qué es eso?
What's this called in
Spanish? ¿Como se llama
esto en español?

Numbers and days
1 un/uno/una
2 dos
3 tres
4 cuatro

5 cinco	101 ciento uno
6 seis	200 doscientos
7 siete	201 doscientos uno
8 ocho	500 quinientos
9 nueve	1000 mil
10 diez	2000 dos mil
11 once	2001 dos mil un
12 doce	2002 dos mil dos
13 trece	2003 dos mil tres
14 catorce	first primero/a
15 quince	second segundo/a
16 diez y seis	third tercero/a
20 veinte	fifth quinto/a
21 veintiuno	tenth décimo/a
30 treinta	Monday lunes
40 cuarenta	Tuesday martes
50 cincuenta	Wednesday miércoles
60 sesenta	Thursday jueves
70 setenta	Friday viernes
80 ochenta	Saturday sábado
90 noventa	Sunday domingo
100 cien(to)	

For a food glossary, see p.156.

SPANISH WORDS AND PHRASES

340

Glossary

Alcázar Moorish fortified palace

Aficionado fan

Ayuntamiento town hall or council

Azulejo glazed ceramic tilework

Auto-de-fé public judgement and execution of heretics by the Inquisition

Avenida (usually abbreviated to avda) avenue

Barrio suburb or neighbourhood

Bodega cellar, wine bar or warehouse

Calle (usually abbreviated to c/) street

Capilla mayor chapel containing the high altar

Capilla real royal chapel

Castillo castle

Castizo authentic *Madrileño*

Chiringuito a makeshift bar

Chotis Madrid's traditional dance

Convento monastery or convent

Coro central part of church built for the choir

Correos post office

Corrida (de toros) bullfight

Cortes Parliament

Custodia monstrance (the ornamental receptacle in which the consecrated host is displayed)

Ermita hermitage

Estanco small shops selling stamps and tobacco, recognizable by their brown and yellow signs bearing the word *Tabacos*

Iglesia church

IVA Spanish equivalent of value-added tax

Madrileño inhabitant of Madrid, or used to describe something pertaining to the city

Mercado market

Mirador viewing point

Monasterio monastery or convent

La Movida a term used to describe the "happening Madrid" of the 1980s, but also signifying areas where there is plenty of nightlife

Mudéjar Muslim Spaniard subject to medieval Christian rule, but retaining Islamic worship; most commonly a term applied to architecture which includes buildings built by Moorish craftsmen for Christian rulers, and later designs influenced by the Moors

Palacio palace

Parador state-run luxury hotel

Paseo promenade; also the evening stroll

Patio inner courtyard

Plateresque elaborately decorative Renaissance style, named for its resemblance to silversmiths' work

Plaza square

Plaza de toros bullring

Posada old name for an inn

Puente bridge

Puerta gateway

Puerto mountain pass

Retablo altarpiece

Sacristía sacristy or sanctuary of a church

Sierra mountain range

Terraza outdoor bar or café annexe, often summer-only

Tertulia semi-formalized discussion group

Turismo tourist office

Verbena traditional street fair

Zarzuela Madrid's own form of light opera

Index

around the world

Alaska ★ Algarve ★ Amsterdam ★ Andalucía ★ Antigua & Barbuda ★
Argentina ★ Auckland Restaurants ★ Australia ★ Austria ★ Bahamas ★
Bali & Lombok ★ Bangkok ★ Barbados ★ Barcelona ★ Beijing ★ Belgium
Luxembourg ★ Belize ★ Berlin ★ Big Island of Hawaii ★ Bolivia ★ Boston
★ Brazil ★ Britain ★ Brittany & Normandy ★ Bruges & Ghent ★ Brussels ★
Budapest ★ Bulgaria ★ California ★ Cambodia ★ Canada ★ Cape Town ★
The Caribbean ★ Central America ★ Chile ★ China ★ Copenhagen ★
Corsica ★ Costa Brava ★ Costa Rica ★ Crete ★ Croatia ★ Cuba ★ Cyprus
★ Czech & Slovak Republics ★ Devon & Cornwall ★ Dodecanese & East
Aegean ★ Dominican Republic ★ The Dordogne & the Lot ★ Dublin ★
Ecuador ★ Edinburgh ★ Egypt ★ England ★ Europe ★ First-time Asia ★
First-time Europe ★ Florence ★ Florida ★ France ★ French Hotels &
Restaurants ★ Gay & Lesbian Australia ★ Germany ★ Goa ★ Greece ★
Greek Islands ★ Guatemala ★ Hawaii ★ Holland ★ Hong Kong & Macau ★
Honolulu ★ Hungary ★ Ibiza & Formentera ★ Iceland ★ India ★ Indonesia
★ Ionian Islands ★ Ireland ★ Israel & the Palestinian Territories ★ Italy ★
Jamaica ★ Japan ★ Jerusalem ★ Jordan ★ Kenya ★ The Lake District ★
Languedoc & Roussillon ★ Laos ★ Las Vegas ★ Lisbon ★ London ★

in twenty years

also look out for our maps,
phrasebooks, music guides
and reference books

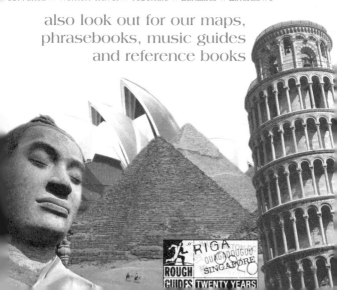

ROUGH GUIDES TWENTY YEARS

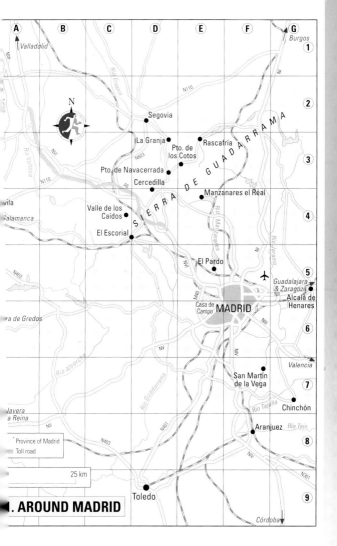

AROUND MADRID

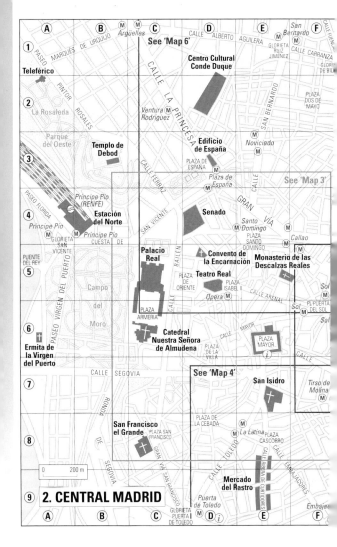

2. CENTRAL MADRID

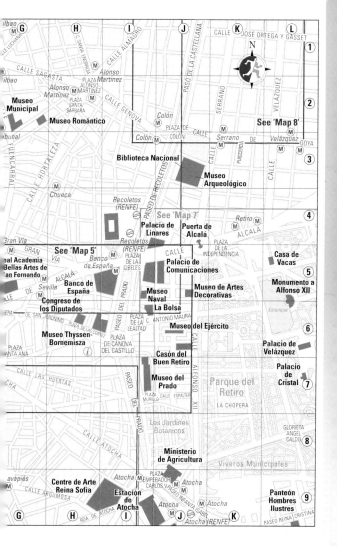

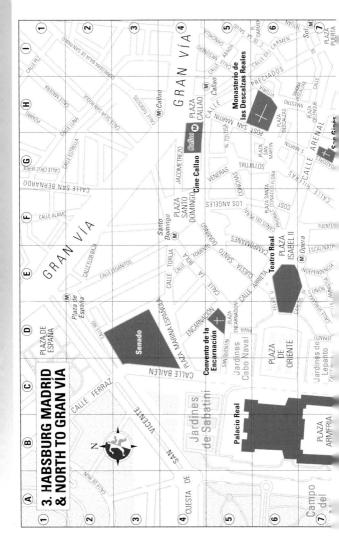

3. HABSBURG MADRID & NORTH TO GRAN VÍA

Monasterio de las Descalzas Reales

Cine Callao

Teatro Real

Convento de la Encarnación

Senado

Palacio Real

San Ginés

GRAN VÍA

PLAZA DE ESPAÑA

PLAZA ARMERÍA

PLAZA DE ORIENTE

PLAZA ISABEL II

PLAZA CALLAO

PLAZA SANTO DOMINGO

PLAZA PUERTA

Jardines de Sabatini

Jardines Cabo Naval

Jardines de Lepanto

Campo del

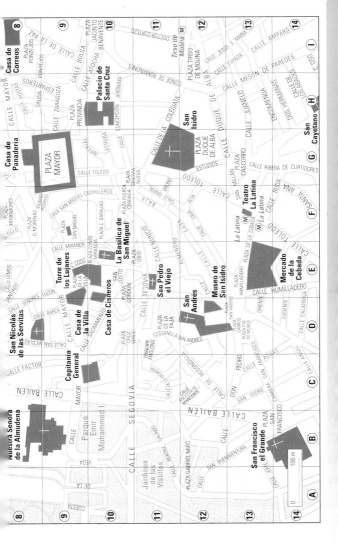

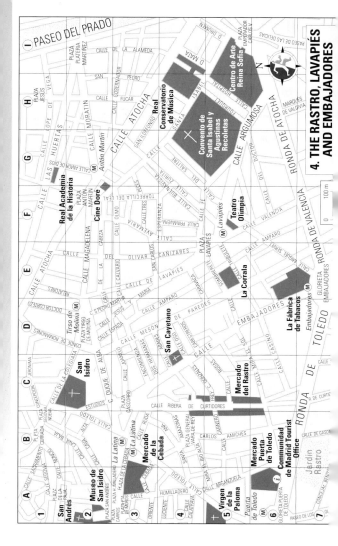

5. SOL, SANTA ANA AND HUERTAS

Museo de Artes Decorativas

Museo Naval

Palacio de Comunicaciones

Bolsa de Madrid

Museo de Ejército

Casón del Buen Retiro

San Jerónimo el Real

CALLE MORETO

CALLE ESPALTER

CALLE VALENZUELA

CALLE ALFONSO XI

CALLE MONTALBAN

CALLE JUAN DE MENA

CALLE ANTONIO MAURA

RUIZ DE ALARCÓN

CALLE FELIPE IV

Fuente de Cibeles

Banco de España

Museo Thyssen-Bornemisza

Monumento a los Caídos por España

Hotel Ritz

Real Academia de la Lengua

Museo del Prado

Puerta de Goya

Puerta de Murillo

PLAZA MURILLO

PASEO DEL PRADO

PLAZA DE LA LEALTAD

CALLE DE ZORRILLA

PLAZA CÁNOVAS DEL CASTILLO

Fuente de Neptuno

PASEO DEL PRADO

ALCALÁ

CUBAS

CALLE DE LOS MADRAZO

MARQUES

CALLE DE CEDACEROS

Círculo de Bellas Artes

Teatro de la Zarzuela

Congreso de los Diputados

PLAZA DE LAS CORTES

DUQUE DE MEDINACELI

PLAZA JESÚS

VEGA

PLAZA LOPE DE VEGA

CALLE MORATIN

CALLE SANTA MARIA

Edificio Metropolis

Iglesia de las Calatravas

GRAN VÍA

Ateneo

Casa de Lope de Vega

Las Trinitarias

CALLE CERVANTES

SAN AGUSTIN

CALLE DE LAS HUERTAS

CALLE SANTA ANA

CALLE ARLABAN

Sevilla

SAN JERÓNIMO

VENTURA VEGA

CALLE PRADO

CALLE LEÓN

Antón Martín

CALLE FDEZ GONZ.

CALLE ECHEGARAY

Teatro de la Comedia

Teatro Español

Real Academia de la Historia

PLAZA ANTÓN MARTÍN

Real Academia de Bellas Artes de San Fernando

PLAZA DE CANALEJAS

CALLE DE LA CRUZ

C. VICTORIA

PLAZA DEL ÁNGEL

San Sebastián

CALLE ATOCHA

CALLE MAGDALENA

Ministerio de Hacienda

Sol

PLAZA PUERTA DEL SOL

CARRERA DE SAN JERÓNIMO

PAS. MATHEU

CALLE ESPOZ Y MINA

NÚÑEZ DE ARCE

PLAZA SANTA ANA

PRÍNCIPE

PLAZA JACINTO BENAVENTE

Teatro Calderón

CALLE CAÑIZARES

CALLE RELATORES

DOCTOR CORTEZO

Tirso de Molina

PLAZA TIRSO DE MOLINA

Casa de Correos

CALLE CARRETAS

CALLE DE LA SAL

CALLE BOLSA

PLAZA PONTEJOS

CALLE CARMEN

CALLE PRECIADOS

PLAZA CARMEN

CALLE TETUÁN

CALLE ABADA

CALLE TRES CRUCES

CALLE DE LA MONTERA

C. VIRGEN DE LOS PELIGROS

CALLE SEVILLA

CALLE DE LA ADUANA

CALLE CABALLERO DE GRACIA

100 m

0   100 yds

N

1 2 3 4 5 6 7

A B C D E F G H I

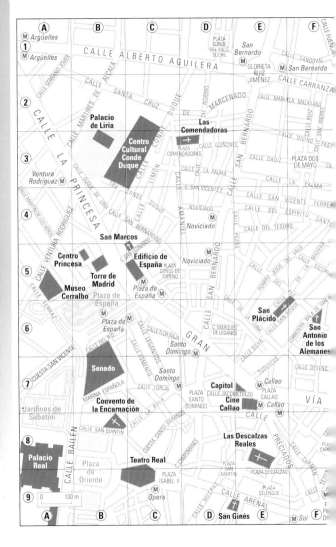

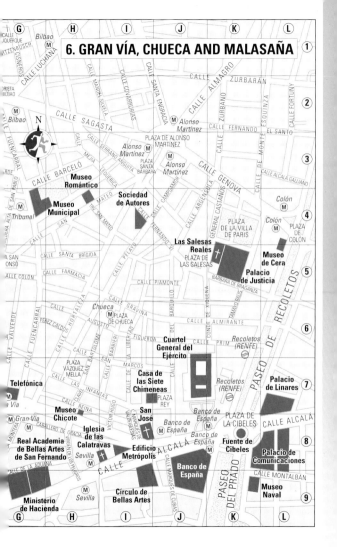

7. PARQUE DEL RETIRO

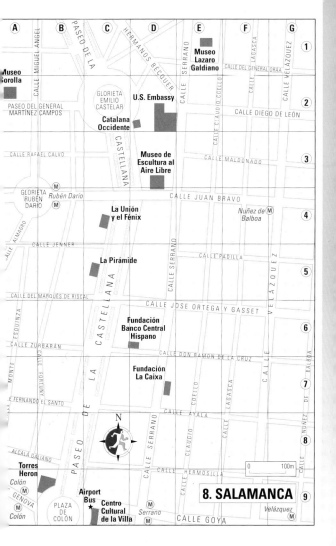

8. SALAMANCA

A · **B** · **C** · **D** · **E** · **F** · **G**

PASEO DE LA · HERMANOS BÉCQUER

Museo Sorolla

CALLE MIGUEL ANGEL

CALLE SERRANO

Museo Lazaro Galdiano

CALLE LAGASCA

CALLE DEL GENERAL ORAA

CALLE VELAZQUEZ

GLORIETA EMILIO CASTELAR

U.S. Embassy

PASEO DEL GENERAL MARTÍNEZ CAMPOS

Catalana Occidente

CALLE CLAUDIO COELLO

CALLE DIEGO DE LEÓN

CASTELLANA

CALLE RAFAEL CALVO

Museo de Escultura al Aire Libre

CALLE MALDONADO

GLORIETA RUBEN DARIO

Ⓜ Rubén Darío

CALLE JUAN BRAVO

CALLE ALMAGRO

La Unión y el Fénix

Núñez de Balboa Ⓜ

CALLE JENNER

La Pirámide

CALLE SERRANO

CALLE PADILLA

CALLE VELAZQUEZ

CALLE DEL MARQUÉS DE RISCAL

CALLE JOSE ORTEGA Y GASSET

CASTELLANA

Fundación Banco Central Hispano

CALLE ESQUINZA

CALLE ZURBARÁN

CALLE DON RAMON DE LA CRUZ

CALLE MONTE

CALLE FORTUNY

Fundación La Caixa

CALLE COELLO

CALLE LAGASCA

CALLE

DE NUÑEZ DE BALBOA

CALLE FERNANDO EL SANTO

CALLE AYALA

N

PASEO DE LA

CALLE SERRANO

CALLE CLAUDIO

CALLE COELLO

CALLE LAGASCA

ALCALA GALIANO

Torres Heron

Colón Ⓜ

GENOVA

Colón Ⓜ

PLAZA DE COLÓN

Airport Bus ★

Centro Cultural de la Villa

Ⓜ Serrano

CALLE HERMOSILLA

0   100m

Ⓜ

CALLE GOYA

Velázquez Ⓜ

1 · 2 · 3 · 4 · 5 · 6 · 7 · 8 · 9

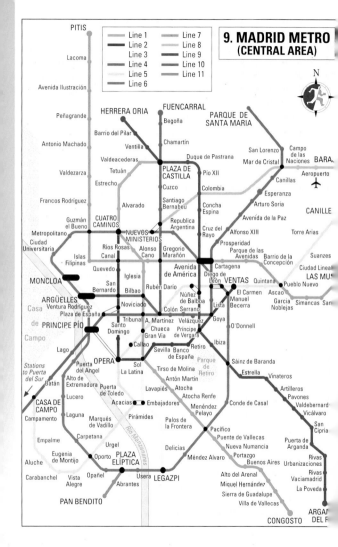